Making Sense of Macroeconomics

Making Sense of Macroeconomics

First Edition

John P. Herzog

University of Dayton

cognella® | ACADEMIC PUBLISHING

Bassim Hamadeh, CEO and Publisher
Jennifer Codner, Acquisitions Editor
Michelle Piehl, Senior Project Editor
Jess Estrella, Senior Graphic Designer
Stephanie Kohl, Licensing Associate
Natalie Piccotti, Senior Marketing Manager
Kassie Graves, Vice President of Editorial
Jamie Giganti, Director of Academic Publishing

Printed in the United States of America.

ISBN: 978-1-5165-3328-2 (pbk) / 978-1-5165-3329-9 (br)

cognella | ACADEMIC PUBLISHING

Contents

Detailed Contents

CHAPTER ONE

Macroeconomics Introduction

IN CHAPTER I, you will begin to understand some of the underlying terms and issues about macroeconomics that will help you to better understand the information presented in later chapters. It will define and give you an overview of why macroeconomics is important to understand. It will also tell you what roles government plays in making it all work.

WHY STUDY ECONOMICS?

First, if you are concerned about whether your job is secure, it may help you to know what the status of our current economy is. If we are having a recession, then it is likely that companies and even government agencies will be cutting back their staffs.

Second, if you are concerned about your retirement investments, such as your 401k, it may help you to know what the status of our current economy is. If we are having a recession, then it is likely that the value of many of your investments has declined.

And third, if you are in business and you are concerned about whether business will be good for you in the near future, it may help you to know what the status of our current economy is. If we are having a recession, then it is likely that your business may not be doing as well as it has been in the past.

Everyone uses economics every day without using that word.

There are many reasons why it is necessary to understand the subject of macroeconomics, but these are the three most common and the three most important.

WHAT IS ECONOMICS?

If you are ***economical***, it means that you are using all the resources you have to the max. You are not wasting them. Using your resources to the max can be for any reason. Everyone has a different perspective on this. You can use them to make yourself financially wealthy. You can use them in the way of talent whether it be in business, theater, social work, or wherever you choose to maximize your creativity. There are many who believe in God and that there is a life that follows this one; therefore, many choose to maximize the use of all of their resources to prepare for that permanent life rather than for temporary things in this life.

Our focus in this book is from the financial perspective. From that standpoint, the formal definition of ***economics*** is that it is the social science concerned chiefly with the description and analysis of the production, distribution, and consumption of goods and services. It is the branch of knowledge that deals with the production, consumption, and transfer of wealth from one person to another or from one organization to another.

The study of economics allows us to have a better understanding of how these things happen.

In the study of ***macroeconomics***, you can learn how governments and societies maximize the use of resources on a national or international level to gain and then keep a healthy economy. It is involved with topics such as the unemployment rate or the inflation rate in our country. The ***unemployment rate*** is the percentage of Americans who are out of jobs who are actively seeking jobs. The ***inflation*** rate is the rate of increases in the average level of prices of goods and services.

When managing the economy, there are three questions that you must answer:

1. What is to be produced with our limited resources?
2. How are we to produce them?
3. For whom do we want to produce them?

While macroeconomics studies these things on a national and international scale, ***microeconomics*** studies them on a more localized, microscopic scale. Microeconomics studies or analyzes the activity of individual organizations and markets. For example, if you are in the pizza business, and if these same three questions would need to be answered by you, you would need to decide if you want to continue to produce and sell pizza, how you would best produce the pizza, and who would likely be buying your pizza?

Why would we want to answer these questions on a national scale?

The answer to that question is that if our country, as a whole, makes products that are not needed or if we make them in a way that wastes resources, there could be a lot of unrest in our country.

For example, many countries in the Middle East produce oil for the world. In doing so, they create many jobs and much of the wealth for their citizens. As a result, their citizens can buy what they need. If, however, the oil was wasted or not used in a way that would create wealth in that part of the world, there would be fewer jobs in those countries, and then poverty and shortages would ensue. People would not be able to get what they need, and their discontent would likely cause social backlash.

WHAT IS THE GOVERNMENT'S ROLE?

Government intervention has increased significantly since the ***Franklin D. Roosevelt (FDR)*** administration that was in office between 1933 and 1945. Prior to FDR's presidency, intervention was seen as needed only for defense, the legal environment, and the postal service. FDR, wanted the federal government to add to its roles the task of stabilizing the economy by direct expenditures (purchases of goods and services and the building of dams and bridges) and income transfers (such as unemployment benefits, welfare, and Social Security).

In general, the government's objective is to make everyone in our country satisfied with the economy by having job stability, meeting needs without shortages, and ensuring reasonable pricing. With the cooperation of economists, it wants to improve a bad economy and maintain a prosperous one.

In other words, the government strives to obtain:

1. Full Employment
2. Price Stability
3. Reasonable Wealth Distribution
4. Economic Growth
5. Stability in all of these things

Legally, it was not the government's job to manage the economy, but when the Great Depression of the 1930s hit us, ***President Herbert Hoover*** was blamed for it and was run out of office. Even though legally it has only been our government's job since FDR's tenure as president to manage the economy, it has been understood that the government must make sure that we have a good economy or one that is prosperous enough to give everyone a job and an acceptable standard of living.

If that doesn't happen, the discontent that a bad economy would cause would likely create a great deal of social unrest. As a result, our government leaders would likely lose their jobs.

Our government wants our country to maximize the use of its resources. If we don't, there will be shortages. Shortages cause high prices. If people can't get what they need, and/or if what they are able to get is expensive, they will be very unhappy.

There is another way of looking at what government is trying to accomplish. We said what it wants to accomplish, but it's also important to know what it does NOT want to happen. Government wants to prevent a depression, a deep recession, a mild recession, stagflation, and unstable prices. If these things do happen, it wants to stop them and get us back to full employment and economic stability. ***Depression*** and ***recession*** are declines in the number of purchases in our country, causing high unemployment. ***Stagflation*** exists when unemployment and inflation are both high. It's bad enough to be out of work, but it's intolerable to be unemployed while being forced to pay high prices for things you need.

If we have a booming economy, the government wants to maintain it. The opposite of stagflation is lower unemployment and lower prices, which is the better of both worlds.

The resources we want to use economically are those used for production. They are called the factors of production, and they are:

1. Land
2. Labor
3. Capital
4. Entrepreneurship

Land is a factor of production for two reasons. First, it is the space we occupy in order to produce goods and services. Second, land is where many products can trace their origins. When you see a component part to a car, for example, the steel and rubber from that part came from resources that come from trees or from the ground.

Obviously, none of those resources will ever be used if we don't take the time to have someone extract them from the land and turn them into something useful. The people, and the time it takes to do that, is what we know as ***labor***. Labor is also used to perform services, such as medical or financial services.

The resource of ***capital*** primarily refers to the tools and equipment that anyone uses to make production happen. Anything from a plow used by a farmer to a conveyor belt in a factory in this context is considered capital. Many *think* of capital as being about money. Others think of it as stocks and bonds. Both of these are correct, but in this context, capital refers to production machinery. Money capital is needed to purchase ***capital equipment***, but in this context, capital will strictly be considered equipment.

Entrepreneurship is what makes the other three factors of production valuable. Nothing happens in an economy until someone steps up to the plate and utilizes those resources to give us the goods we need and the jobs we seek.

The problem is that there is a limit to the quantity available of these resources; hence, they can become scarce, causing shortages of goods and services. As a result of scarcity, to say yes to producing one thing often means saying no to producing another. This is called ***opportunity cost***.

Opportunity cost is not a bad thing. College students may say no to taking a job that pays the minimum wage in order to go to college. Over a four-year period, their sacrifice could add up to over $60,000 of income thrown away. Is that bad? Not really.

College students are very wise to turn down that 60,000 dollars in the hopes of going to college first, betting that a degree that will help them earn far more than that and make up for that loss of that $60,000 in the long run.

It works the same way in production. If you choose to make cars with all of the resources you have, there would be nothing left with which you could produce any other product or service, such as refrigerators, perhaps.

Which one would you choose to produce? If you are in business to make a profit, it would most likely be the one that brings you the most profit.

The ***Production Possibilities Curve*** shows you your production possibilities, and it will help you to decide *what* you will produce. It is the combination of things you could likely produce at a given time with the resources you have. For example, looking at the chart in Figure 1-1 below, suppose you decide to produce only cars using all of your resources. That means you could produce no refrigerators because you would have used up all of your resources to produce the cars. Therefore, the coordinate representing production of both items would be at Point Y, right on the Y axis: only cars would be produced and no refrigerators.

However, if you decide you would like to produce at least a few refrigerators, then you would have to give up producing some of the cars. Your new coordinate could likely then be at Point B. Perhaps you choose to produce even more refrigerators. Once again, you would have to produce even fewer cars, and your coordinate could

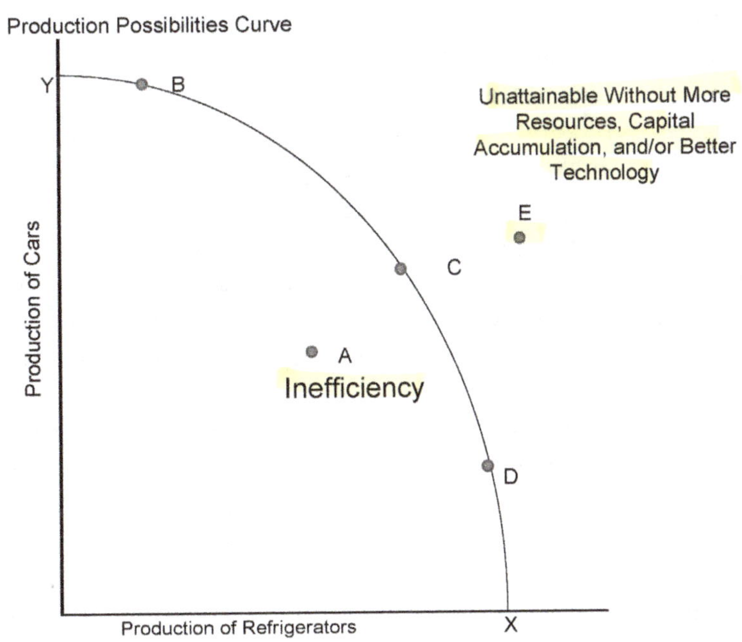

FIGURE 1.1A Production Possibilities Curve

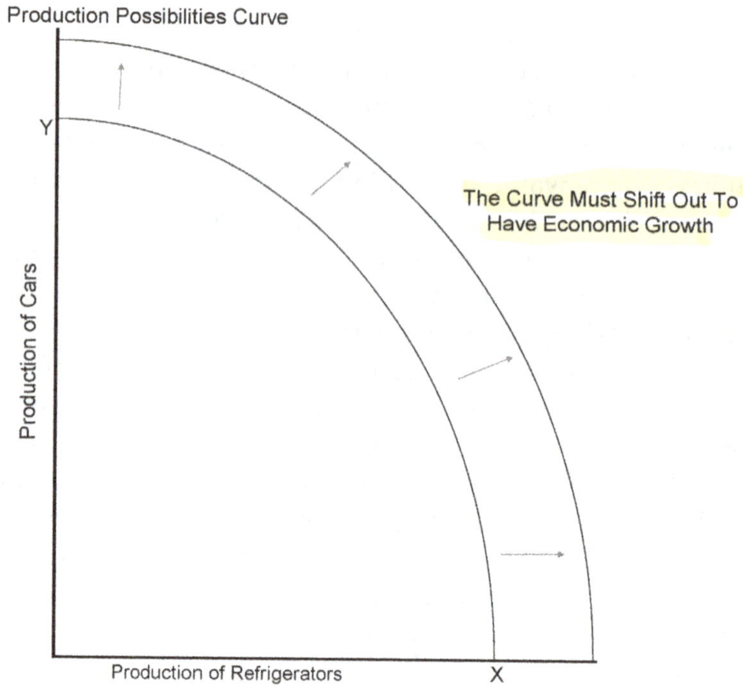

FIGURE 1.1B Production Possibilities Curve

likely then be at Point C. Maybe you choose to produce still even more refrigerators. Again, you would have to produce even fewer cars, and your coordinate could likely then be at Point D. On the other hand, you may choose to produce fewer quantities of *both* the cars and refrigerators. In other words, you may choose not to use all of your resources. You may then be producing at Point A, inside the Production Possibilities Curve.

Point A represents waste. If you don't use all of your resources, you can't get many of them back in time. For example, if you do not use the labor of all of your employees today, tomorrow you can't hire someone to fill the time you wasted today. Waste is often unhealthy for society. As mentioned before, waste often means fewer goods are being produced and shortages may occur.

Why would anyone want to produce at Point A? It may be that the producer has no choice. If there is high unemployment in our economy, he or she would produce at Point A because he or she may not be able to sell the items produced if output was increased. Later in this book, we will discuss the many things that motivate producers to reduce production and to not use all of their resources.

To produce outside of the Production Possibilities Curve is not possible. Why? Because you would not have enough resources to do so. Point E, for example, is a point of production that is unattainable with what you now have to work with.

The only way that you could produce at the level of Point E would be to shift the entire curve outward or to the right. This can be done if you obtain more resources, make better use of the resources you have, or become more efficient.

So how does one do that? There are several options.

First you can use technology to improve your output. ***Technology*** often, but not always, requires more capital equipment. Some refer to this as ***capital accumulation***. Technology can also come in the form of ideas that yield a better way of accomplishing the same things. If I can produce something today in ten steps that used to take twenty steps, then technology is at work even if it's just figuring out a better way.

If you don't shift that curve outward, or to the right, you are never going to have ***economic growth***. Your level of output, and likely profits, would remain the same (see Figure 1-1A).

Production possibilities on a national scale, therefore, are very important to our economic stability, as well. The government wants to make sure that all of us are using all of our resources to avoid social shortages and high prices. It also wants us to shift our Production Possibilities Curve outward. If we don't, there will be no economic growth in our own firms, thus, the country will have no economic growth either. That means that as more people enter the workforce, there will not be enough jobs for them, and we will find ourselves with high unemployment.

The government will do all it can to prevent any shortages of goods, resources, and jobs.

SHORTAGES CAUSE HIGHER PRICES

If you want to sell the only gallon of milk that exists in the entire state, I guarantee you that there would be many people willing to pay you far more for that milk than the current prices charged at the supermarket.

When both shortages and higher prices emerge, we will have a very unhappy society, and there will be a great deal of social unrest.

GOVERNMENT INTERVENTION

In this book, we will explore the different ways that government can intervene to achieve the objectives of which we have spoken.

There are those, however, who believe that government should not get involved. It is believed by many that when the government tries to regulate an economy, it always fails to achieve its goals while making things worse.

One of them was ***Adam Smith (1726–1790)*** who wrote ***The Wealth of Nations*** in 1776 in which he discussed ***The Invisible Hand Theory***. He felt that the answers to the questions of what, how, and for whom things are to be produced should be answered by the free market and not by the government. He felt that the as long as there is money to be made by producing something that people want and are willing to pay dearly for, those things will be provided, not because the producers of those things care about society but because of their greed for money. He believed that the process of self-correction in the economy would happen automatically as if there were an invisible hand making it happen.

The theory is now called the *market mechanism*. If consumers demand fewer cars and more refrigerators, fewer cars and more refrigerators will be produced; thus, workers who produced cars will then shift to other jobs, such as producing refrigerators, thereby, changing the mix of output. Government doesn't have to tell you to produce fewer cars if people have stopped buying them nor does it need to tell you to produce more refrigerators if they are very popular. People are smart enough to cash in on the things people want and are willing to pay dearly for as well as to stop making the things that are not needed. This natural shift from producing one thing and then to another is the invisible hand at work, managing the economy. It just happens to work itself out. In this scenario, therefore, the questions would be answered as follows:

What will be produced? Refrigerators.

How? With use of those who are skilled at producing refrigerators and are willing to produce them for the prices consumers are willing to pay.

For whom? For those willing to pay a price for them that generates adequate profits for the producers.

Notice, therefore, the essential element of the market mechanism is the ***price signal***. People will not produce refrigerators for you unless you are willing and able to pay them the price that will give them the profits they want.

Adam Smith believed that these questions are better answered by those who are in engaged in the free market rather than to have government decide.

THE ECONOMIC ENVIRONMENT

There are many countries in the world besides America that are predominately free-market societies. Many of those same countries, however, have a very imbalanced economic status, with only 1 or 2% of the people owning nearly all of the wealth and the remaining 98% of the people living in total poverty. So, if we are also a free market, why do we not have such problems? Many believe, for example, that our antitrust laws, which prohibit people from conspiring to monopolize a market, are what help us to have a better distribution of wealth and income than the other countries. Therefore, many believe that there is some level of need for regulations.

While many economists don't always agree, there is evidence that productivity and prosperity, along with acceptable wealth and income distribution, usually don't happen without some level of involvement by government regulations.

In any case, the government must also create an economic environment that is perceived by producers as friendly and cooperative with them rather than hostile.

It is believed by many economists that it is very important for the rich to pay their fair share of taxes. They also believe that it is extremely important that businesses are held in check with certain regulations to keep them from doing harmful things such as exploiting consumers with high prices, exploiting workers with low wages, hurting the environment, and more.

The bottom line is that these economists want a government that taxes and regulates businesses when it is appropriate without being perceived as being hostile toward business owners and producers by overtaxing or overregulating them. Businesses now work in a global economy. Many of them can sell Americans their products without having to set up shop here. If they do find another country with lower taxes and fewer regulations, they can move their operations to those countries where taxes are easier to pay and where it is easier and less expensive to comply with their regulations. Many often have done so. When businesses move to those countries, they take their jobs with them. Therefore, it has been found that when government is seen as hostile toward business, it has often created a great deal of unemployment.

Many economists believe that there has to be some level of standards set by government. If a firm threatens to leave our country because the government insists on safe and livable working conditions and fair wages, then such a firm would not be missed if it left the country. Few people would want to work for terrible pay in a place that has horrible or unsafe working conditions.

Many feel that there needs to be a balance: we should not over tax or over regulate business, but we also must not under tax or under regulate them.

What regulations we impose must also be enforced. Many economic fiascos have happened in the past because of firms breaking laws without government taking them to task for it.

When we try to set a balance, it is very hotly debated by conservative and liberal economists and politicians as to where that balance is.

There are other areas where the government can play a role to enhance business operations and productivity.

These are the things that our government typically provides for our economy such as:

a. Providing the legal framework
b. Protecting the environment
c. Protecting consumers
d. Protecting labor
e. Protecting infrastructure (such as our highways, bridges, airports to ensure adequate facilities to facilitate sales and production)
f. Providing services (emergency services, law enforcement, military, and more)

WHAT KIND OF AN ECONOMY DO WE HAVE?

ECONOMIC MYTH #1	The United States operates in a pure free-market economy.

If you are doing business in this country, you are working in an economy that is predominately a free market, but the United States does not operate completely in a ***free-market economy***. That would be an economy in which private business provides for all of our needs with no goods or services provided by the government. The reason that we are not a pure or completely free-market economy is that there are many things that society needs that the free market system cannot provide. That is known as ***market failure***.

Every society has a different economic system. Some gravitate more toward having a pure free market while others gravitate toward pure ***Socialism*** where the government decides what, how, and for whom all things will be produced.

It is important to know what economic system it is in which you are working whether you are doing business here or abroad. We are in a global economy, which means we can do business in any country we want to as long as its economic system will allow it. Even if that country does allow it, its regulations and government involvement will likely differ from ours here in the United States.

There is also a government system known as ***Communism***. While Communism and Socialism share many similarities, they are not the same. Many argue that Communism is actually a form of Socialism that is much more extreme.

Communism is an economic and political system while Socialism is only concerned with the economy. It is believed, therefore, that a certain degree of Socialism can exist within more than one political system including ***Capitalism***. Capitalism is another term for an economic system embraced by countries that would prefer to allow private individuals to control industries and trade at a profit rather than to have them controlled by the government. Socialism also maintains that personal ownership is allowed while Communism does not. Socialism promotes the idea that people should be able to make choices in areas such as their religion or education but Communism does not.

Therefore, let's focus more on Socialism and how it works in relationship to the free market.

It is often referred to as a ***planned economy***, a ***central economy***, or a ***command economy*** where a centralized entity, such as the government, decides what will be produced, how, and for whom. The only way that it can succeed is if the government truly knows what people want and don't want to buy.

For example, some have referred to the term socialized medicine. Many people feel that it is a type of Socialism where, once again, the government answers those three economic questions by creating a national health care system.

Over many, many years, some countries have moved from one end of the continuum toward Socialism while others have moved to the other end of the continuum toward a free market. A country tends to move toward the free market when it appears that the government isn't making enough of the necessary goods for the public. On the other hand, a country may move toward Socialism if it appears that we are having market failure where the free market fails to give society all that it needs. Examples of these needs that the free market usually can't provide at a profit are our military services, highways, and emergency services. No entrepreneurs are likely to be able to make those things available at a profit; therefore, the government needs to pass the hat (by charging taxes) to create them. That is why we say that the United States is in a ***mixed economy*** due to market failure in that the free market cannot satisfy all of society's needs.

In some countries, it has been known that their economy has drifted back and forth from a Socialist economy to a free-market system as societies or leaderships see fit.

The United Kingdom, for example, has ***socialized medicine***. It took some time to achieve that and to get it to the point that it is today. Some argue that it still isn't satisfying needs while some disagree. Still others argue that other societies need to do what the U.K. has done. Regardless of where you are on this debate, it shows how countries move up and down the continuum.

The United States has far more goods provided by the private sector than it does by the government, so our mixed economy would put us the right of the center of the continuum between Socialism and a free-market society.

Government failure exists, too, however. There are times the government has failed to create good economic conditions with its economic policies of intervention, and it has also failed, at times, to produce what we need in high enough quantities, at an affordable cost, or in a timely fashion.

WHAT IS REQUIRED FOR A GOOD ECONOMY?

If all of the people in our country only buy necessities such as, food, shelter (by renting), and clothing from one another, it would not be enough to create an economy with full employment. An economy must also have sales of other items that are beyond necessities, such as new homes, cars, appliances, and clothing. It must also have sales of capital equipment for businesses.

Therefore, economists, in cooperation with government policy, are aimed toward stimulating purchases in these areas.

ECONOMIC MYTH #2	It is desired to have zero inflation or even declining prices.

To have zero inflation would discourage growth. The way that happens is something that will be discussed later.

When we reach full employment, it is imperative that demand for goods and services does not surpass the supply of them. If that happens, shortages would be the result, and shortages can cause higher prices. Therefore, the only way that we can have full employment and stable prices is to find a way to slow down economic growth when we reach full employment in order to give producers the ability to catch up with demand. We don't want to stop growth or reduce the number of items sold in this country; we just want to slow down its growth rate.

THE WEAKNESS OF ECONOMIC THEORY

Economic theory exists when people, usually economists, prescribe what society needs to do to reach economic objectives. The theories we discuss here will prescribe the cause and effect of different actions and strategies. It's often thought of as financial physics. They are often used to make predictions that use the concept known as ***ceteris paribus*** which means nothing else changes. For example, economists say that if prices go up, purchases will decline, *ceteris paribus*. In other words, if prices go up, purchases will decline if nothing else changes. The problem with such thinking is that seldom does one thing happen without others simultaneously changing.

Another problem exists in that once theories are applied, reality, in the form of politics and imperfect knowledge, hint at the flaws in those theories.

ECONOMIC MYTH #3	The condition of the economy can always be attributed to the action of those currently in office.

There is also a reality known as ***legislative lag*** that exists. It takes time to decide on what policies we should use when the economy is at a given status. Whenever a theory is prescribed, and policy is set, it then takes time to pass legislation or apply the regulations of that theory. Once you do, it then takes time to implement those theories. From there, it takes time for passed and implemented policy to have an effect on the economy. This process has often taken two years or more. Therefore, economic conditions we are experiencing now, may be the result of policy set years ago. Also, government officials in office today may implement a policy that does not take effect for a couple of years, long after they have left office.

ECONOMIC MYTH #4	Politicians feel that their first priority is to maintain a good economy and to engage in good economics.

Economic theory is only good if politicians apply the right theory at the right time rather than engage more in their own political agendas. Unfortunately, many politicians practice good politics before they practice good economics. It is usually in their interest to do good economics to get reelected but not always. Things such as fiscal restraint (discussed later) which often cuts programs in the federal budget may be needed for the economy, but it won't happen if politicians fear that it would hurt their reelection bids.

THE MIDTERM ELECTION PROBLEM

There are times that an administration is blamed for a bad economy that it didn't cause while at other times an administration may be given credit for a good economy it didn't create. Every time there is a presidential election, the party that wins the White House is highly scrutinized for its policies in the way of managing the economy. Sometimes, as mentioned earlier, it can take nearly two years from legislative lag for economic policies to take effect. The midterm elections are two years after the presidential election. Since the president is not up for reelection at that time, if the economy is not doing well by then, the party of the current president in the White House will likely lose members of Congress in those elections even though it may have good policies in place that simply have yet to take effect.

THE MAIN ECONOMIC THEORIES AREN'T RIGHT OR WRONG

Economic theories exist that prescribe what economic policies should be implemented to manage the economy. Economic theoriesare like medication. None of the theories are necessarily right or wrong; you simply have to apply the right theory to the right economic condition be it to stop a mild recession (a small decline in output by our country's producers and jobs), deep recession (a huge decline in output and jobs), depression (an astronomical decline in output and jobs), or unreasonable inflation. For example, for someone to say that aspirin doesn't work would be correct if he or she were using it to cure cancer. Aspirin does work if it is used at the right time. In the same way, many politicians will say that some of the economic theories don't work. However, it is more appropriate to say that each of them does work when they are used at the right time.

These economic theories and conditions will be defined later.

Chapter 1 Review

QUESTIONS TO THINK ABOUT

1. Why study economics?
2. What is economics?
3. When managing the economy, what are the three questions that you must answer?
4. What is the government's role in macroeconomics?
5. What is the focus of this book?
6. What do economists feel is the ideal economic environment?
7. What are the things that our government typically provides for our economy?
8. What kind of an economy do we have?
9. What is required for a good economy?
10. What level of inflation is preferred?
11. Explain the weakness of economic theory.
12. Explain the midterm election problem.
13. What are the myths described in this chapter?

TERMS/PEOPLE TO KNOW

Adam Smith

Capital

Capital Accumulation

Capital Equipment

Central Economy

Ceteris Paribus

Command Economy

Communism

Depression

Economic Growth

Economic Theory

Economical

Economics

Entrepreneurship

Franklin D. Roosevelt (FDR)

Free-Market Economy

Government Failure

Inflation

Labor

Land

Legislative Lag

Macroeconomics

Market Failure

Microeconomics

Mixed Economy

Opportunity Cost

- Planned Economy
- President Herbert Hoover
- Price Signal
- Production Possibilities Curve
- Recession
- Socialism
- Socialized Medicine
- Stagflation
- Technology
- The Invisible Hand Theory
- The Market Mechanism
- The Wealth of Nations
- Unemployment Rate

CHAPTER TWO

The What, How, and for Whom Goods are Being Produced

CHAPTER I GAVE you some of the basic concepts of macroeconomics while Chapter 2 will make you more familiar with how we determine the current status our economy compared to other countries.

WHAT WE PRODUCE

The monetary value (plus taxes and not including subsidies) of the ***final goods*** of what a nation produces, *and ultimately sells* over a given period of time (quarterly or annually), is known as ***gross domestic product (GDP)***. The key word here is "final goods." If your firm buys a component part and adds value to it by putting it on a product and then reselling it, such goods would not be considered a final good but, rather, an ***intermediate good***. For example, if a car manufacturer buys tires and add them to one of their assembled cars, those tire are considered intermediate goods. The reason that those types of goods are not counted in GDP is that doing so would be counting them twice, once at their purchase by the manufacturer and, then, second when the manufacturer sells the product to which that component part was added.

TABLE 2.1 Goods

Tires	Cars
Steering Wheels	Vans
Headlights	Trucks

Gross domestic product is added up by knowing the purchase price of goods within four different categories:

1. (C) ***Consumer Goods***—Anything purchased by a citizen for personal use.
2. (I) ***Investment Goods***—Purchased by a business for business but not added to a product for resale to its customers. These investments are not to be confused with investments in things such as stocks or bonds. They are called investment goods because businesses hope to enhance their profits by purchasing them, and it is their hope that the money they spend for them (or invest in them) will reduce costs and increase profits and income just as anyone would with any investment.
3. (G) ***Government***—Any and all spending by the federal government except for transfer payments. Transfer payments are those made to citizens for economic aid. They include things such as welfare, unemployment, and Social Security payments (or money transfers) to those in need or entitled to them. These are not counted in GDP.

(X_n) ***Net Exports***—Consumer goods and investment goods mentioned above that are sold to anyone outside of our country minus any imports we may have purchased from other countries. This number has been negative for many years because the money value of what we have imported is far greater than the money value of the goods and services that we have exported.

Up until the early 1990s, the government's focus was more toward the measure of ***gross national product (GNP)***. It measures income of people in this country. For the most part, income of Americans as measured by GNP should be the same as GDP because every time you purchase something it becomes someone's income. However, income may reflect more than that. For example, there are many who earn dividends and interest from investments they made in foreign firms. The profits from those firms are not derived from production that create jobs here.

Another way of defining GNP is by taking GDP and adding net income of Americans that they receive from outside our country.

The measure of GDP is very important because it tells us the status of our economy. Earlier, it was mentioned that a recession is a small decline in output by our country's producers and jobs, deep recession is a huge decline in output and jobs, and a depression is an astronomical decline in output and jobs.

When GDP falls for two consecutive quarters, it is then determined by economists that a recession exists. At that point, unemployment, bankruptcies, and foreclosures will rise while company profits and prices will fall. You are not really recovered from a recession until you have returned to the GDP you once had before the recession. A recession is not truly completely over until your economy reaches full employment. ***Full employment*** is not necessarily zero unemployment. That is something that will be studied later.

Recession is also described not only by the change in GDP but also by the time it takes to recover from it. In Figure 2-1, you will see the different shapes that depict the

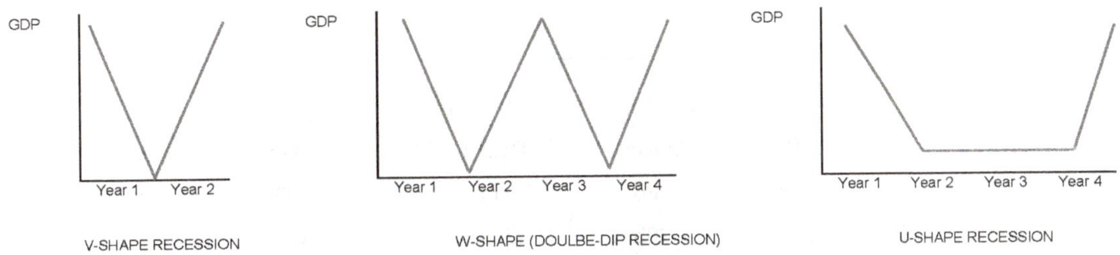

FIGURE 2.1 V-Shape Recession, W-Shape Recession, U-Shape Recession

length of time that various recessions lasted. ***The v-shaped recession*** is one that lasts only a short period of time. It is called that because GDP is shown to be dropping on a chart and then rising very quickly. ***The w-shaped recession or double-dip recession*** implies that the recession ended but was then quickly followed by another recession. That is similar to what happened in 2001. As we were recovering from a slight recession during 2001, 9/11 then occurred. That sent us right back into another recession. ***The u-shaped recession***, on the other hand, implies that there was only one recession but that it took more than a year for the economy to recover from it.

Recessions have also been categorized by the level of unemployment that it causes. A mild recession may cause unemployment to rise perhaps 6 to 8% while some feel that a deep recession causes unemployment to reach 10% or beyond

If the total GDP is not adjusted for inflation, is it called ***nominal GDP***. GDP has often risen without an increase in the actual number of goods and services sold or produced and, therefore, without an increase in job creation. That can happen if inflation is high, thus, artificially raising GDP figures. That's why economists prefer to use ***real GDP***, which gives you those production and purchase totals after factoring in inflation and removing the inflated numbers to get a better understanding of the quantity of goods that were produced and purchased and how many jobs were created. Table 2-2 shows those figures over the last few decades.

If GDP in your country is greater than that of another country, it doesn't always mean that your country's economy is doing better. It can often be because the population in your country is different than that of another.

In 2016, for example, China had a much higher GDP than that of the U.S., but the population of China is so much greater than that of the United States. It is misleading to look at only those figures and to conclude that China had a stronger economy. Table 2-3 shows figures from 2016 with China at the top.

That is why economists prefer to measure ***GDP per capita***. It is equal to GDP divided by the total of men, women, and children in that country. During 2016, the U.S. had more than $57,000 in GDP per person or per capita but China's was less than $9,000. In a sense, it is saying that income for each American was $57,000 that year while for each Chinese citizen it was only $9,000. Table 2-4 shows that China was not even among the top ranked countries when calculating GDP per capita.

TABLE 2.2 GDP Trends

U.S. REAL GDP SINCE 1929

Date	Real GDP	Date	Real GDP	Date	Real GDP
2016	16.85 trillion	1986	7.94 trillion	1956	2.84 trillion
2015	16.55 trillion	1985	7.71 trillion	1955	2.78 trillion
2014	16.22 trillion	1984	7.40 trillion	1954	2.61 trillion
2013	15.79 trillion	1983	7.00 trillion	1953	2.54 trillion
2012	15.38 trillion	1982	6.49 trillion	1952	2.53 trillion
2011	15.19 trillion	1981	6.59 trillion	1951	2.40 trillion
2010	14.94 trillion	1980	6.50 trillion	1950	2.27 trillion
2009	14.54 trillion	1979	6.50 trillion	1949	2.00 trillion
2008	14.58 trillion	1978	6.42 trillion	1948	2.04 trillion
2007	14.99 trillion	1977	6.02 trillion	1947	1.96 trillion
2006	14.72 trillion	1976	5.73 trillion	1946	1.96 trillion
2005	14.37 trillion	1975	5.49 trillion	1945	2.22 trillion
2004	13.95 trillion	1974	5.36 trillion	1944	2.24 trillion
2003	13.53 trillion	1973	5.46 trillion	1943	2.07 trillion
2002	12.96 trillion	1972	5.25 trillion	1942	1.77 trillion
2001	12.71 trillion	1971	4.91 trillion	1941	1.49 trillion
2000	12.68 trillion	1970	4.71 trillion	1940	1.27 trillion
1999	12.32 trillion	1969	4.72 trillion	1939	1.16 trillion
1998	11.77 trillion	1968	4.62 trillion	1938	1.08 trillion
1997	11.21 trillion	1967	4.40 trillion	1937	1.11 trillion
1996	10.74 trillion	1966	4.29 trillion	1936	1.06 trillion
1995	10.28 trillion	1965	4.10 trillion	1935	0.94 trillion
1994	10.05 trillion	1964	3.78 trillion	1934	0.86 trillion
1993	9.65 trillion	1963	3.60 trillion	1933	0.78 trillion
1992	9.41 trillion	1962	3.42 trillion	1932	0.79 trillion
1991	9.02 trillion	1961	3.28 trillion	1931	0.90 trillion
1990	8.91 trillion	1960	3.08 trillion	1930	0.97 trillion
1989	8.85 trillion	1959	3.06 trillion	1929	1.06 trillion
1988	8.61 trillion	1958	2.92 trillion		
1987	8.29 trillion	1957	2.85 trillion		

Source: U.S. Bureau of Economic Analysis.

TABLE 2.3 GDP Trends by Country

World	115,165,700
China	21,417,150
European Union	19,721,689
United States	18,569,100
India	8,702,900
Japan	5,266,444
Germany	4,028,362
Russia	3,397,368
Brazil	3,141,333
Indonesia	3,032,090
United Kingdom	2,796,732
France	2,773,932
Italy	2,312,559

Source: https://en.wikipedia.org/wiki/List_of_countries_by_GDP_(nominal).

TABLE 2.4 GDP Capita Trends by Country

Qatar	127,660
Luxembourg	104,003
Singapore	90,151
Macau	87,855
Brunei	76,884
Kuwait	71,887
Norway	69,249
Ireland	69,231
United Arab Emirates	67,871
Switzerland	59,561
San Marino	59,058
Hong Kong	58,322
United States	57,436
Saudi Arabia	55,158

Source: https://en.wikipedia.org/wiki/List_of_countries_by_GDP_(PPP)_per_capita.

Per Capita GDP helps to make numbers practical to analyze a country's economic status, but it has its weaknesses.

First of all, it is not an indicator of the actual distribution of the wealth. For example, it appears, at first, that each person in the United States is earning over $57,000. But that is only an average. There are many who earn far less than that while others earn millions of dollars per year.

Second, wealth is not only measured by income. A person's wealth can include a savings account at the bank, stocks, bonds, cars, homes, and much more. Sometimes people gain this wealth from generations of money that has been passed down many times. GDP does not address such things.

HOW WE PRODUCE

After studying what we produce, we then study how we produce by analyzing our productivity. ***Productivity*** is measured by taking output and dividing it by the number of inputs used to produce it: inputs such as labor hours or capital equipment.

The U.S. and other developed nations (such as Canada, Japan, and the European Community) have higher productivity with labor because they have organizations that are ***capital intensive***. That means that through the use of capital equipment we produce more goods for every hour of labor we employ. Manufacturers tend to have operations that are very capital intensive as they use a great deal of equipment and automation while industries such as the service sector (accountants, physicians and such) are more ***labor intensive***, using more people than equipment for production.

Over the years, the United States has dominated the world in this regard. While many other countries have made huge improvements and strides in productivity and the use of capital equipment, the U.S. is still the leader.

Labor intensive industries, or countries that tend to be more labor intensive than capital intensive, utilize what is called ***human capital***. That is the level of skills and knowledge your human workforce has. Cheaper help is not always better help. The U.S. has the advantage here, too, with labor in our country being among the best educated and skilled for production.

Another thing that we have going for us in the U.S. is ***factor mobility***: the ability for our workforce to shift from one firm to another when its existing employers have slower or negative growth or when layoffs ensue. Skills that workers use in one organization can often be plugged into that of another who may be needing more workers. This helps to keep productivity in our country higher and can help reduce unemployment.

Chapter 2 Review

QUESTIONS TO THINK ABOUT

1. What is gross domestic product, and how does it indicate our current economic condition?
2. How does the United States stand worldwide regarding GDP?

TERMS TO KNOW

Capital Intensive

Consumer Goods

Double-Dip Recession

Factor Mobility

Final Goods

GDP Per Capita

Government

Gross National Product (GNP)

Human Capital

Intermediate Good

Investment Goods

Labor Intensive

Net Exports

Nominal GDP

Productivity

Real GDP

U-Shaped Recession

V-Shaped Recession

W-Shaped Recession

CHAPTER THREE

The Circular Flow

CHAPTER 3 GIVES you an overview of how the economy works on an ongoing basis. The concept of the circular flow is one that will be discussed often in later chapters, and so it is also important to focus on that concept here.

THE PROCESS

When a sale is made, there is always a process that takes place.

Step 1: If am a consumer, I will likely take my money and go looking for a business from whom I can buy a product or service. That business will be in the ***product market***.

Step 2: That product market will direct me to a business from which I would buy the product or service.

Step 3: I would then make the purchase of a product or service from the business I feel would best serve me.

Step 4: The business who serves me will buy their resources from people like you and I when they:

a. Pay us for the land we own (paying rent for the use of the land).
b. Pay us for our labor (paying a wage to one of us to produce the good or service for the product market).
c. Buy capital equipment from one of us.
d. Pay us part of the business's profits if we are the entrepreneurs of the business.

Once someone like you or I is paid, we can once again become consumers, and we can take our money and buy more things from the product market. At that point, the process starts all over again.

This process is known as the ***circular flow***. It must go around and around as long as possible and as strong as possible or our economy could likely fall on bad times. Please see Figure 3-1.

Sometimes, however, the circular flow can spring a leak. Just like the plumbing in your house, if the leak isn't fixed or if the water that leaked out isn't somehow reinjected, eventually your pipes will have no more water to circulate, and they would dry up. We never want to see our economy dry up. We must keep the circular flow moving.

What kind of a ***leakage*** could occur?

The first is *taxes*. When you are paid, you are not able to spend all of your money because a large part of that income must be paid to the government. So that money is leaked out of the flow. How is that money reinjected?

Taxes find their way back into the circular flow when the government takes your tax money and buys things from the product market just as a consumer would. They buy office equipment, cars, buildings, and much more. It can also pay money directly to landlords for land, to workers for labor, to those selling capital equipment, or to those in business who take care of some of the things government needs.

Another leak comes from *savings*. If people put money aside in their savings accounts after they have earned it, the money won't be spent and that would create another leakage in the circular flow.

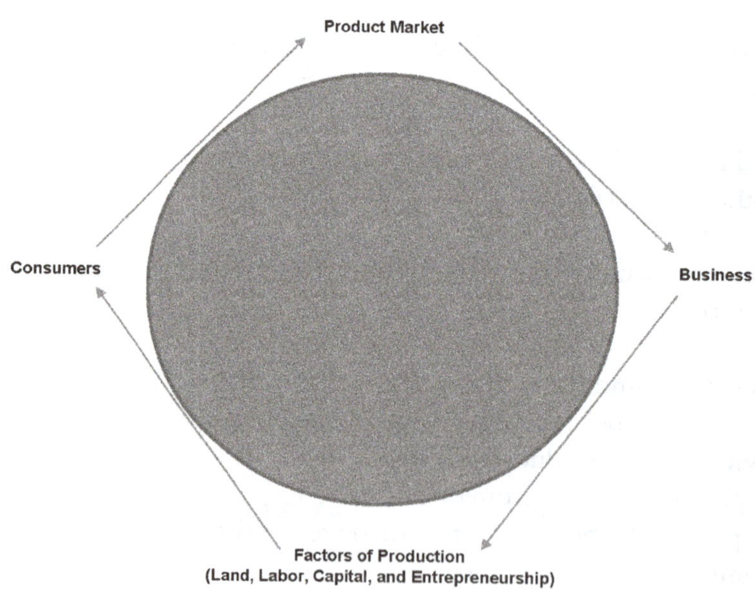

FIGURE 3.1 The Circular Flow

Savings find their way back into the circular flow, however, as long as people who save money put them into financial institutions such as banks, mutual funds, or investment firms that sell stocks and bonds. When that happens, those financial institutions turn right around and make that money available to those who need it to buy homes, cars, appliances, capital equipment for business, and much more.

The final major leakage from the circular flow comes from *imports*. If people are buying goods from other countries and not from here, that money, once again, escapes from the American circular flow. The reinjection of that money then comes from exports that we sell to people abroad.

There is a problem here. As mentioned earlier, the dollar value of the products we sell or export from our country and sell to people in other countries are far fewer than the imports we purchase. For many years, the reinjection of our exports to compensate for lost sales in our imports has not been adequate.

So, then, why doesn't the circular flow of our country dry up?

One major reason is that the ***reinjections*** of government spending and loans from banks more than make up for the import/export leakages. The government spends much more than it receives in tax revenue. Also, when you put money in banks, much more money is created by those deposits than the deposits themselves. Does that sound impossible? Later you will see how it is, in fact, possible and happens all the time.

Chapter 3 Review

QUESTIONS TO THINK ABOUT

1. Describe the circular flow in your own words.
2. How can we better fix the leakages in the circular flow?

TERMS TO KNOW

Leakages

Reinjections

CHAPTER FOUR

The Laws of Supply and Demand

NOW THAT THE circular flow has been discussed in Chapter 3, it will become easier to understand the concepts of supply and demand. Here in Chapter 4, supply and demand is discussed in great detail. Just like the circular flow, you will hear these terms often in future chapters. If you ever study Microeconomics, you will study it there, too. Supply and demand concepts are at the heart of many financial principles and are, thus, very important to understand. That is why this in-depth discussion is provided.

DEMAND

To ***demand*** something means that:

1. You want it.
2. You have the means to purchase it (meaning you have the money to buy it, or you have enough credit in order to borrow enough to buy it).
3. You can and will take the action to buy it.

All three of these things must happen if demand is to take place.

Demand is defined as the ability and willingness of a given person or entity to buy given quantities of a good or service at a given price (*Ceteris Paribus*). The ***law of demand*** basically states that as sellers continue to raise their prices, the quantity demanded of those goods and services will decline. The opposite is also true. Lower prices will bring an increase in the demand of goods and services.

There are two reasons for this. The first is called the ***income effect***. Everyone has a limit to what he or she can afford because we all have a limit to our income. Even the richest people in the world have limits to what they can purchase. Therefore, if prices go up, people cannot afford to buy as much, thus, demand will fall. The second reason that fewer goods and services are purchased from you as a producer with your higher prices is the ***substitution effect***. If you are a producer or seller and if you charge more and more for your goods and services, your customers will look for another way, a less expensive way, to satisfy their needs. They will find other goods or substitutes (***substitute goods***) to do so. Substitutes could be one of your competitors' goods or services or something that will satisfy the same need.

For example, back in the late 1970s, many people became overwhelmed by the increases in energy costs. Unfortunately, the utility companies had no competitors. Therefore, many, many consumers began to look for other ways to heat their homes. They used products such as kerosene stoves and fireplace inserts. As a result, the energy companies experienced a significant decline in sales. The sellers of those products were not direct competitors to the utility companies, but they still satisfied the same need.

Let's take a look at an example of how a typical firm's demand for its product or service might work.

Suppose you are a consumer. The schedule below could be an example of how many slices of pizza you might buy from me in a given year if I am selling pizza. This would be an ***individual consumer's demand***.

TABLE 4.1A Price Per Slice

PRICE PER SLICE	$5	$4	$3	$2	$1
DEMAND	1	2	3	4	5

Now assume that 10,000 consumers like you are in a given market area that become potential buyers or demanders of a given pizza place. The schedule below could then be an example of how much pizza a given pizza firm may have demanded from it during a given year. This would be called the ***firm's demand***.

TABLE 4.1B Price Per Slice

PRICE PER SLICE	$5	$4	$3	$2	$1
DEMAND	10,000	20,000	30,000	40,000	50,000

Now assume that there are 10,000 pizza parlors in the country. The schedule below would show how much pizza would be demanded in our country. This would be known as the ***market demand*** for the pizza industry.

TABLE 4.1C Price Per Slice

PRICE PER SLICE	$5	$4	$3	$2	$1
DEMAND	100,000,000	200,000,000	300,000,000	400,000,000	500,000,000

Now assume that there are 100,000 different industries with average prices such as these in the country. The schedule below would show how much would be demanded in our country's entire economy. This would be known as the ***aggregate demand*** for our entire country. Aggregate demand, therefore, is the same as gross domestic product (GDP).

TABLE 4.2 Average Price Per Unit

AVERAGE PRICE PER UNIT	$5	$4	$3	$2	$1
DEMAND	10 Trillion	20 Trillion	30 Trillion	40 Trillion	50 Trillion

If we were to graph the aggregate demand of the data shown in the schedule above, you would be creating what is called the ***Aggregate Demand Curve***. It would look something like what you see in Figure 4-1.

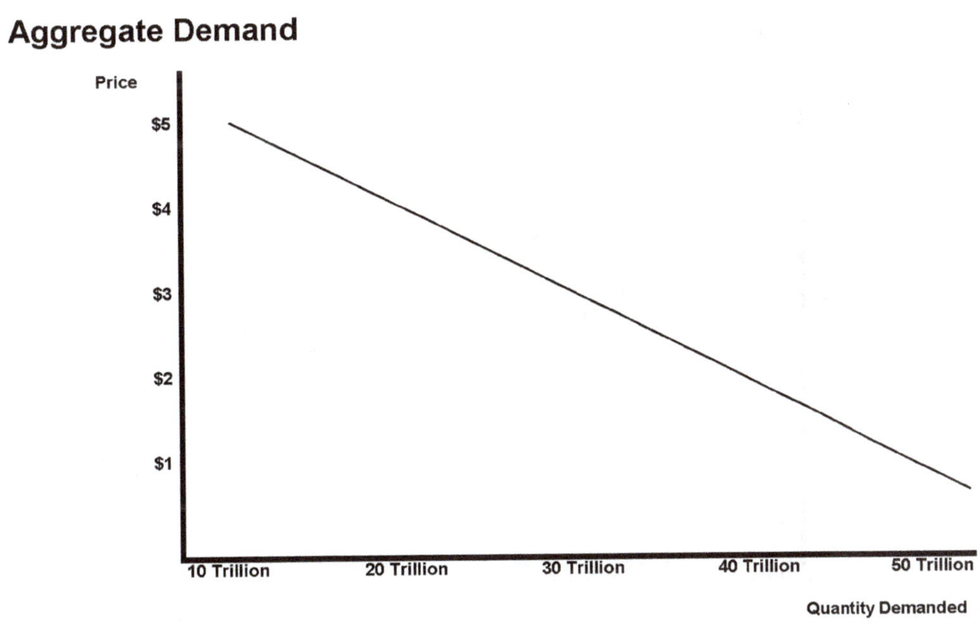

FIGURE 4.1 Aggregate Demand Curve

Therefore, the first major determinant of demand is the price that producers charge. If the average price that all producers charge for each item sold drops from $5 down to $4, the aggregate demand would increase to $20 trillion. As the average prices in our country would continue to change, either going down or up, the aggregate demand would move up and down along the curve. Therefore, the only thing that causes aggregate demand to move along the Aggregate Demand Curve is a change in the average price charged by producers in this country.

There are other determinants of demand besides that of the prices charged by producers.

TASTE (LIKING OR DISLIKING OF AMERICAN PRODUCTS)

Suppose, for example, that people stop liking American products. Suppose that they feel that there are products better than ours around the world. Even if our prices remain the same, demand for our products would decline. If the average price of goods and services is approximately $4, then demand could possibly decline to Point D or somewhere in that vicinity as is illustrated in Figure 4-2 below. If the average price of goods and services is approximately $3, then demand could possibly decline to Point E or somewhere in that vicinity. If the average price of goods and services is approximately $2, then demand could possibly decline to Point F or somewhere in that vicinity.

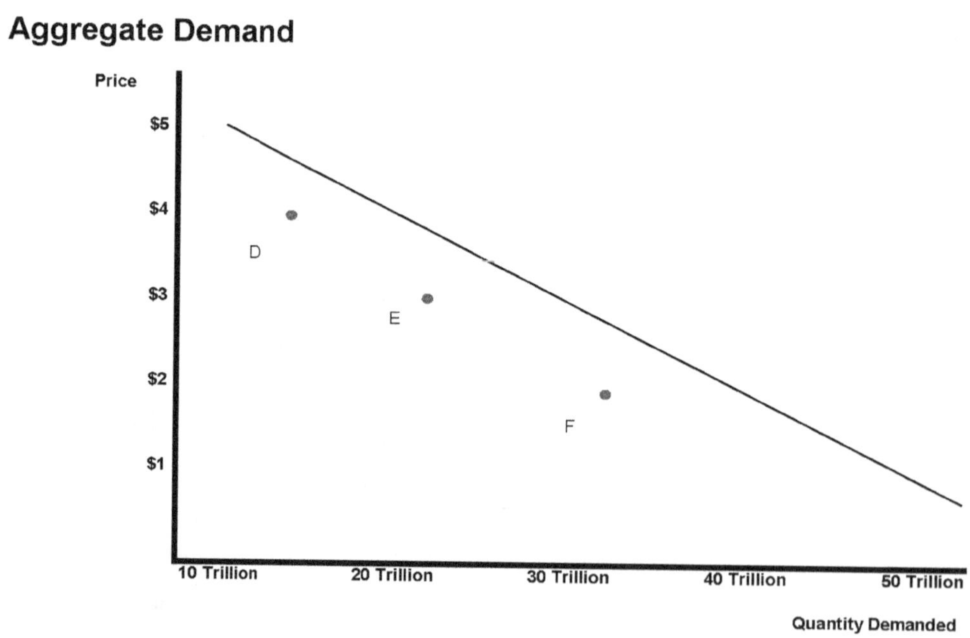

FIGURE 4.2 Aggregate Demand Curve (Liking/Disliking)

If you connect those three coordinates D, E, and F, you would have a new demand curve. In other words, if fewer people like American products, the Aggregate Demand Curve for America would shift to the left as seen in Figure 4-3. That is bad news because aggregate demand is the same as GDP. That could cause a recession.

This happened in the late 1970s when our American cars got very low gas mileage and it was perceived that they were poorly built, requiring a great deal more maintenance. At that time, aggregate demand in America shifted to the left.

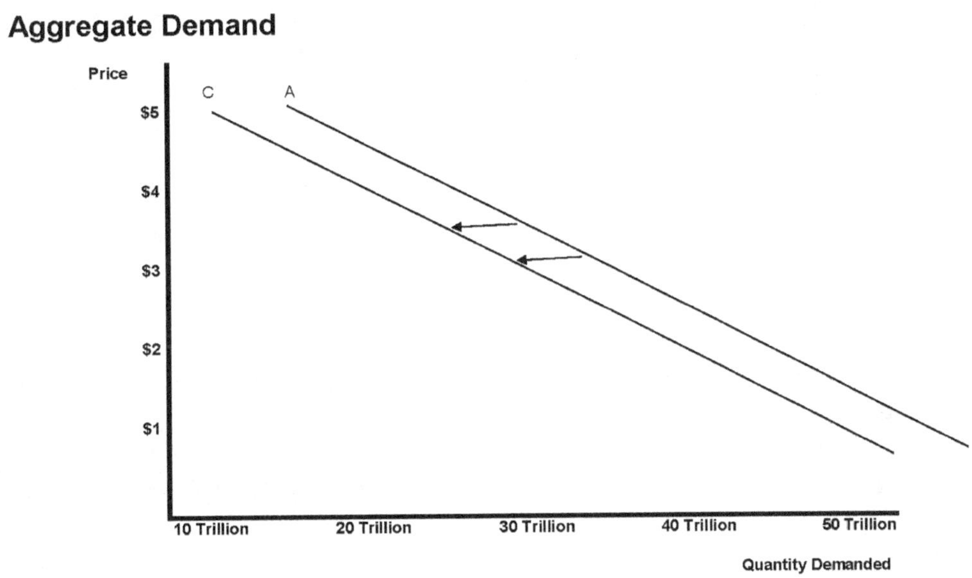

FIGURE 4.3 Aggregate Demand Curve Shift Left (Liking/Disliking)

The opposite is also true. Suppose, for example, that people began liking American products more. Suppose that they feel that American products are better than all other products around the world. Even if our prices remain the same, demand for our products would increase. Our Aggregate Demand Curve will then shift to the right from point A to B as seen in Figure 4-4. That would increase GDP and, hopefully, bring us out of a recession or stabilize an already prosperous time. That is good news!

In the early 1980s, American cars were dramatically improved, and gas mileage on those cars skyrocketed, shifting our Aggregate Demand Curve outward.

INCOME

Now suppose that the income of our families in America began to decline. American customers would have less money to spend. Even if our prices remain the same,

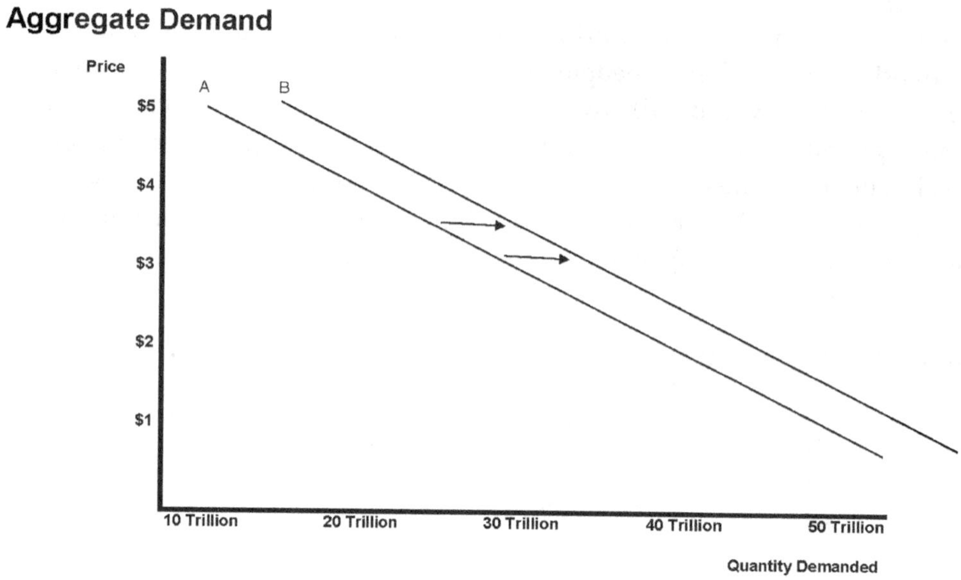

FIGURE 4.4 Aggregate Demand Curve Shift Right (Liking/Disliking)

demand for our products would decline. If the average price of goods and services is approximately $4, then demand could possibly decline to Point D or somewhere in that vicinity as seen in Figure 4-5 below. If the average price of goods and services is approximately $3, then demand could possibly decline to Point E or somewhere in

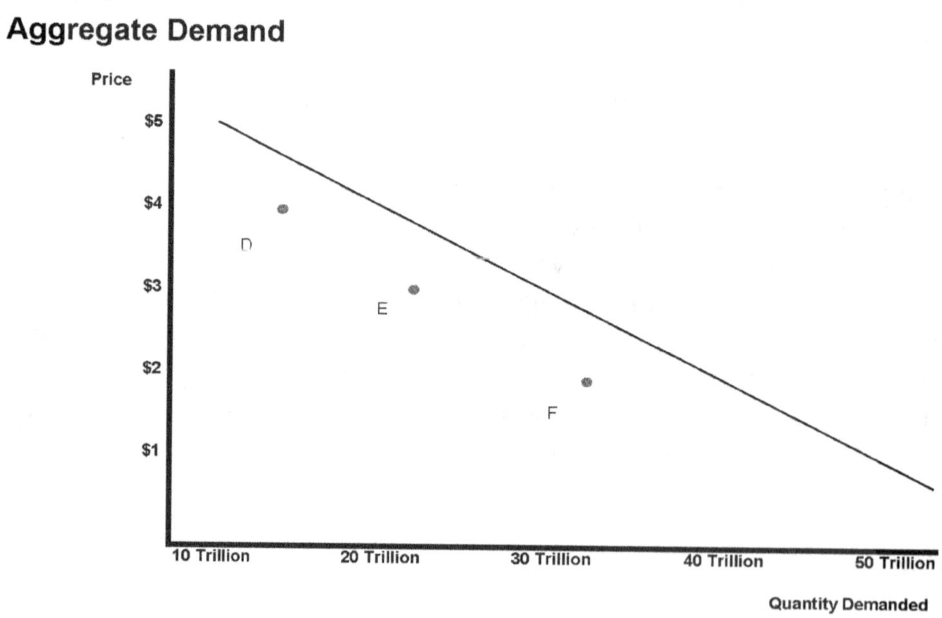

FIGURE 4.5 Aggregate Demand Curve (Income)

that vicinity. If the average price of goods and services is approximately $2, then demand could possibly decline to the Point F or somewhere in that vicinity.

Now, if you connect those three coordinates, you would have a new demand curve. In other words, if the income of American families or for people around the world declines, the Aggregate Demand Curve for America would shift to the left from Point A to Point C as seen in Figure 4-6. Again, that is bad news because aggregate demand is the same as GDP. That could also cause a recession.

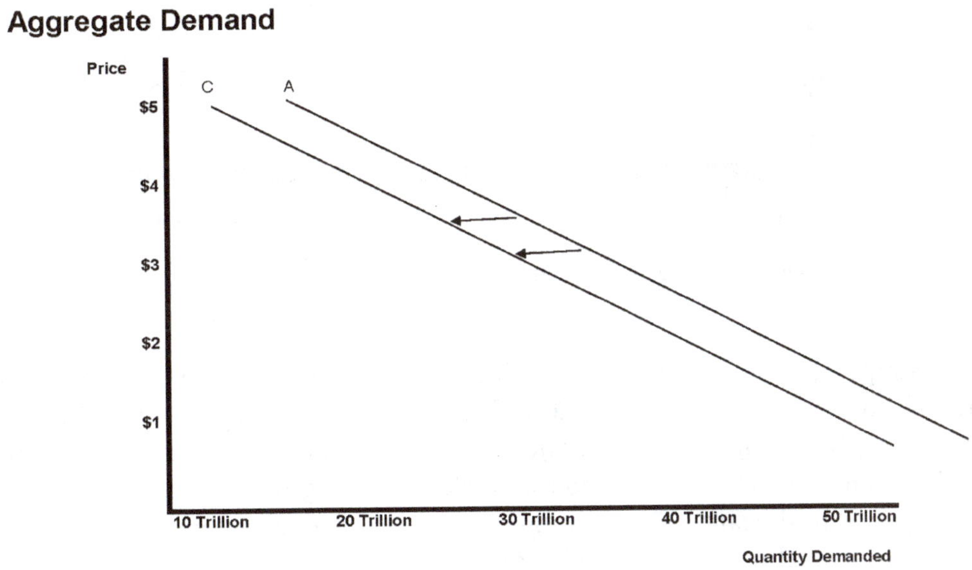

FIGURE 4.6 Aggregate Demand Curve Shift Left (Income)

The opposite is also true. Suppose, for example, that people in America and/or our international customers begin to earn higher income. Even if our prices remain the same, demand for our products would increase. Our Aggregate Demand Curve will then shift to the right from point A to B as shown in Figure 4-7. That would increase GDP and, hopefully, bring us out of a recession or stabilize an already prosperous time. That is good news!

OTHER GOODS: SUBSTITUTE GOODS

We have spoken about the idea of the substitution effect. If people find other, better, less expensive goods around the world to satisfy needs instead of using our products, those products would be referred to as ***substitute goods***.

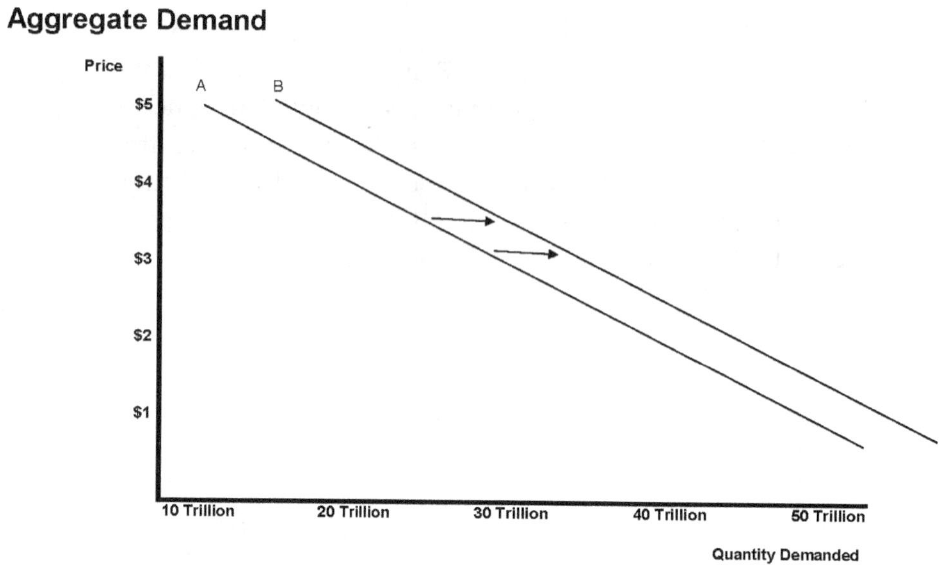

FIGURE 4.7 Aggregate Demand Curve (Income)

Now, suppose, for example, that the price of those substitute goods declined while quality of those goods was perceived as being relatively the same as ours. *Also assume that prices for American good remain unchanged*. That would make those goods more attractive than ours to buyers around the world, including Americans. This is exactly what happened in the late 1970s. Foreign cars were less expensive than ours. Even if our prices remain the same, demand for our products would decline. If the average price of goods and services is approximately $4, then demand could possibly decline to Point D or somewhere in that vicinity as seen in Figure 4-8 below. If the average price of goods and services is approximately $3, then demand could possibly decline to Point E or somewhere in that vicinity. If the average price of goods and services is approximately $2, then demand could possibly decline to Point F or somewhere in that vicinity.

Once again, if you connect those three coordinates, you would have a new demand curve. In other words, if people can buy products just as good as American products at a much lower price, the Aggregate Demand Curve for America would shift to the left from Point A to Point C as seen in Figure 4-9. That is bad news because this means that aggregate demand will fall, and, once again, we could have a recession.

The opposite is also true. Suppose, for example, that prices for *foreign/substitute goods* rise *while the prices of American goods remain the same*. Demand for our products would increase. Our Aggregate Demand Curve will then shift to the right from point A to B as seen in Figure 4-10. That would increase GDP and, hopefully, bring us out of a recession or stabilize an already prosperous time. Good news again!

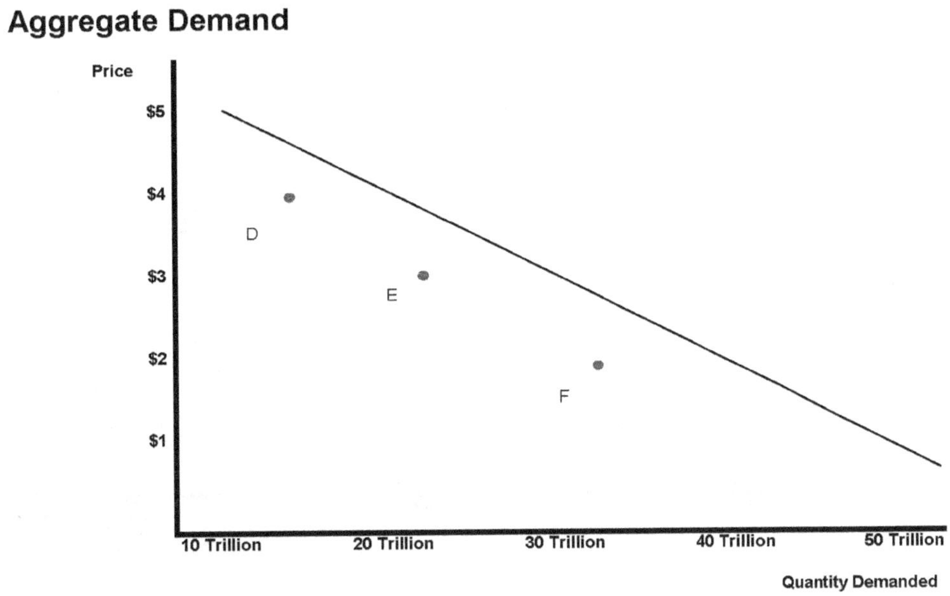

FIGURE 4.8 Aggregate Demand Curve (Substitute Goods)

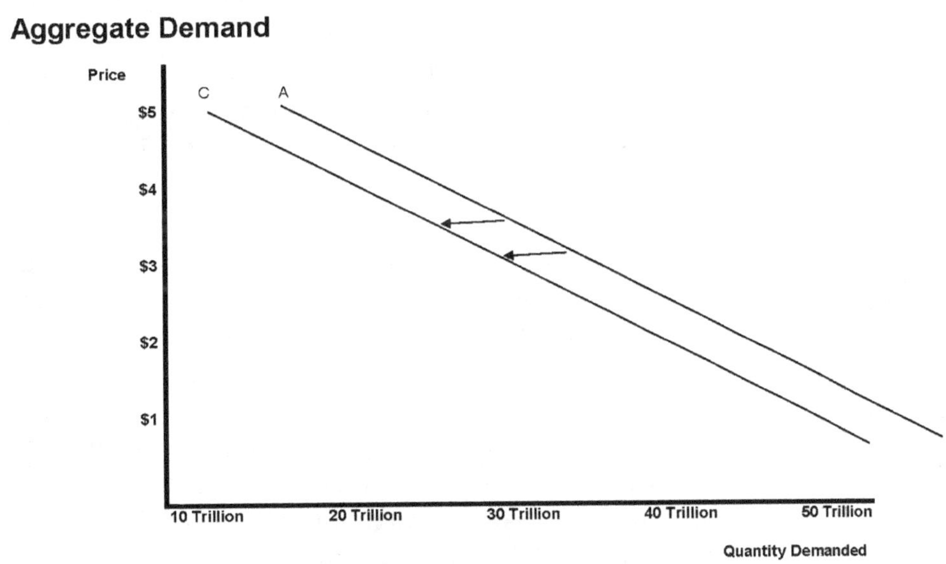

FIGURE 4.9 Aggregate Demand Curve Shift Left (Substitute Goods)

COMPLEMENTARY GOODS

There are many goods out there that require the purchase of another good or service in order to own and operate them.

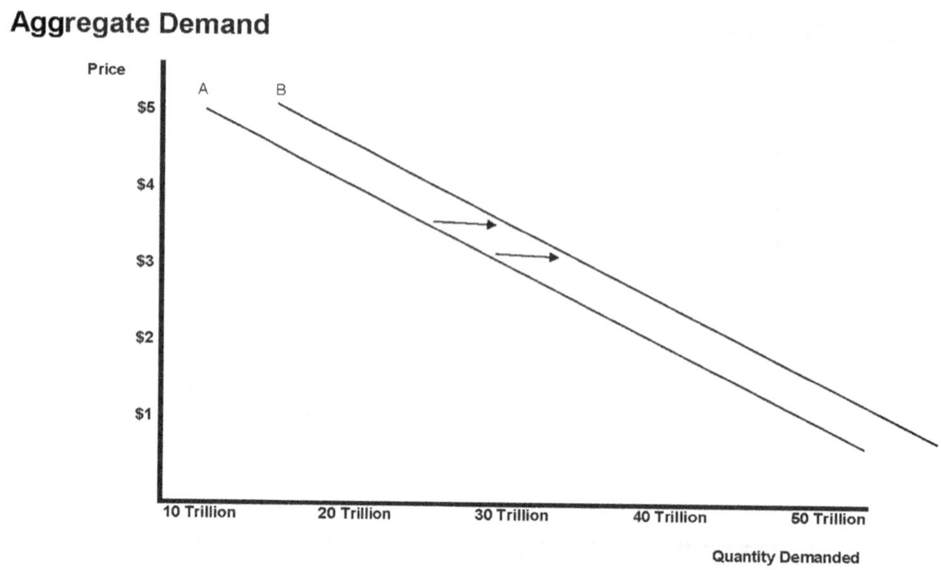

FIGURE 4.10 Aggregate Demand Curve (Substitute Goods)

For example, you are not likely to own a telephone if there is no telephone service or network available. At the same time, you would not need to have access to a telephone network if you do not have a telephone. Another example would be cars, lawnmowers, or any gasoline-driven product. You can't operate them without gasoline, and you would not have much use for gasoline without those products. These are called ***complementary goods***.

If the price of a complementary good rises, then it becomes more expensive to own the product that requires it. For example, if the price of gasoline goes sky-high, the sales for cars would decline because the cost of owning cars would rise. The same would be true for telephone service. Few telephones would be purchased if people could not afford the access to a telephone network.

Now suppose, for example, the price of those complementary goods increases significantly. *Also assume that prices for American cars or telephones remain unchanged*. Once again, that is exactly what happened in the late 1970s. The price of gasoline soared, causing the demand for American cars to fall. Even if our prices remain the same, demand for our products would decline. If the average price of goods and services is approximately $4, then demand could possibly decline to Point D or somewhere in that vicinity as seen in Figure 4-11 below. If the average price of goods and services is approximately $3, then demand could possibly decline to Point E or somewhere in that vicinity. If the average price of goods and services is approximately $2, then demand could possibly decline to Point F or somewhere in that vicinity.

If you connect those three coordinates, you would have a new demand curve. In other words, if the price of goods that are complementary to American products goes

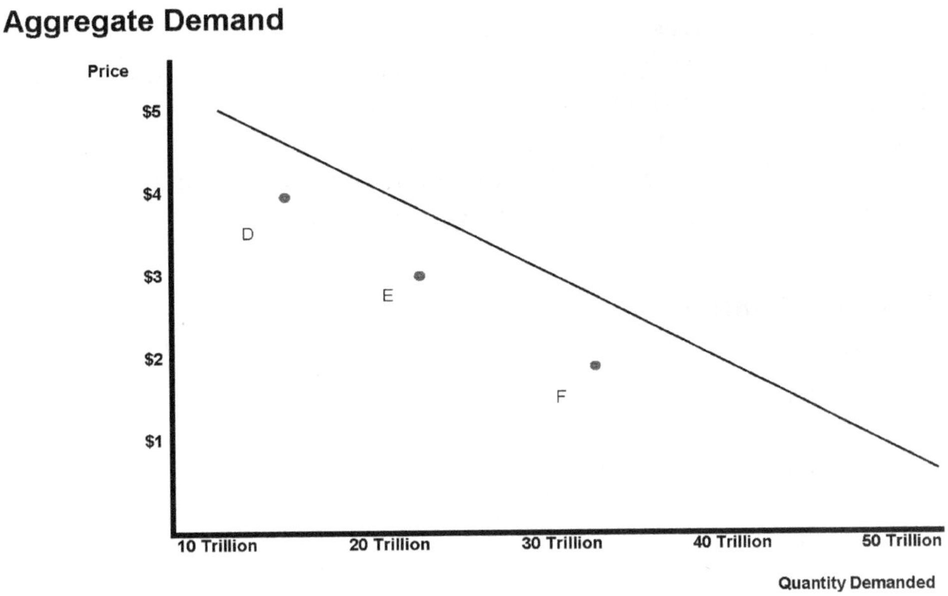

FIGURE 4.11 Aggregate Demand Curve (Complementary Goods)

up, the Aggregate Demand Curve for America would shift to the left from Point A to Point C as seen in Figure 4-12. Again, that is bad news because a drop in aggregate demand means we could be heading toward a recession.

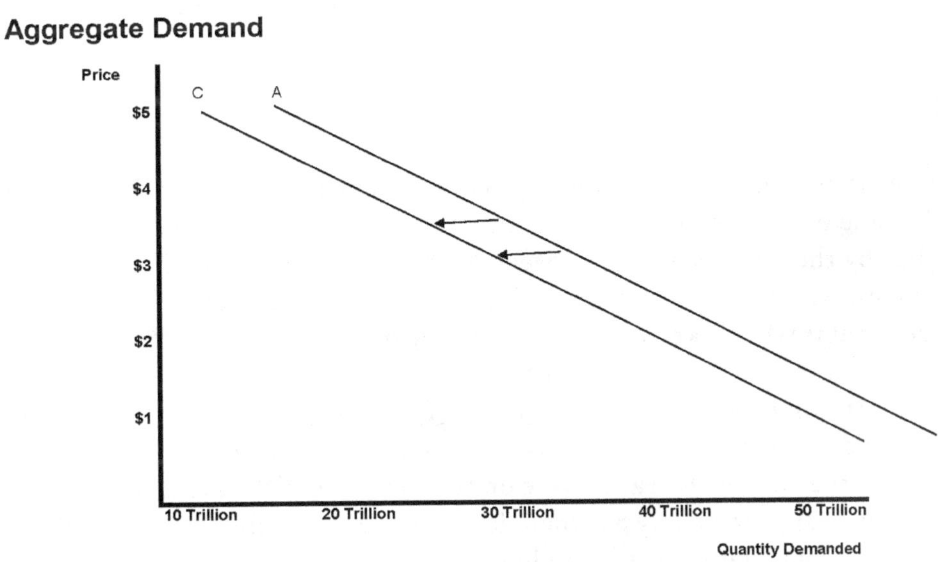

FIGURE 4.12 Aggregate Demand Curve Shift Left (Complementary Goods)

The opposite is also true. Suppose, for example, that prices for gasoline or telephone network services *decline while the prices of American cars and telephones do not.* Even if our prices remain the same, demand for our products would increase. Our Aggregate Demand Curve will then shift to the right from point A to B as seen in Figure 4-13. That would increase GDP and, hopefully, bring us out of a recession or stabilize an already prosperous time. Happy, happy, happy!

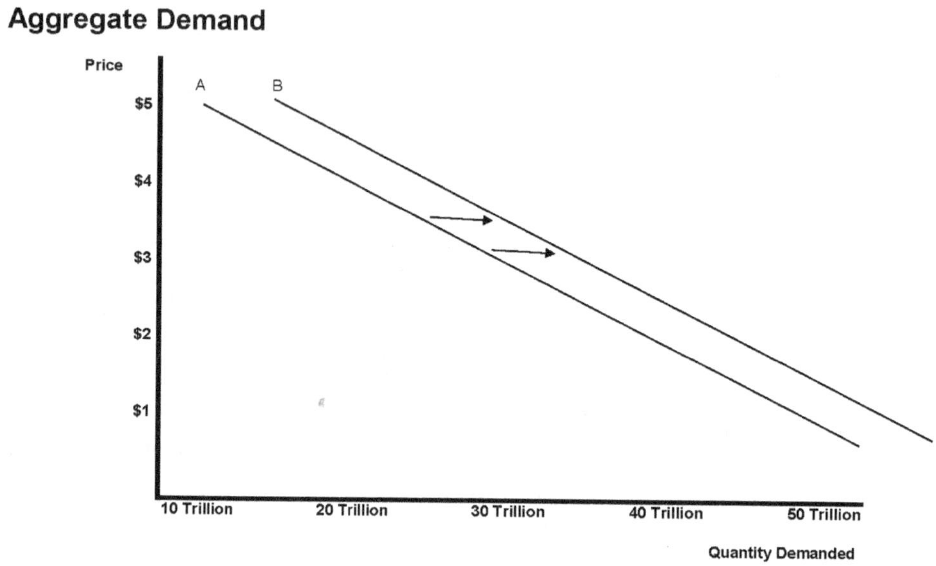

FIGURE 4.13 Aggregate Demand Curve Shift Right (Complementary Goods)

TAXES

Before we discuss taxes, we must define income in a little more depth. ***Personal income*** is the income of households in our country. That is income received not by a corporation but by the owners and employees of those organizations. If the government lowers taxes, American consumers will have more income to spend. The opposite is also true. That is what is known as ***disposable income***: income of each household after it has paid its taxes to the government.

If taxes are increased and *prices for American goods remain unchanged*, demand for goods and service from Americans will decline. Once again, that is exactly what happened in the late 1970s. Taxes were on the increase. If the average price of goods and services is approximately $4, then demand could possibly decline to Point D or somewhere in that vicinity as seen in Figure 4-14 below. If the average price of goods and services is approximately $3, then demand could possibly decline to Point E or somewhere in that vicinity. If the average price of goods and services is approximately $2, then demand could possibly decline to Point F or somewhere in that vicinity.

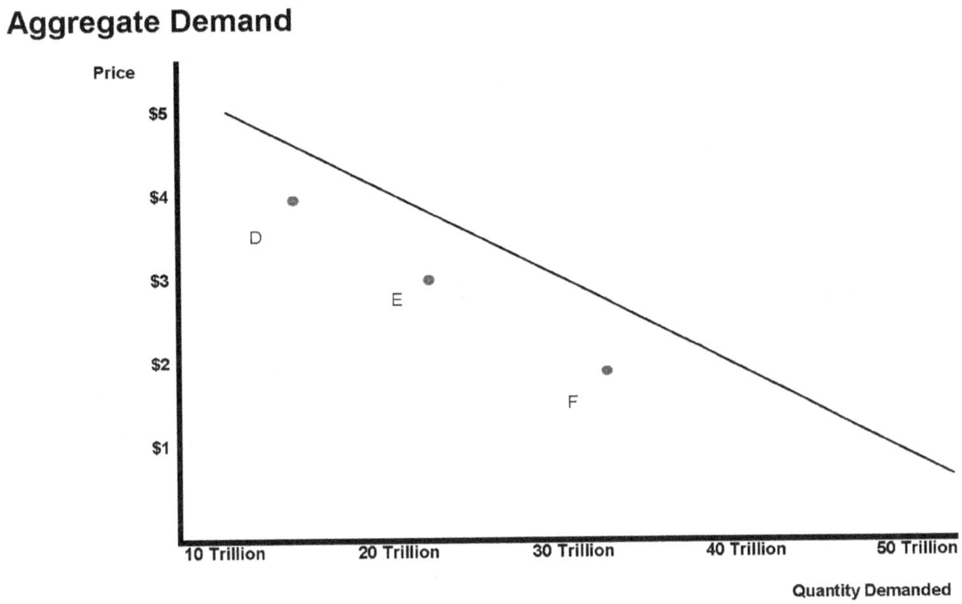

FIGURE 4.14 Aggregate Demand Curve (Taxes)

If you connect those three coordinates, you would have a new demand curve. In other words, if taxes rise, the Aggregate Demand Curve for America would shift to the left from Point A to Point C as seen in Figure 4-15. Bad news, again. That could also cause a recession.

The opposite is also true. Suppose, for example, that taxes in this country are reduced *while the prices of our products do not change*. Demand for our products would increase. Our Aggregate Demand Curve will likely shift to the right from point A to B as seen in Figure 4-16. That would increase GDP and, hopefully, bring us out of a recession or stabilize an already prosperous time. More happy news!

GOVERNMENT SPENDING

Sometimes our federal government feels that it has too much money being spent on programs that are no longer needed. Sometimes the money for such projects simply runs out. On other occasions, politicians feel that our deficit is getting too high. State governments are not permitted to engage in deficit spending, thus if their tax collection fall, they must cut their spending to balance their budgets. In any of these

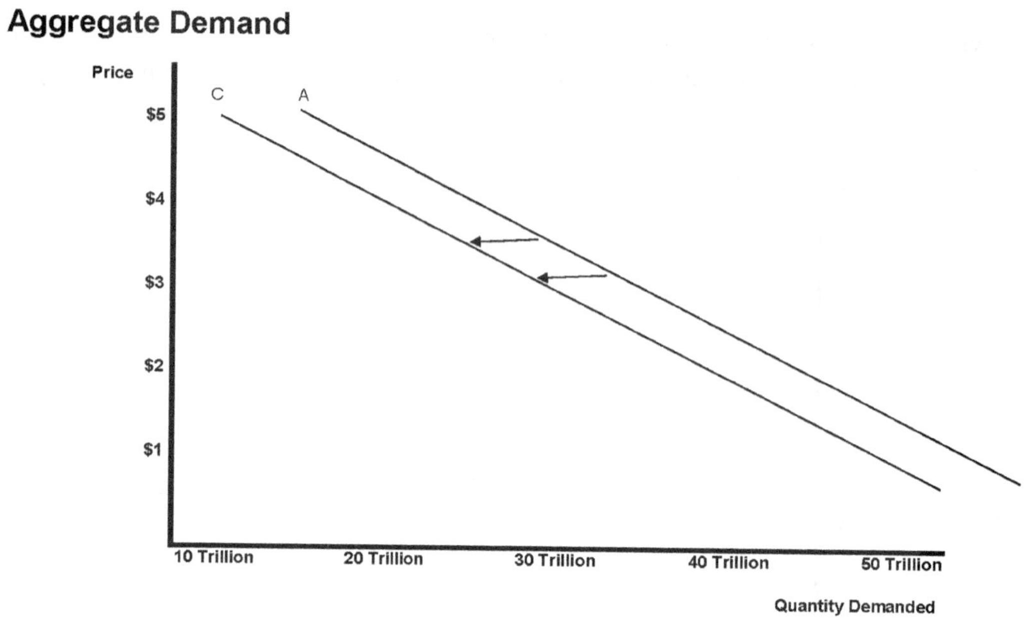

FIGURE 4.15 Aggregate Demand Curve Shift Left (Taxes)

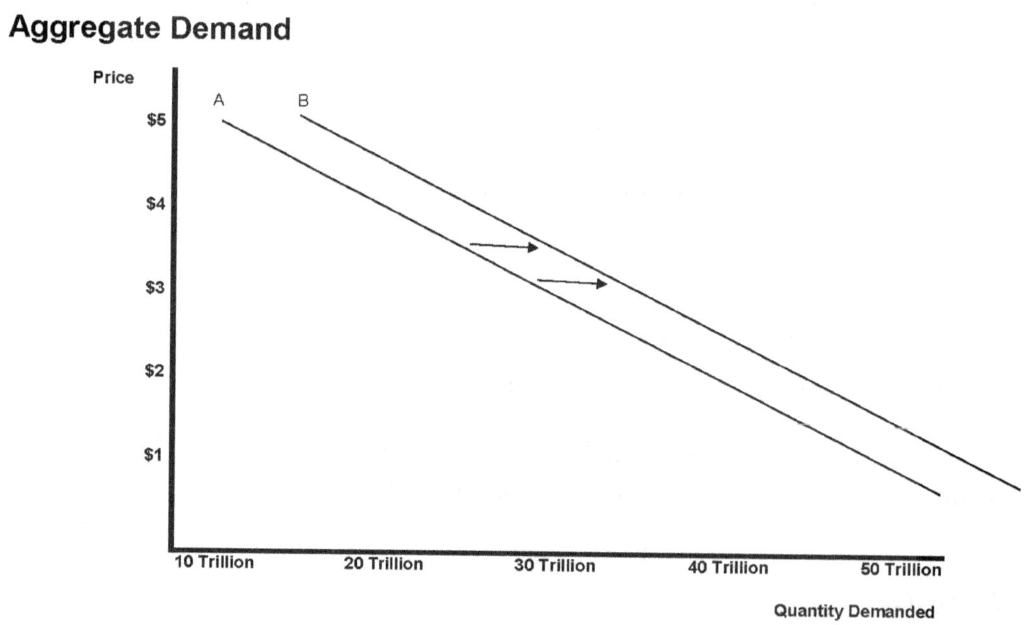

FIGURE 4.16 Aggregate Demand Curve Shift Right (Taxes)

cases, the government may decide it's time to reduce spending to help balance the budget (something that will also be discussed later). When it feels the need to reduce spending, GDP will llikely decline because government spending (G) is part of GDP or aggregate demand. If the average price of goods and services is approximately $4, then demand could possibly decline to Point D or somewhere in that vicinity as shown in Figure 4-17 below. If the average price of goods and services is approximately $3, then demand could possibly decline to Point E or somewhere in that vicinity. If the average price of goods and services is approximately $2, then demand could possibly decline to Point F or somewhere in that vicinity.

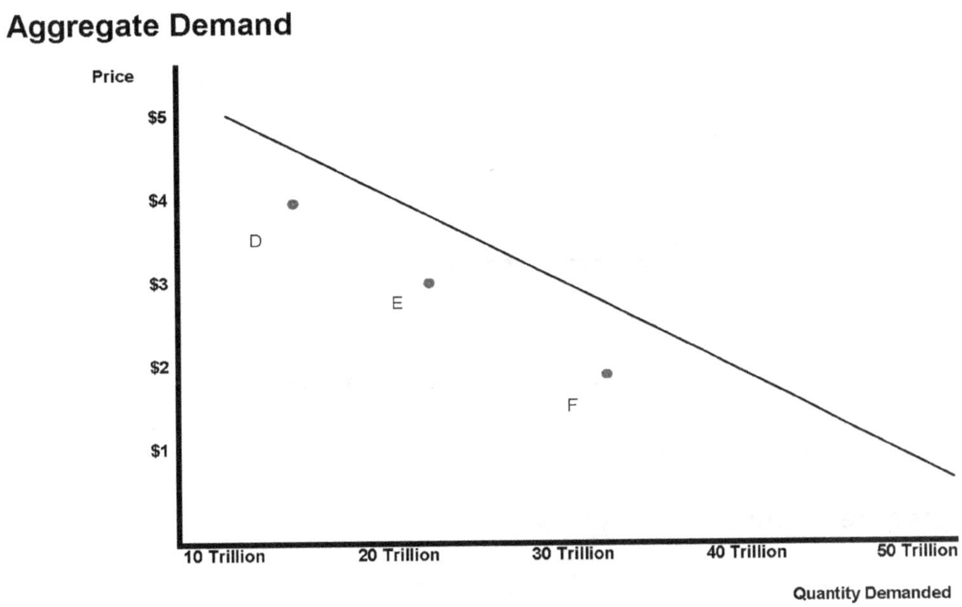

FIGURE 4.17 Aggregate Demand Curve (Government Spending)

If you connect those three coordinates, you would have a new demand curve. In other words, if government spends less, the Aggregate Demand Curve for America would most likely shift to the left from Point A to Point C as shown in Figure 4-18.

The opposite is also true. Suppose, for example, that the government decides it needs to spend more. Over the years, the federal government has often tried to buy its way into prosperity. Sometimes it finds that it needs to spend more money on projects that are very important such as unemployment benefits and welfare for the needy. It may choose to give more money to education or to grants that would help our society. Even if our prices remain the same, demand for our products would increase. Our Aggregate Demand Curve will then shift to the right from Point A to B shown in Figure 4-19. That would increase GDP and, hopefully, bring us out of a recession or stabilize an already prosperous time. Happy days are here again!

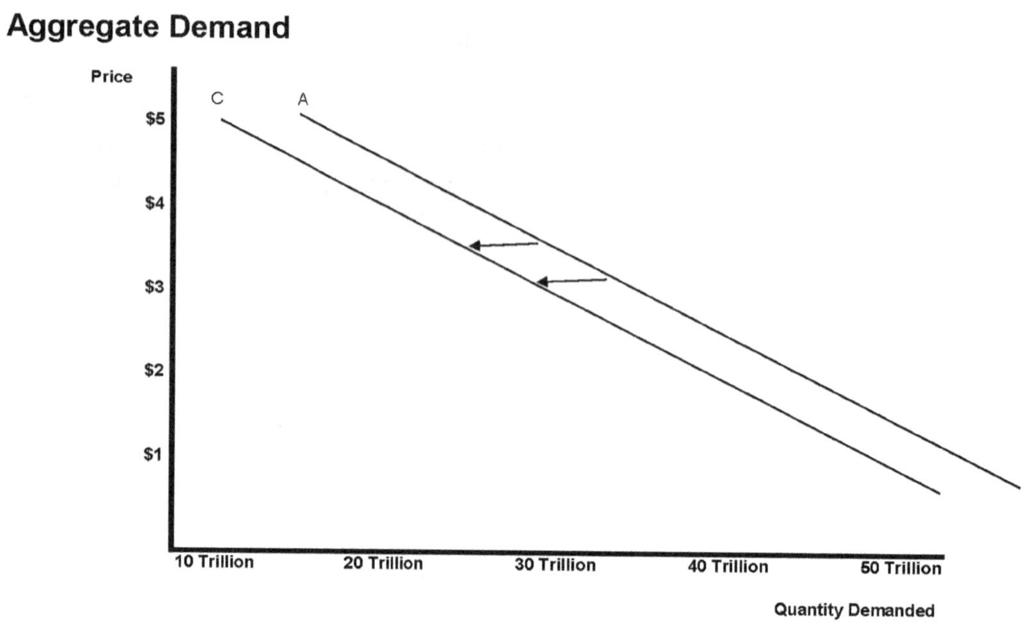

FIGURE 4.18 Aggregate Demand Curve Shift Left (Government Spending)

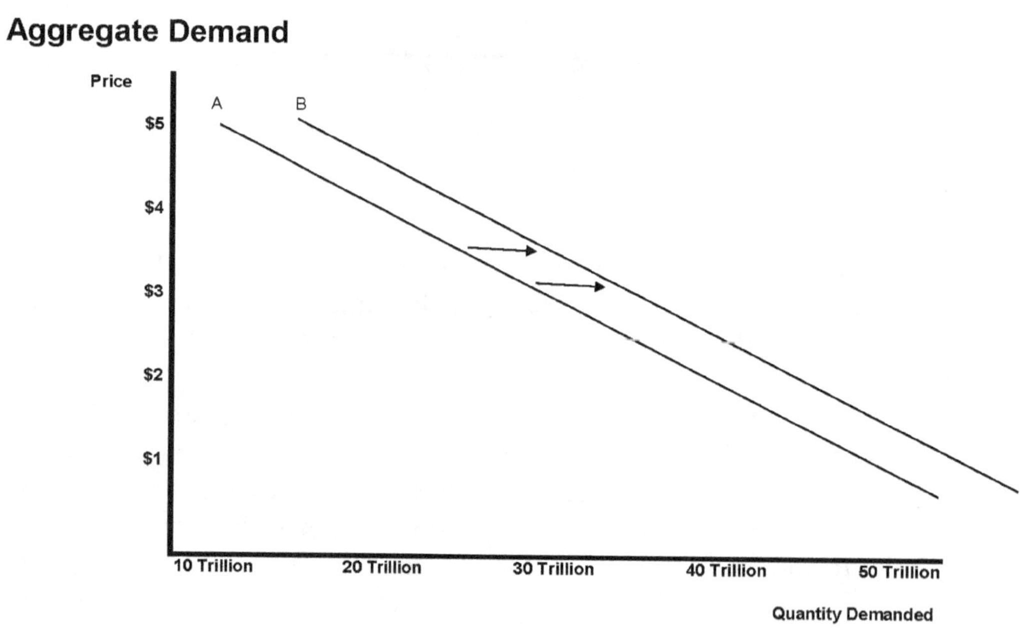

FIGURE 4.19 Aggregate Demand Curve Shift Right (Government Spending)

THE MONEY SUPPLY

There is always a certain amount of money at the disposal of people who want to spend it for day-to-day needs or to buy something more expensive such as a house, car, or a major appliance. The average person typically doesn't have the ability to pay cash for a house, car, or major appliance. Therefore, he or she often chooses to borrow in order to make those purchases. The government often takes measures to keep that kind of money less available if it feels that the economy is expanding too quickly, beyond that of the amount of available goods. . When the economy expands too quickly, it can cause shortages, which cause higher prices or ***inflation***. Therefore, the government can reduce that money supply by raising interest rates. Doing so makes loan payments higher and out of reach for many. The government can also simply print less money at the United States Mint (more on that later, too). There are other measures it can take to reduce the money supply, andthat will be discussed later.

If the government reduces the money supply, there will likely be fewer purchases of houses, cars, and appliances. If the average price of goods and services is approximately $4, then demand could possibly decline to Point D or somewhere in that vicinity as shown in Figure 4-20 below. If the average price of goods and services is approximately $3, then demand could possibly decline to Point E or somewhere in that vicinity. If the average price of goods and services is approximately $2, then demand could possibly decline to Point F or somewhere in that vicinity.

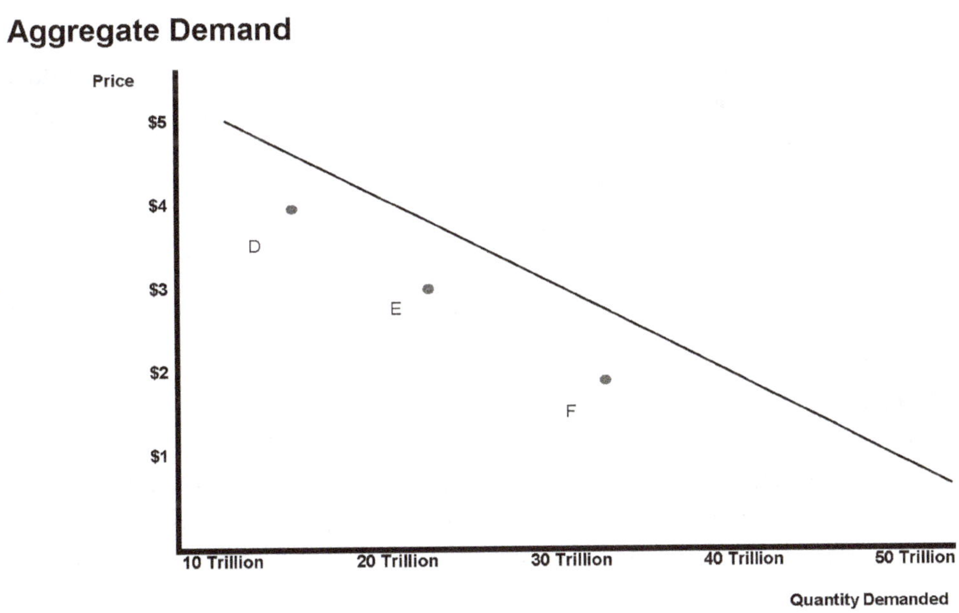

FIGURE 4.20 Aggregate Demand Curve (Money Supply)

If you connect those three coordinates, you would have a new demand curve. In other words, if government reduces the money supply, the Aggregate Demand Curve for America could shift to the left from Point A to Point C as seen in Figure 4-21.

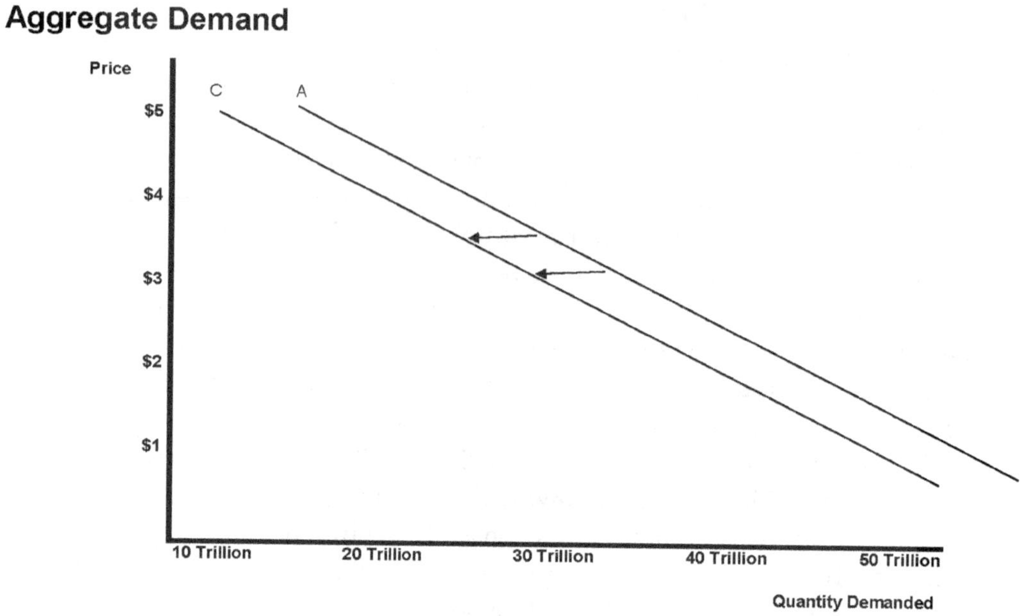

FIGURE 4.21 Aggregate Demand Curve Shift Left (Money Supply)

The opposite is also true. Suppose, for example, that the government takes measures to increase the money supply if the economy is not expanding fast enough. More people will then buy more cars, homes, and appliances. Even if our prices remain the same, demand for our products would increase. Our Aggregate Demand Curve will then shift to the right from Point A to B (see Figure 4-22). That would increase GDP and, hopefully, bring us out of a recession or stabilize an already prosperous time. Good news, good news, good news!

EXPECTATIONS

If you expect that the foreseeable future is bleak regarding the economy, and you, therefore, feel that there is a chance that you could lose your job, you will not likely buy things unless you absolutely need them. The purchases of homes, cars, and appliances will often decline.

It has often been said that when the economy gets a cold, Detroit gets pneumonia. That's because the automotive industry is a major provider of jobs there. When people

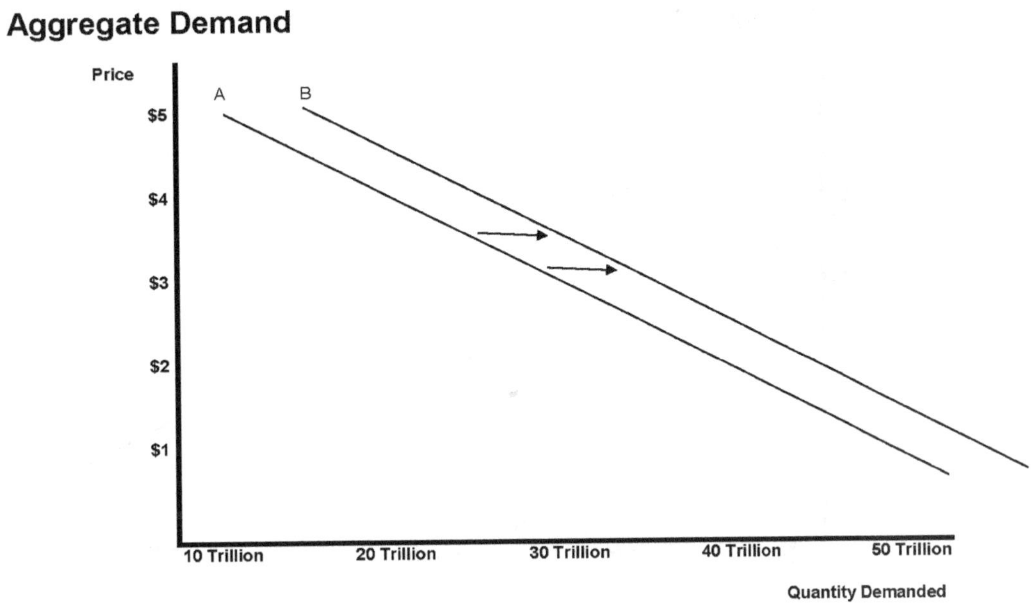

FIGURE 4.22 Aggregate Demand Curve Shift Right (Money Supply)

expect a bad economy, they stop buying cars. Detroit, as well as other towns that depend on car manufacturing jobs, will then see much higher unemployment than other parts of the country that do not rely on car sales. Businesses would also likely buy less in the way of capital equipment. They are not going to expand their output capacities if they feel that business is about to take a bad turn. An expected drop in consumer spending (C) would cause a drop in business investment (I), both of which are major components of GDP.

If the average price of goods and services is approximately $4, then demand could possibly decline to Point D or somewhere in that vicinity as illustrated in Figure 4-23. If the average price of goods and services is approximately $3, then demand could possibly decline to Point E or somewhere in that vicinity. If the average price of goods and services is approximately $2, then demand could possibly decline to Point F or somewhere in that vicinity.

If you connect those three coordinates, you would have a new demand curve. In other words, if expectations for the foreseeable future of our economy are pessimistic, then the Aggregate Demand Curve for America would shift to the left from Point A to Point C shown in Figure 4-24.

The opposite is also true. Suppose, for example, the outlook of the economy looks very good. More people may then buy cars, homes, and appliances. Businesses would also likely buy more in the way of capital equipment. If they feel that higher spending by consumers is here to stay in the future, they will buy capital equipment to expand output in order to cash in on consumers' increase in spending. An expected

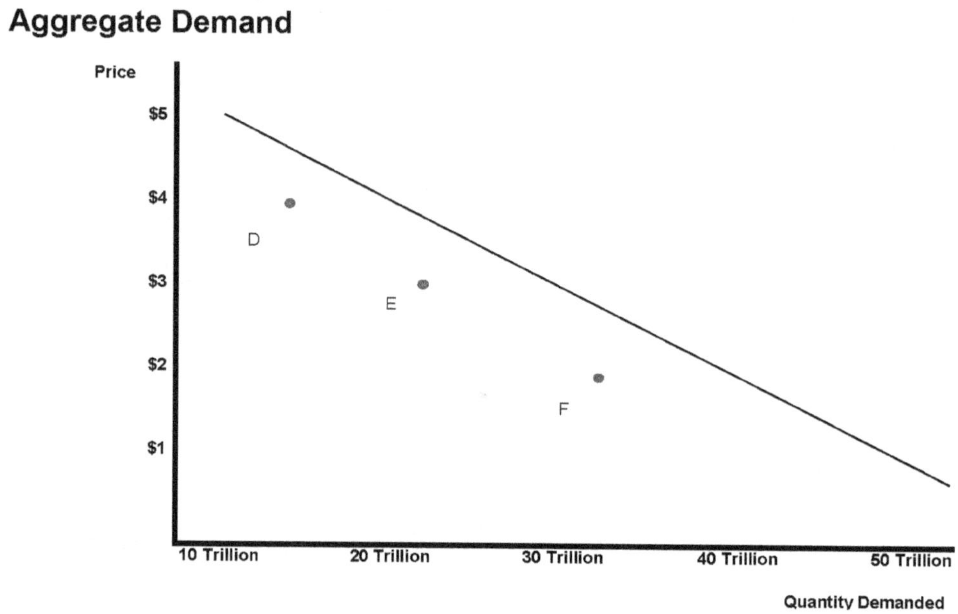

FIGURE 4.23 Aggregate Demand Curve (Expectactions)

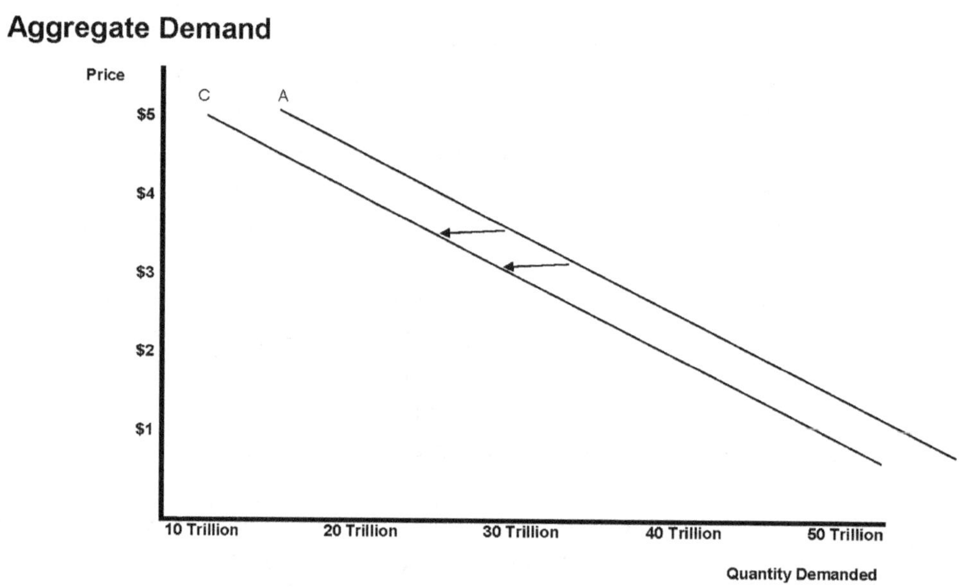

FIGURE 4.24 Aggregate Demand Curve Shift Left (Expectactions)

increase in consumer spending (C) could cause an increase in business investment (I), both of which are major components of GDP.

Even if our prices remain the same, demand for our products would increase. Our Aggregate Demand Curve will then shift to the right from Point A to B as you can see in Figure 4-25. That would increase GDP, and, you guessed it, hopefully, bring us out of a recession or stabilize an already prosperous time. More good news!

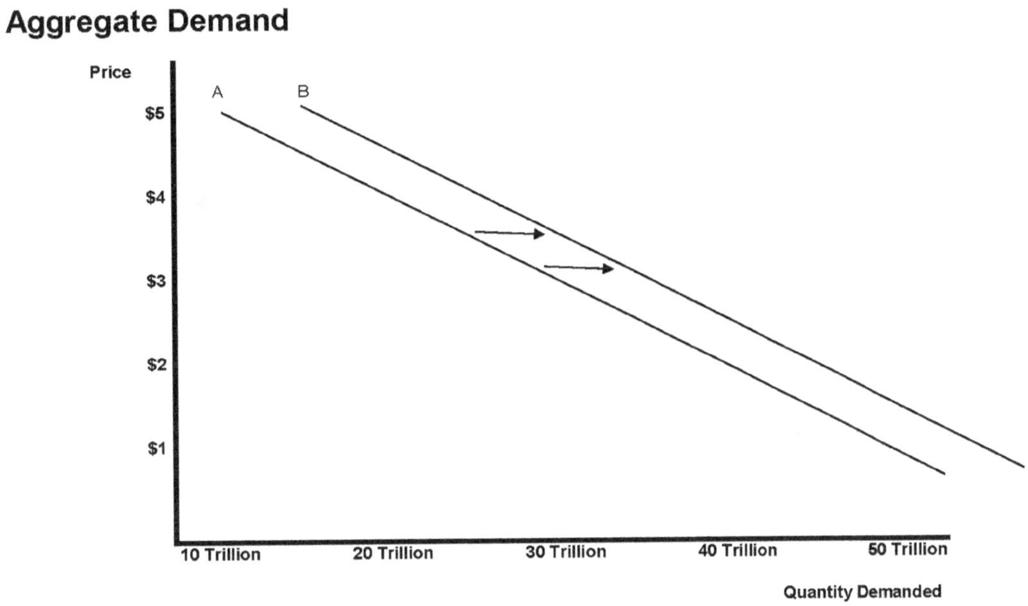

FIGURE 4.25 Aggregate Demand Curve Shift Right (Expectactions)

NUMBER OF BUYERS

Many believe that a higher population can hurt society, but when our population declines, so, too, does the number of potential buyers of our goods and services, bringing aggregate demand down.

If the average price of goods and services is approximately $4, then demand could possibly decline to Point D or somewhere in that vicinity as seen in Figure 4-26. If the average price of goods and services is approximately $3, then demand could possibly decline to the Point E or somewhere in that vicinity. Do you feel like you've heard this before? If the average price of goods and services is approximately $2, then demand could possibly decline to the Point F or somewhere in that vicinity.

If you connect those three coordinates, you would have a new demand curve. In other words, if population decreases, the Aggregate Demand Curve for America would shift to the left from Point A to Point C as shown in Figure 4-27.

The opposite is also true. Suppose, for example, that we see a major increase in population. Even if our prices remain the same, demand for our products would increase. Our Aggregate Demand Curve will then shift to the right from Point A to B. That would increase GDP and make our economy better or more stable as illustrated in Figure 4-28.

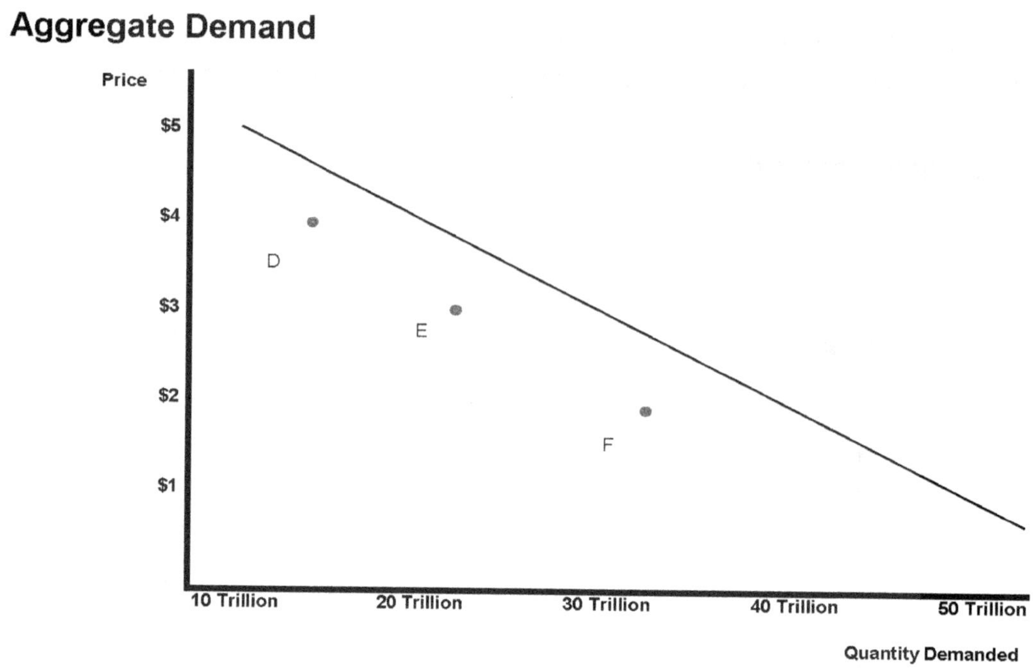

FIGURE 4.26 Aggregate Demand Curve (Number of Buyers)

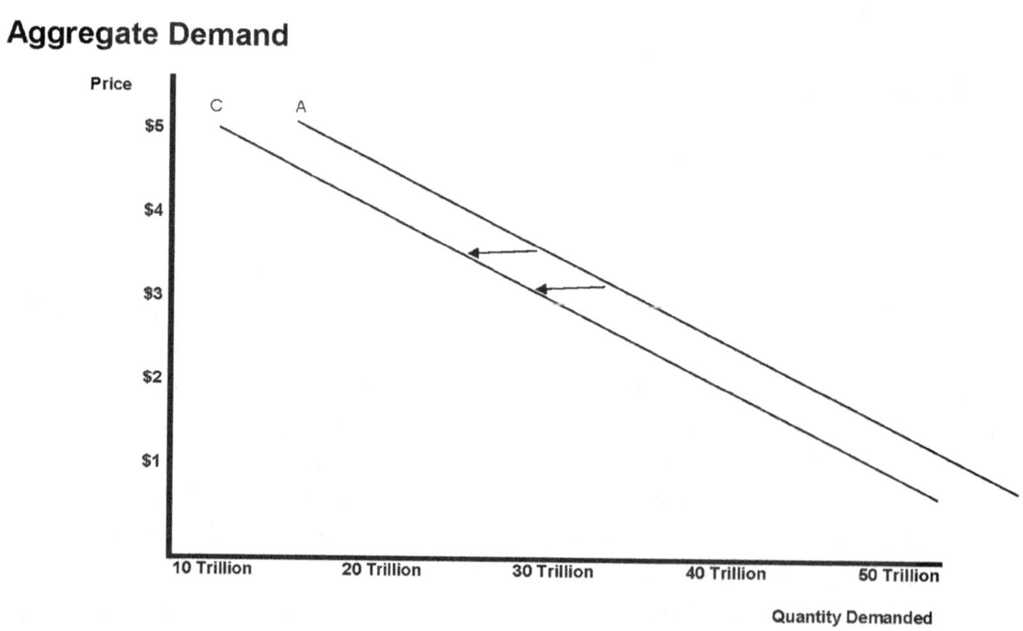

FIGURE 4.27 Aggregate Demand Curve Shift Left (Number of Buyers)

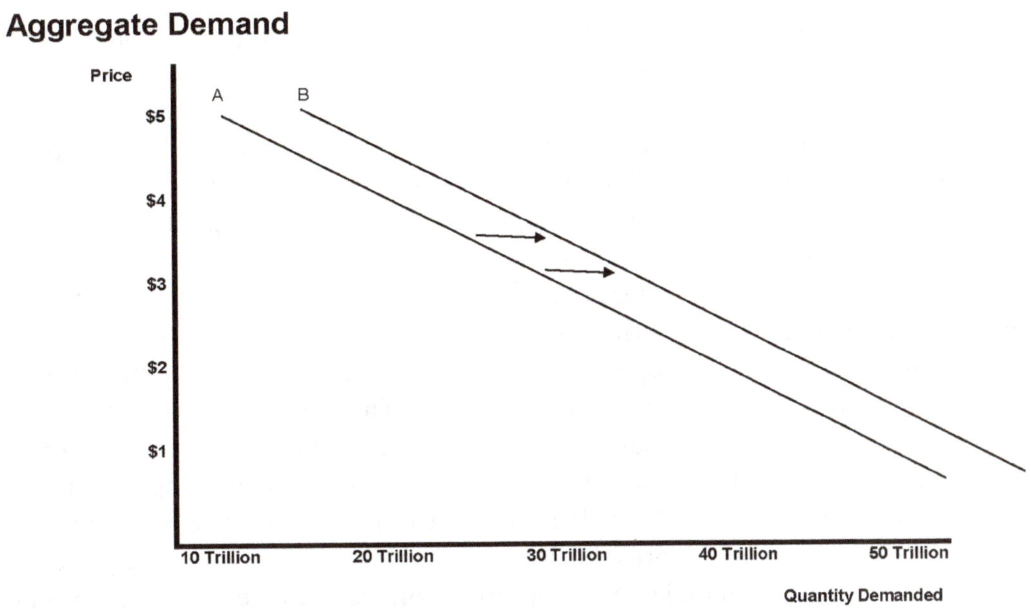

FIGURE 4.28 Aggregate Demand Curve Shift Right (Number of Buyers)

SUMMARY OF DETERMINANTS OF DEMAND

- Prices of producers move demand along the Aggregate Demand Curve.
- The remaining determinants of overall demand will shift the curve. Those determinants are mainly:
  - Tastes
  - Income
  - Other Goods (Substitute and Complementary)
  - Lower/Higher Taxes
  - More/Less Government Spending
  - More/Less Money Injected into the Money Supply
  - Expectations
  - Number of Buyers

WHEN DEMAND IS THE INDEPENDENT VARIABLE

Up until now, we have been discussing what will happen to demand if prices and other determinants of demand would change.

What happens to prices, however, when demand is the independent variable? In other words, what happens to prices when demand changes?

If demand rises, it will typically drive prices up, as well. One of the reasons for this is that higher demand can possibly create a shortage if producers can't keep up with that demand. As mentioned earlier, shortages cause higher prices and/or inflation. Another reason is that when a product is popular, many want to get their fair share of it. People don't want to be left out. If everyone is buying a product, it's only wise in the minds of many that they want to be in with everyone else during such a fad. Such rushes to buy hot products drive up prices.

There have been times when stocks, for example, had high prices, not so much because they were good investments but because the other available investments, such as bonds, were very unpopular. Therefore, many investors chose stocks as the lesser evil, driving up the prices, erroneously making people think that those stocks were making great returns.

The opposite is also true. When demand for things fall, there is often a surplus of goods in warehouses and stores. Stores start having sales to get those unpopular goods out of their stores to make room for more. During the recession of 2008, many businesses had to lower their prices to entice buyers to come back to them because so many people were out of work. Housing during that time also saw prices plummet. People knew that demand for them was very low; therefore, people chose not buy homes until they believed that housing prices had bottomed out. They wanted to get the lowest prices possible.

TABLE 4.3

High Demand Causes High Prices	Low Demand Causes Low Prices

SUPPLY

Now we move our discussion toward the concept of supply.

If a person is to ***supply*** something, that means that he or she is willing and able supply it, produce it, or make it available for someone (most likely for purchase).

In order to supply something, therefore, you must:

1. Be willing to supply/produce it.
2. Be able to supply/produce it.
3. Be prepared to take the action to supply/produce it.

Supply is defined as the ability and willingness to sell or produce given quantities of a good or service at a given price (Ceteris Paribus).

The ***law of supply*** says that if the price that people are willing to pay a producer goes up, the producer is likely to supply more. It's the price signal. Higher prices paid to you for what you do motivates you to produce more. Not only are you motivated to do so but the higher price paid to you makes it more likely that you can produce it at a higher profit.

The opposite is also true. If people are no longer willing to pay you a high price for what you produce, you are not motivated to produce as much. In fact, you may not even be able to afford to produce at all without losing money.

Let's return to the pizza producer.

If you feel that you would be willing to supply perhaps 50,000 slices of pizza during any given year if people are willing to pay you $5 for each of them, then the grid below may be a schedule that would describe how much you would be willing to supply as the market price for your pizza slices changes. This would be the ***firm's supply***.

TABLE 4.4A Price Per Slice

PRICE PER SLICE	$5	$4	$3	$2	$1
DEMAND	50,000	40,000	30,000	20,000	10,000

Now assume again that there are 10,000 pizza parlors in the country. The schedule below would show how much pizza would be supplied in our country. This would be known as the ***market supply*** for the pizza industry.

TABLE 4.4B Price Per Slice

PRICE PER SLICE	$5	$4	$3	$2	$1
DEMAND	500,000,000	400,000,000	300,000,000	200,000,000	100,000,000

Now assume that there are 100,000 different industries with average prices such as these in the country. The schedule below would show how much would be supplied in our country's entire economy. This would be known as the ***aggregate supply*** for our entire country. Aggregate supply, therefore, is the same as gross domestic product (GDP) as long as all that is supplied is also demanded.

TABLE 4.5 Price Per Unit

AVERAGE PRICE PER UNIT	$5	$4	$3	$2	$1
DEMAND	50 Trillion	40 Trillion	30 Trillion	20 Trillion	10 Trillion

If we were to graph the aggregate supply from the schedule above, it would create what we would call the Aggregate Supply Curve, which would look something like Figure 4-29.

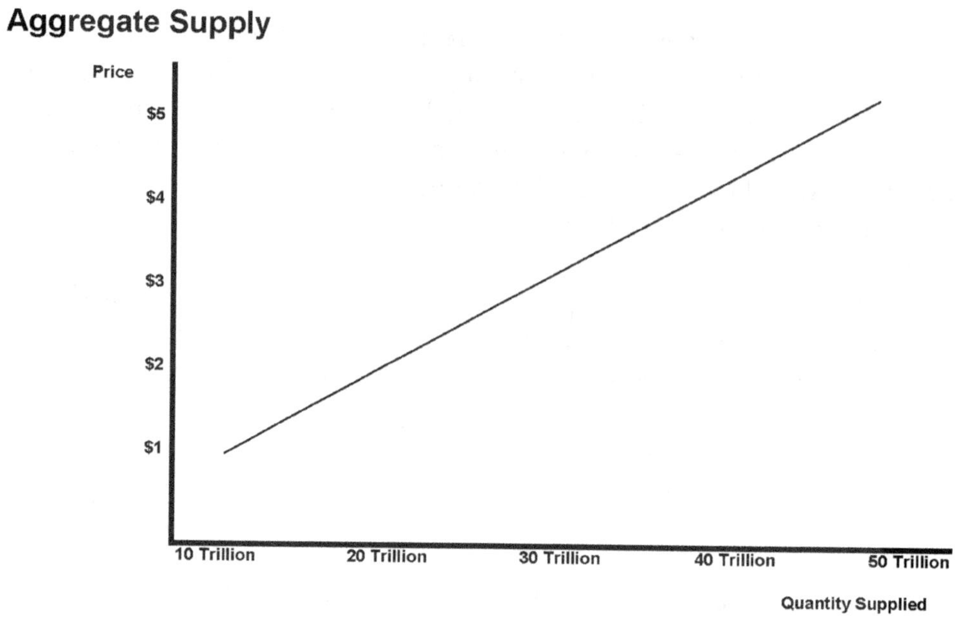

FIGURE 4.29 Aggregate Supply Curve

Therefore, the first major determinant of supply is the price that consumers are willing to pay producers. If the average price paid to all producers drops from $5 each down to $4 each, the aggregate supply would decrease to $40 trillion. As the average prices in our country would continue to change, either going down or up, the aggregate supply would move up and down *along* the Aggregate Supply Curve. Therefore, the only thing that causes aggregate supply to move along the curve is a change in the average price paid to producers in this country.

There are other determinants of supply besides that of the prices paid to producers.

TECHNOLOGY

Suppose, for example, that people around the country begin to find more efficient ways to increase their output by the use of technology. Even if the market prices paid to producers remain the same, supply for our products would increase. If the average price paid for our goods and services is approximately $4, then supply could possibly increase to Point G or somewhere in that vicinity as seen in Figure 4-30. If the average price paid for goods and services is approximately $3, then supply could possibly increase to Point H or somewhere in that vicinity. If the average price paid for goods and services is approximately $2, then supply could possibly increase to Point I or somewhere in that vicinity.

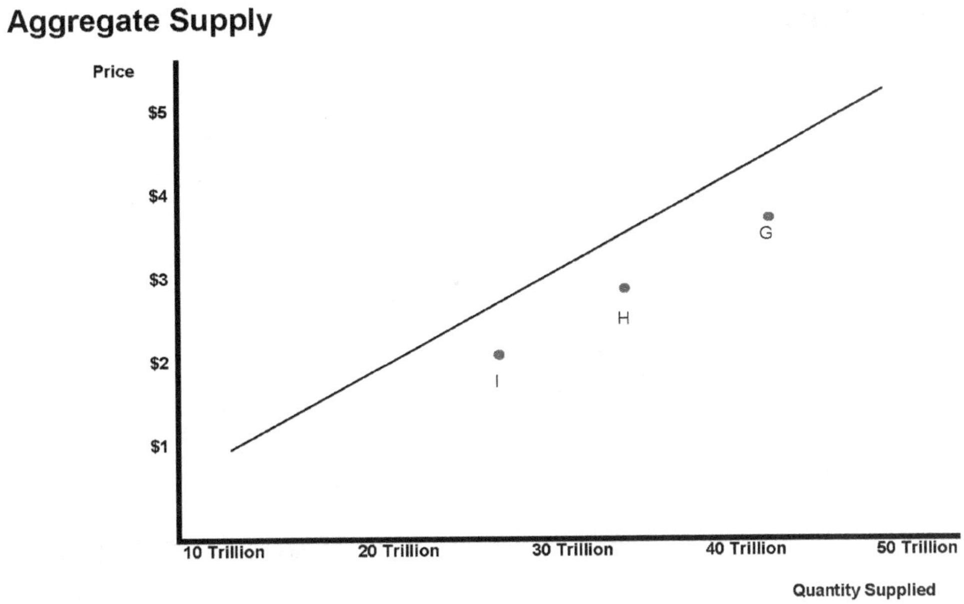

FIGURE 4.30 Aggregate Supply Curve (Technology)

If you connect those three coordinates, you would have a new supply curve. The supply curve has, thus, been shifted outward or to the right, which is what you see in Figure 4-31. In other words, if more technology is used in our country, supply (or output) would increase from Point X to Point Y. That is good news for consumers. They are less likely to face shortages of goods and services, therefore, there is a good chance that prices will remain stable. It also is good news for workers because as producers supply more goods, they will likely hire more workers to do it, along with the purchase of capital equipment. More production helps the economy. Also remember that aggregate supply can equal GDP.

Some may ask what would make the Aggregate Supply Curve shift to the left as a result of a change in technology. The only time that technology would drive the supply curve to the left, or reduce supply, would be if existing technology is abandoned or removed from our businesses, but this is not likely to happen.

ECONOMIC MYTH #5	Technology and automation reduces employment.

There are those who believe that more machinery, automation, and technology put people out of work. In reality, technology and automation have created far more jobs

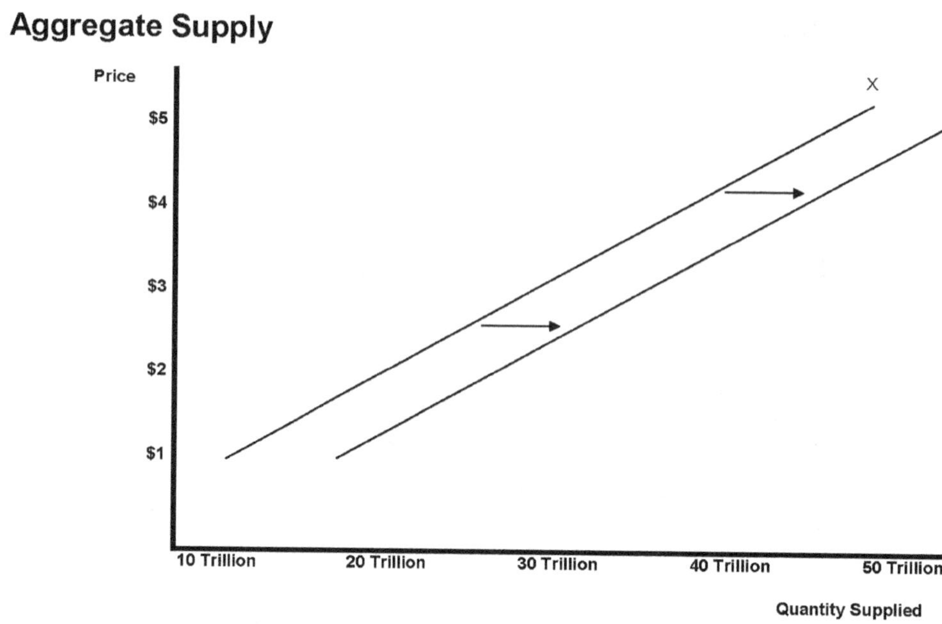

FIGURE 4.31 Aggregate Supply Curve Shift Right (Technology)

than they have cost. There are three reasons for this. First, machinery and technology aren't free. Businesses' purchases of machines, computers, and software create jobs. Second, many American firms would have closed their doors by now without technology and machinery. We are in a global economy, and firms in other countries use them all the time. If we don't match their use of it, their costs will be well below ours, and we could never compete. Finally, businesses obtain technology, not to put people out of work but to make them more productive. They usually want to get more units produced from the same number of workers, rather than the same amount of output from fewer workers. More output per worker keeps costs down so that your employer can stay in business.

It is also important to note here that not only do economists tell us that technology creates more and not fewer jobs, but those jobs pay more than the jobs of yesteryear. Using this technology requires more skills that make workers more valuable and thus eligible for higher pay. Many workers who lose jobs to technology often lose them when they refuse to learn the newer skills to use the new technology.

FACTOR COSTS

If the cost of doing business declines, that is an indication that the ***factor costs*** (costs of the factors of production such as land, labor, and capital), which are the costs of our resources, are going to fall, as well. That's good news for producers because their profits per unit of output can rise even if their prices don't. They are then motivated to produce and supply more. If the average price paid for our goods and services is approximately $4, then supply could possibly increase to Point G or somewhere in that vicinity as shown in Figure 4-32. If the average price paid for goods and services is approximately $3, then supply could possibly increase to Point H or somewhere in that vicinity. If the average price paid for goods and services is approximately $2, then supply could possibly increase to Point I or somewhere in that vicinity.

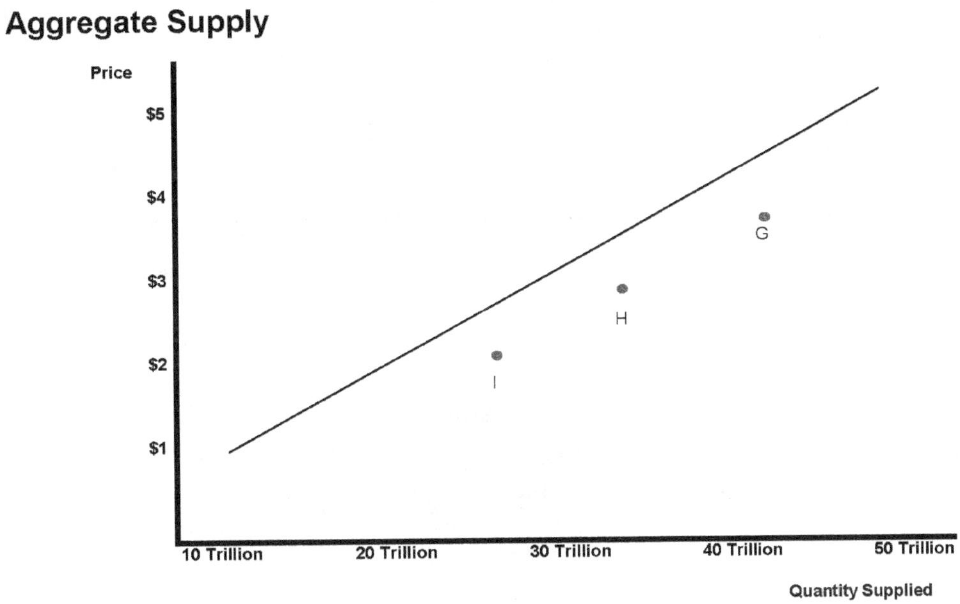

FIGURE 4.32 Aggregate Supply Curve (Factor Costs)

If you connect those three coordinates, you would have a new supply curve. In other words, if more and better technology is available and used by producers in our country, supply (or output) would increase, thus, shifting the Aggregate Supply Curve to the right from Point X to Point Y as you can see in Figure 4-33. That is good news for consumers and workers. Again, more output usually means that more jobs may be created in order to make the increase in output possible.

The opposite is also true. If the cost of doing business goes up, that is an indication that the costs of factors of production are going to rise, as well. If producers aren't being paid higher prices, their profits for each unit of production they make are going to fall. When producers' profits per unit of production fall, they are then less motivated to produce and the Aggregate Supply Curve would be shifted to the left from Point X to Point Z as seen in Figure 4-34.

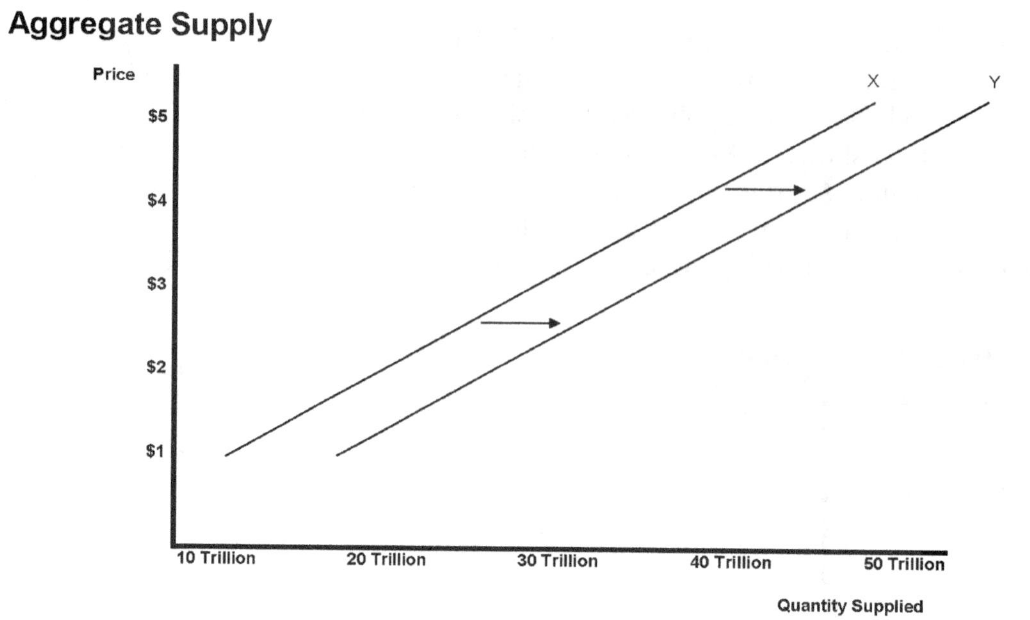

FIGURE 4.33 Aggregate Supply Curve Shift Right (Factor Costs)

That is bad news for both consumers and workers. With a cut in production (or supply), fewer goods are available, and shortages can result; thus, higher prices may ensue. Cuts in production also cause layoffs and unemployment.

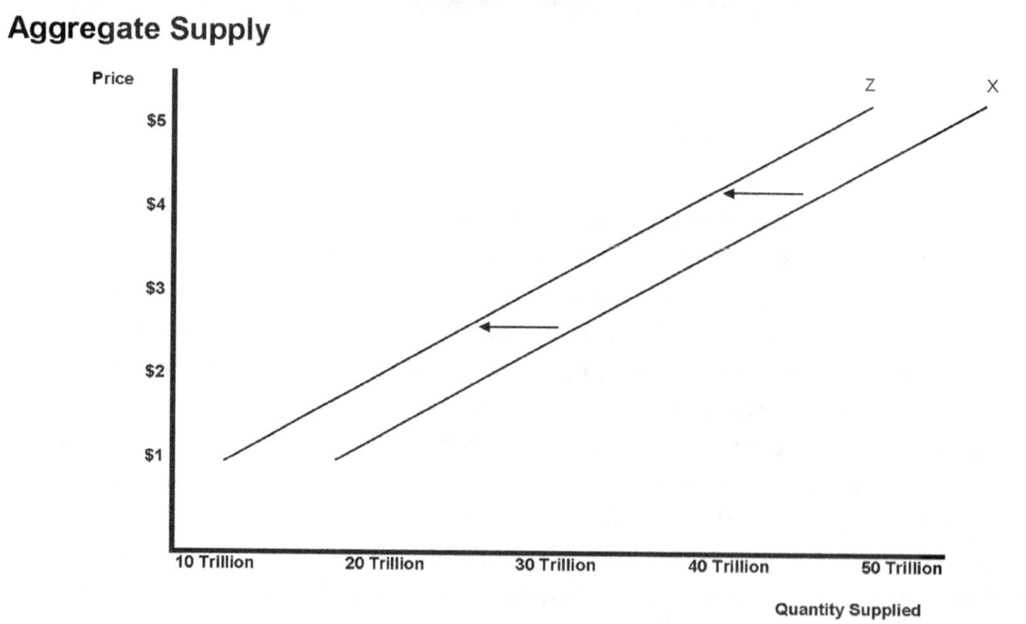

FIGURE 4.34 Aggregate Supply Curve Shift Left (Factor Costs)

TAXES

ECONOMIC MYTH #6	Lowering taxes for businesses is wrong as it gives big corporate fat cats more money while not giving any benefit to the middle class.

Many people oppose the lowering of taxes for businesses. They fear that businesses would not be paying their fair share of taxes. Something that must be considered here is that, first, 80% of the businesses in existence in this country are *small businesses*. They are not "big corporate fat cats" who crush the middle class. The overwhelming majority of these businesses are run by small owners, often running a family business and the like. Second, if the country is experiencing high unemployment, the lowering of taxes can put many of these unemployed people back to work.

Lower taxes are good motivators for producers to increase output. Even if the price that businesses collect per unit of sale stays the same, they get to keep more of the profits they earn. Politicians of both political parties have proposed legislation, voted for legislation, and implemented legislation granting tax cuts for businesses over the years, especially during times of high unemployment.

If the average price paid for our goods and services is approximately $4, then supply could possibly increase to Point G or somewhere in that vicinity as shown in Figure 4-35. If the average price paid for goods and services is approximately $3, then

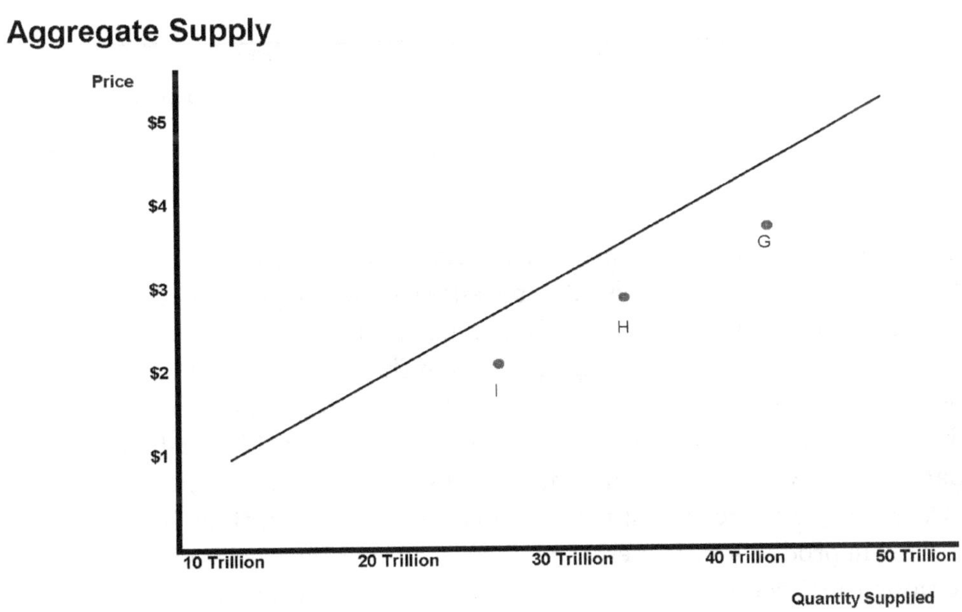

FIGURE 4.35 Aggregate Supply Curve (Taxes)

supply could possibly increase to point H or somewhere in that vicinity. If the average price paid for goods and services is approximately $2, then supply could possibly increase to the point of Point I or somewhere in that vicinity.

If you connect those three coordinates, you would have a new supply curve, shifting the Aggregate Supply Curve to the right from Point X to Point Y as seen in Figure 4-36. In other words, if taxes are lowered by the government, supply (or output) would increase. Once again, that is good news for consumers and workers. More output leads to more available goods, lower prices, and more jobs.

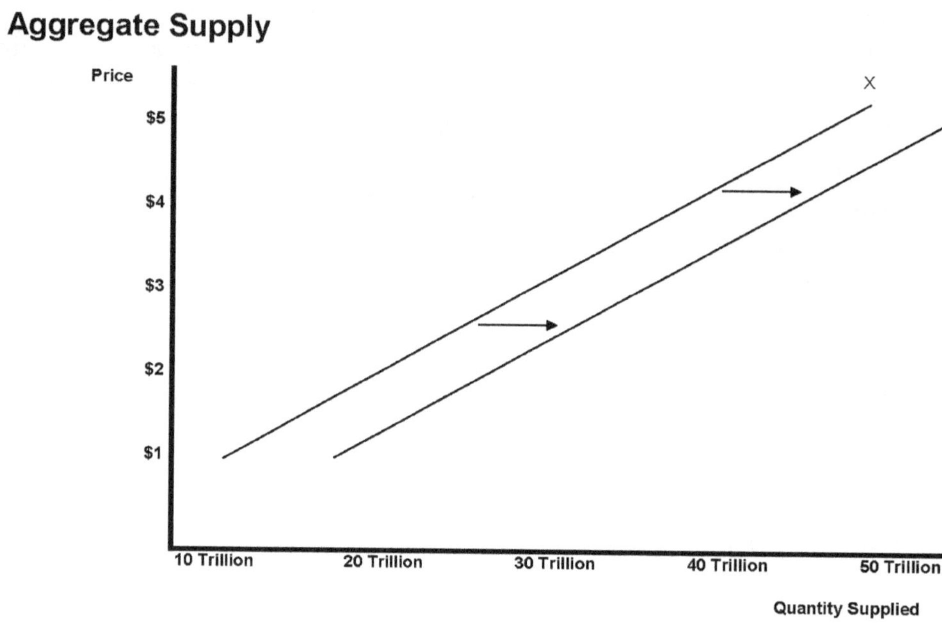

FIGURE 4.36 Aggregate Supply Curve Shift Right (Taxes)

The opposite is also true. When the government raises taxes, producers are less motivated to supply goods and services because they don't get to keep as much of their profits. Some say, "Why bother working so hard and producing so much if the government is going to take such a huge portion of the profits away?" As a result, there is a very strong chance that production will be cut. That would shift the Aggregate Supply Curve to the left from Point X to Point Z as seen in Figure 4-37.

That is bad news for both consumers and workers. With a cut in production (or supply), fewer goods are available and shortages can begin; thus, higher prices may ensue. Cuts in production, as mentioned before, also cause layoffs and unemployment. At the same time, people are often less inclined to work that extra job at night or on the weekends with higher taxes. The middle class can then be hurt, too. When fewer people are willing to supply their labor hours to businesses, this can cause a drop in supply, as well, because businesses will have fewer people to fill existing positions. Fewer people working also means that income will decline, but cause a decline in GDP or aggregate demand.

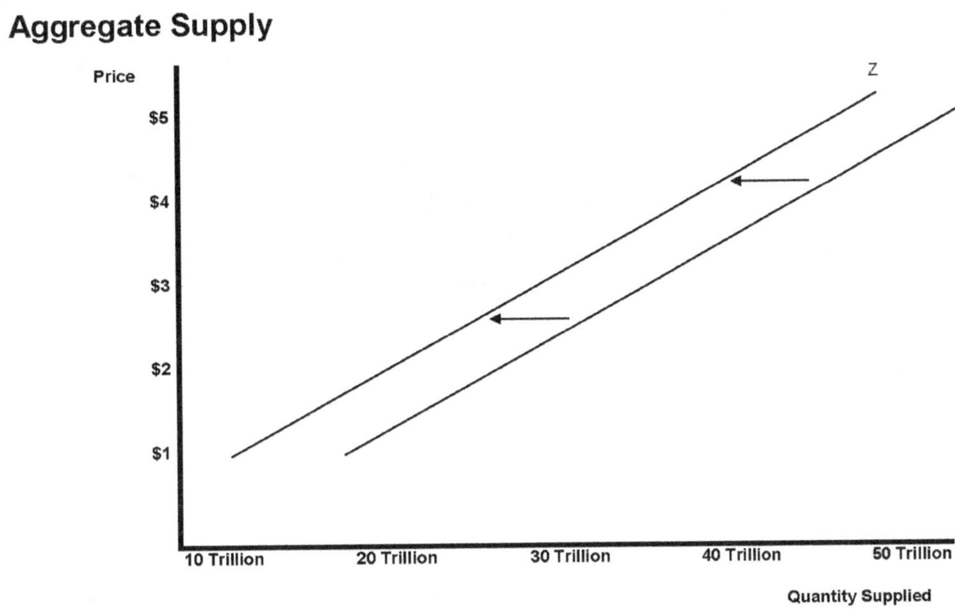

FIGURE 4.37 Aggregate Supply Curve Shift Left (Taxes)

REGULATIONS

ECONOMIC MYTH #7	Deregulation only makes society less safe.

Deregulation is an attempt to remove any and all of the *unreasonable*, unnecessary regulations that are imposed by governments that are not effective. Deregulation is not always a bad thing as long as the regulations that have been cut back or removed have been proven to be ineffective toward making society better. Many regulations were removed by the government over the years, and it actually helped rather than hurt society.

Both political parties have sponsored a great deal of deregulation. Jimmy Carter was the president who really began a wave of deregulation in many industries, and that wave has continued through many presidential administrations since.

It is often difficult and expensive to comply with many of the regulations imposed by governments over the years. If doing so makes producers feel that it just isn't worth the trouble to produce their products or services, they will simply stop producing. When the government chooses to ease regulations, producers are often inclined to increase output. Even if the price collected per unit of sale stays the same, fewer regulations make it more likely that producers can more afford to products and/or that it will be easier to produce.

If the average price paid for our goods and services is approximately $4, then supply could possibly increase to Point G or somewhere in that vicinity as you can see in Figure 4-38. If the average price paid for goods and services is approximately $3, then supply could possibly increase to Point H or somewhere in that vicinity. If the average price paid for goods and services is approximately $2, then supply could possibly increase to Point I or somewhere in that vicinity.

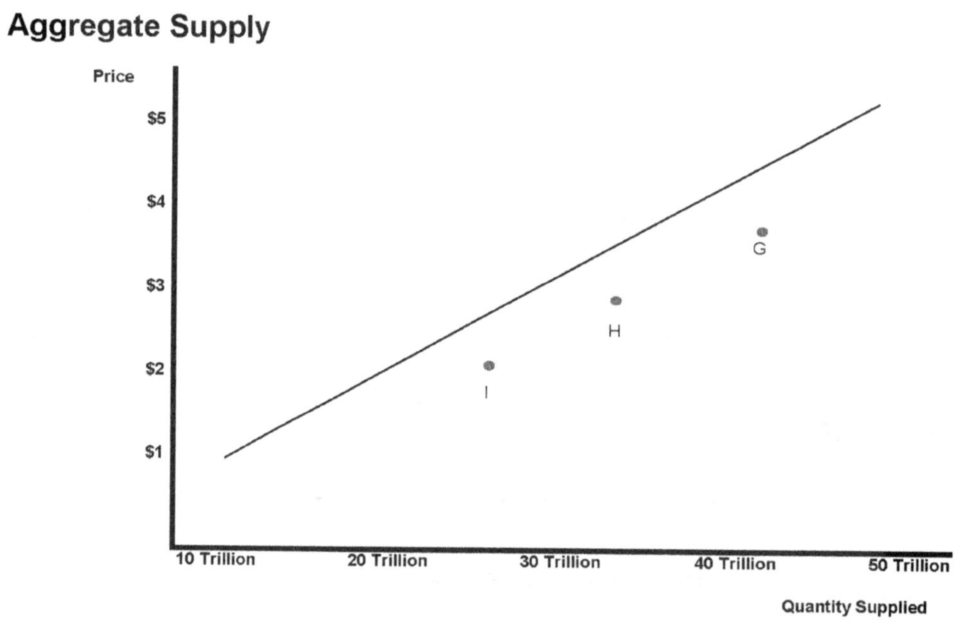

FIGURE 4.38 Aggregate Supply Curve (Regulations)

If you connect those three coordinates, you would have a new supply curve, thus, shifting the Aggregate Supply Curve to the right from Point X to Point Y a seen in Figure 4-39. In other words, deregulation in our country can help supply (or output) to increase. You guessed it. Once again, that is good news for consumers and workers.

The opposite is also true. When the government imposes more regulations, producers are less motivated to supply goods, and there is a very strong chance that production will be cut. That would shift the Aggregate Supply Curve to the left from Point X to Point Z as seen in Figure 4-40.

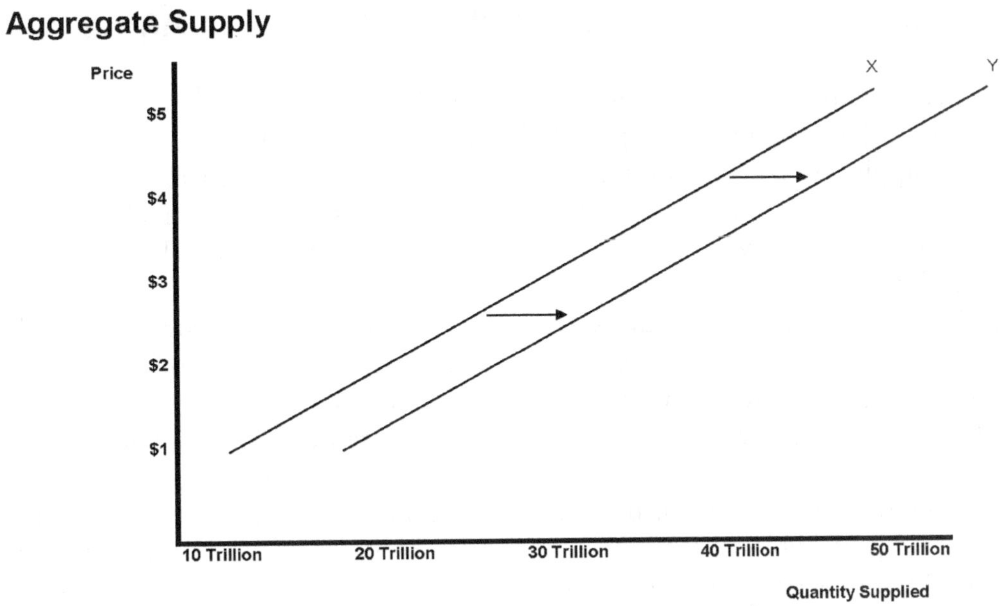

FIGURE 4.39 Aggregate Supply Curve Shift Right (Regulations)

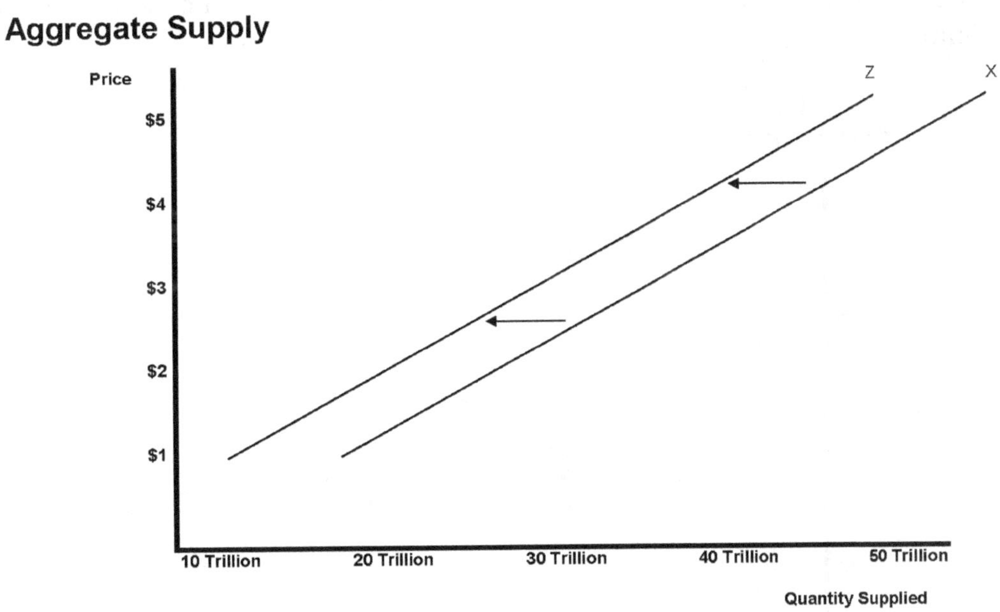

FIGURE 4.40 Aggregate Supply Curve Shift Left (Regulations)

Once again, both consumers and workers may suffer. With a cut in production (or supply), fewer goods are available, and shortages and, thus, higher prices may again ensue. Cuts in production also cause layoffs and unemployment.

SKILLS/KNOWLEDGE AND MAXIMIZATION OF THE USE OF HUMAN CAPITAL

People are more productive if they are better at doing their jobs. They can become better at their jobs and more competent through education and training. When this happens, supply will increase in this country. That is one of the reasons government often takes measures to make sure that our education system effectively increases skills. It puts people to work who otherwise could not find a job if they lacked the skills needed.

President Bill Clinton gave huge tax breaks to corporations and small businesses who opted to pay the tuition charged to their employees who were enrolled in colleges to get their degrees. Many economists agree that it created a significant increase in output, thus, keeping prices stable and making sure that all consumers had the goods they needed.

If the average price paid for our goods and services is approximately $4, then supply could possibly increase to Point G or somewhere in that vicinity as is illustrated in Figure 4-41 as a result of better education and training. If the average price paid for goods and services is approximately $3, then supply could possibly increase to Point H or somewhere in that vicinity. If the average price paid for goods and services is approximately $2, then supply could possibly increase to Point I or somewhere in that vicinity.

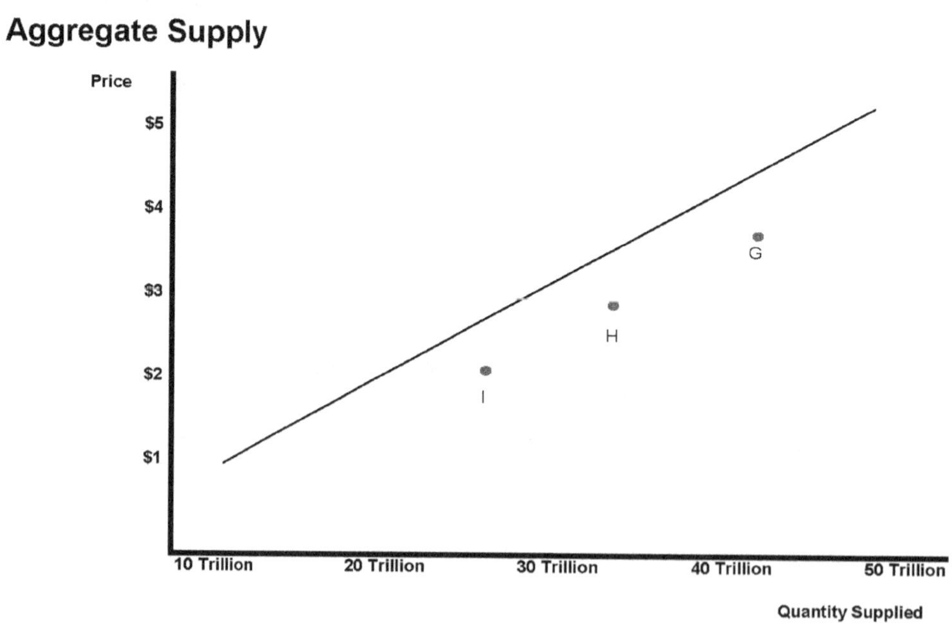

FIGURE 4.41 Aggregate Supply Curve (Skills/Knowledge/Human Capital)

If you connect those three coordinates, you would have a new supply curve. In other words, if more and better education and training is utilized in our country, supply (or output) would increase, thus, shifting the Aggregate Supply Curve to the right from Point X to Point Y which is shown in Figure 4-42. Once again, that is good news for consumers and workers.

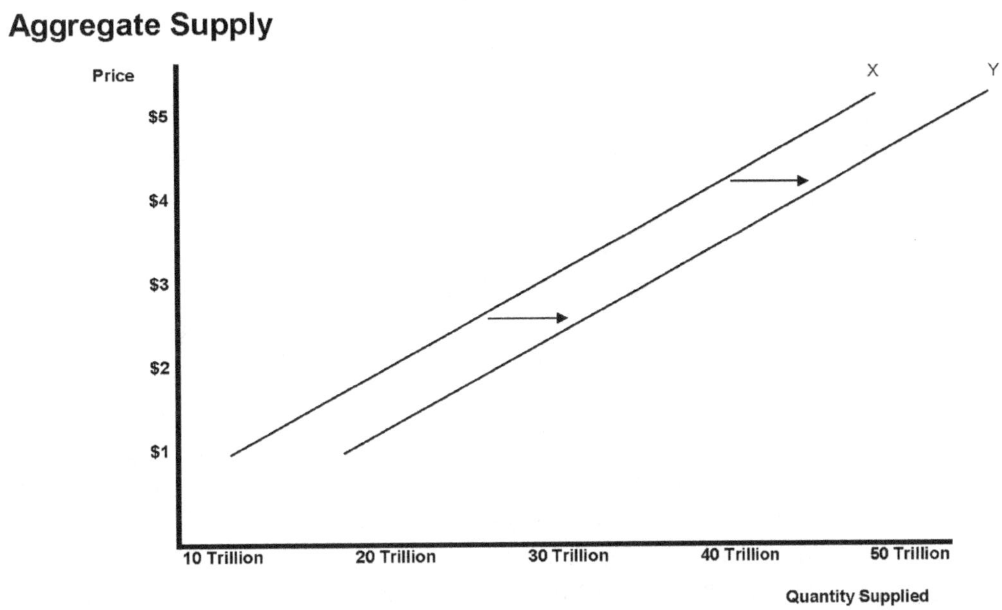

FIGURE 4.42 Aggregate Supply Curve Shift Right (Skills/Knowledge/Human Capital)

The opposite is also true. When the government chooses to reduce funding of education, of if less training and education is available to our workforce, it tends to become less efficient. Output or supply is then reduced, and the Aggregate Supply Curve would shift left from Point X to Point Y as seen in Figure 4-43. It also becomes more difficult for people to find jobs if they lack the skills needed to get employment.

That is bad news for both consumers and workers for reasons mentioned earlier.

SUBSIDIES

There are some industries that cannot get the output needed because they are so competitive. An example of that would be the farming industry. If the market price of corn is too low, many farmers will not produce the corn because they will lose money or they will not be able to earn the profits they need to make it worth their while. When this happens, the government will often ask, "What price do you need

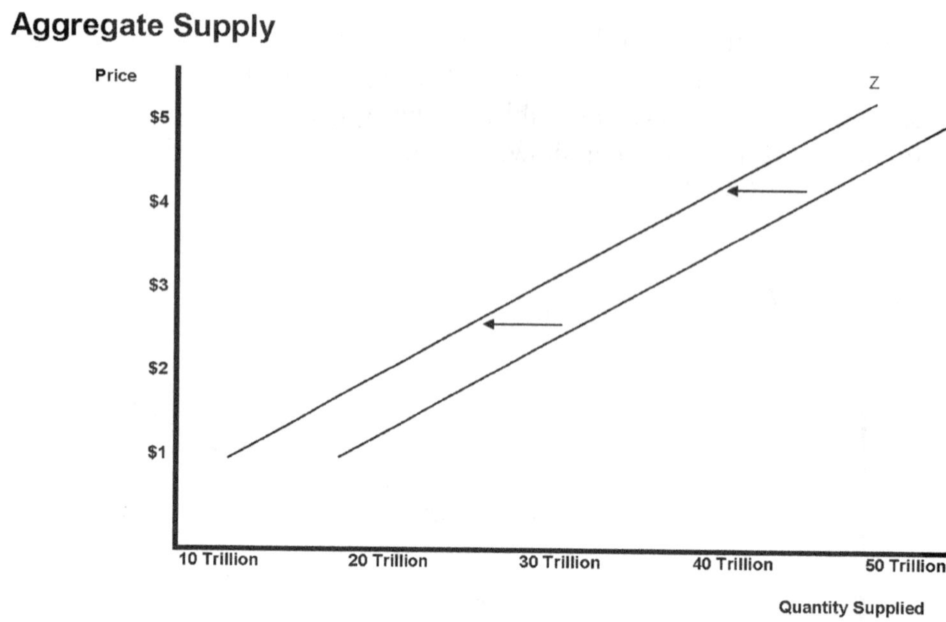

FIGURE 4.43 Aggregate Supply Curve Shift Left (Skills/Knowledge/Human Capital)

per bushel of corn in order to make a profit?" Suppose the going price is $4 per bushel, but the farmers would need $5 per bushel to make a profit. The government will not stand for shortages in food. That would cause major social uproar. Therefore, the government may be inclined to pay the farmers the extra dollar they need in order to produce the corn at the profit they desire. Such an act by the government is called a ***subsidy***.

When the government offers subsidies to producers, the supply of those goods and services will increase.

If the average price paid for our goods and services is approximately $4, then supply could possibly increase to Point G or somewhere in that vicinity as seen in Figure 4-44. If the average price paid for goods and services is approximately $3, then supply could possibly increase to Point H or somewhere in that vicinity. If the average price paid for goods and services is approximately $2, then supply could possibly increase to Point I or somewhere in that vicinity.

If you connect those three coordinates, you would have a new supply curve. In other words, if more subsidies are made available by our government, aggregate supply (or output) would increase, and the Aggregate Supply Curve would shift out from Point X to Point Y as seen in Figure 4-45. Consumers have more goods with stable prices, and workers are less likely to lose their jobs.

The opposite is also true. When the government chooses to reduce subsidies in their budget, output or supply is then reduced. Aggregate supply would shift from Point X to Point Z (see Figure 4-46).

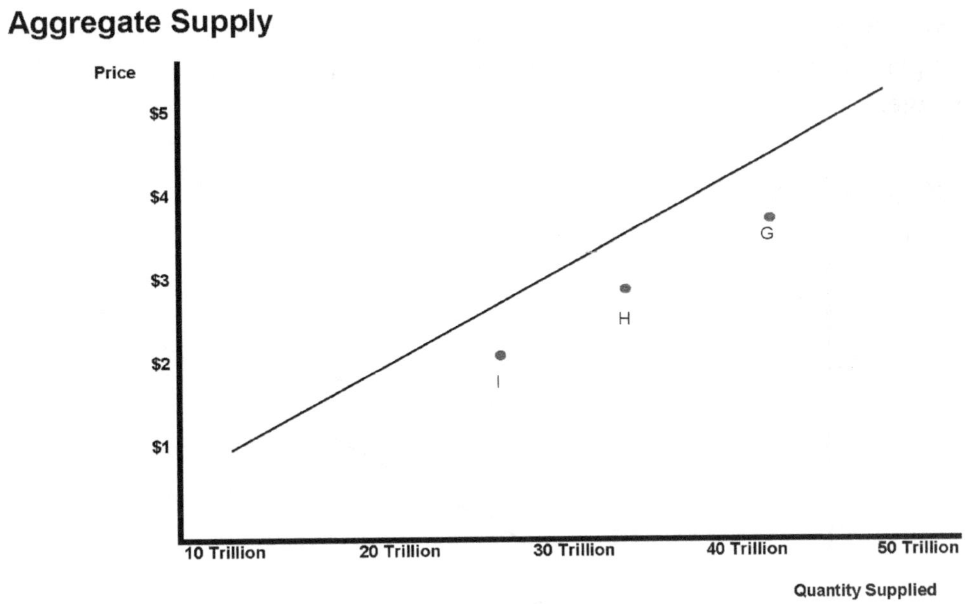

FIGURE 4.44 Aggregate Supply Curve (Subsidies)

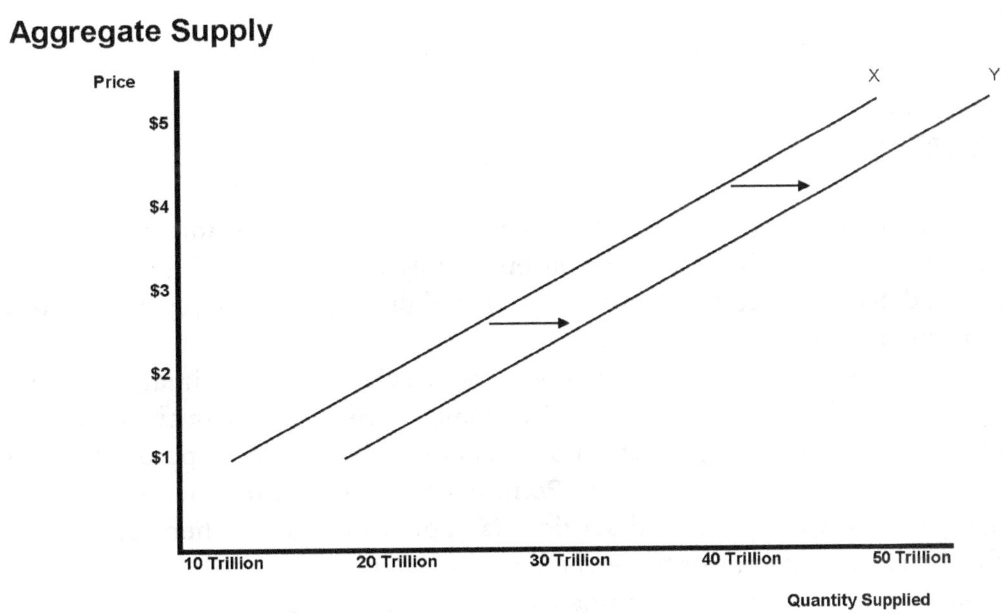

FIGURE 4.45 Aggregate Supply Curve Shift Right (Subsidies)

That is bad news for both consumers for reasons of fewer goods available and higher prices. It could also mean that needed goods, such as corn, could suffer a shortage.

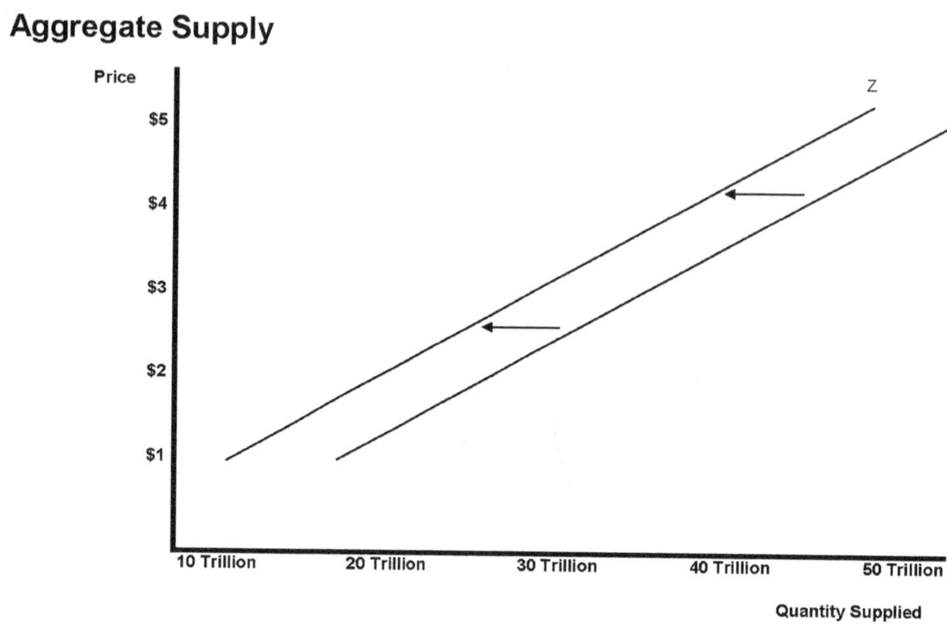

FIGURE 4.46 Aggregate Supply Curve Shift Left (Subsidies)

EXPECTATIONS

If you are a producer and if you expect the economy to boom in the foreseeable future, you may be inclined to increase your output/supply in order to cash in on the good times ahead. Such expectations will likely compel producers to supply more of whatever they are producing and selling.

If the average price paid for our goods and services is approximately $4, then supply could possibly increase to Point G or somewhere in that vicinity as portrayed in Figure 4-47. If the average price paid for goods and services is approximately $3, then supply could possibly increase to Point H or somewhere in that vicinity. If the average price paid for goods and services is approximately $2, then supply could possibly increase to Point I or somewhere in that vicinity.

If you connect those three coordinates, you would have a new supply curve; thus, the Aggregate Supply Curve will shift out from Point X to Point Y (see Figure 4-48). In other words, if better expectations or optimism toward the economy increases, supply (or output) would increase. You guessed it. That is good news for consumers and workers.

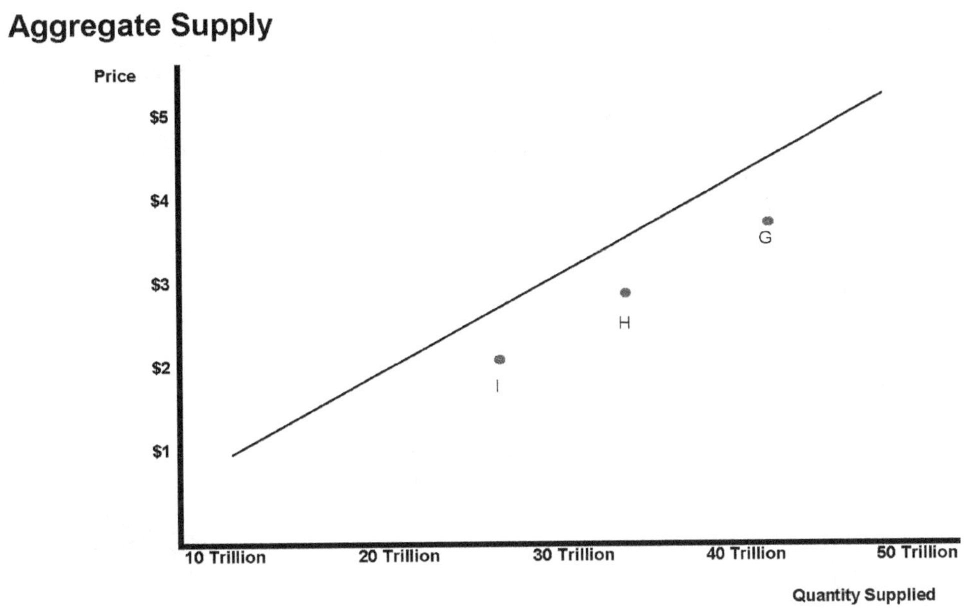

FIGURE 4.47 Aggregate Supply Curve (Expectations)

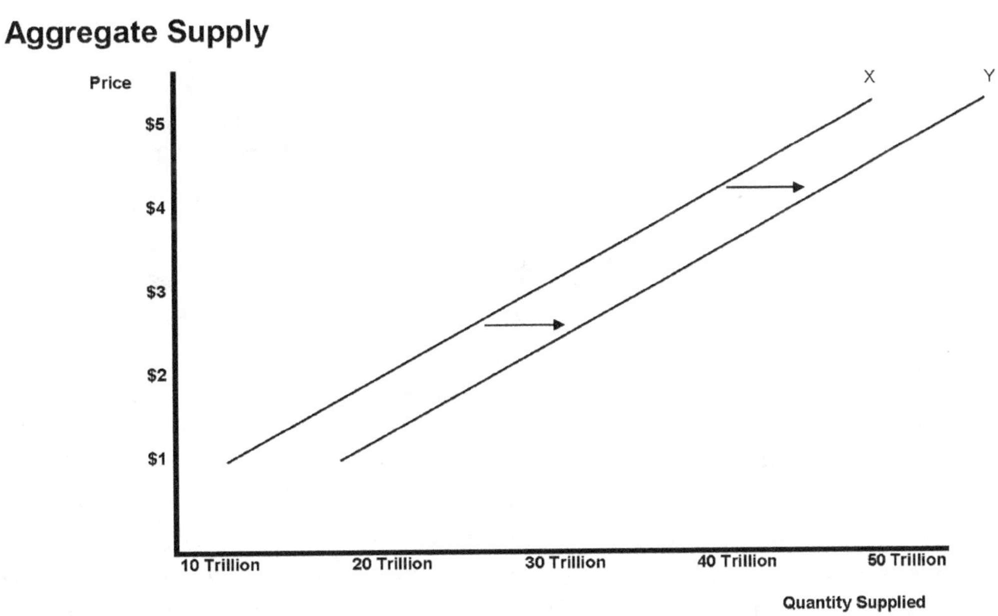

FIGURE 4.48 Aggregate Supply Curve Shift Right (Expectations)

The opposite is also true. When times look bleak in the days, weeks, months, or even years ahead, producers are less inclined to produce as many goods as they have been for fear that those goods will have no buyers.

That is bad news for workers who could lose their jobs as a result of a drop in supply/output/production.

Pessimism can kill an economy!

Such a drop in output or supply would shift the Aggregate Supply Curve to the left from Point X to Point Z as seen in Figure 4-49.

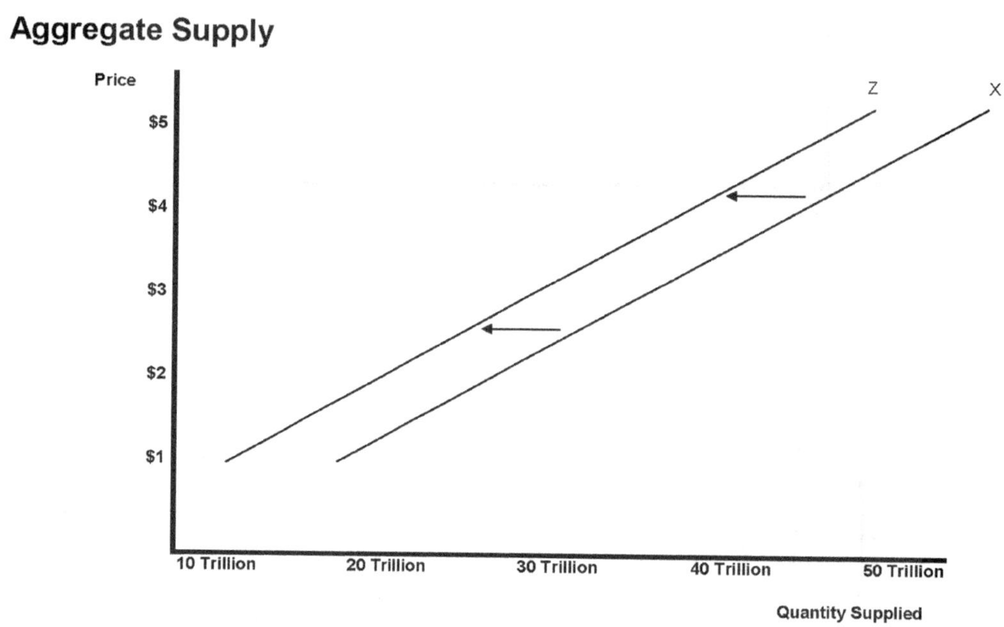

FIGURE 4.49 Aggregate Supply Curve Shift Left (Expectations)

INFRASTRUCTURE

Our country cannot supply goods and services if there are no means of getting the products and services to customers. The ***infrastructure*** of our country, therefore, plays a major role in that. It is a combination of roads, highways, computer networks, internet access, buildings, power supply, and any other items that are necessary for our country to stay connected or to expedite the completion of purchases of goods and services around the country. As we improve these things, keeping them in better repair, more efficient, and more effective, supply can then increase.

If the average price paid for our goods and services is approximately $4, then supply could possibly increase to Point G or somewhere in that vicinity as seen in Figure 4-50. If the average price paid for goods and services is approximately $3, then supply could possibly increase to point H or somewhere in that vicinity. If the average price paid for goods and services is approximately $2, then supply could possibly increase to Point I or somewhere in that vicinity.

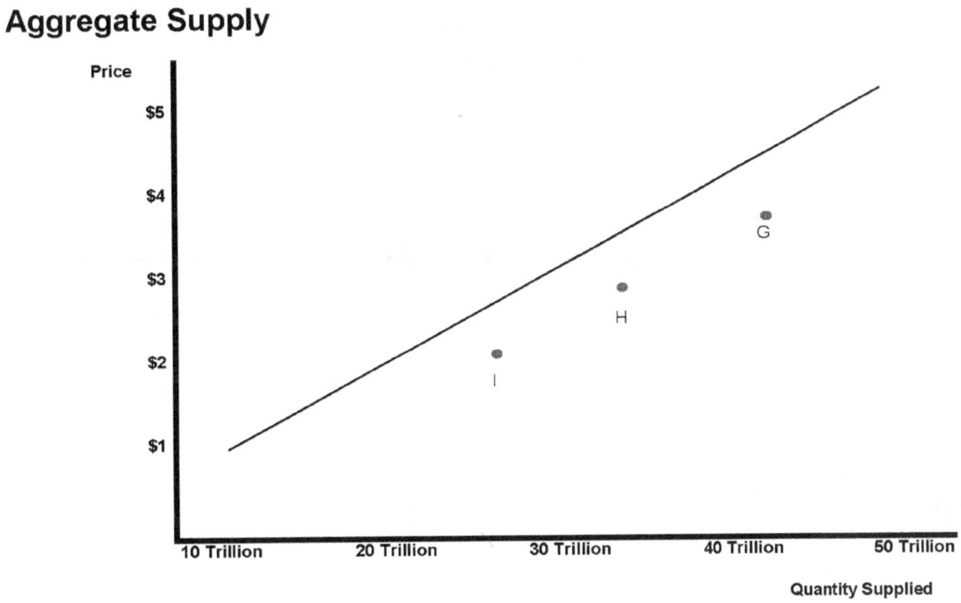

FIGURE 4.50 Aggregate Supply Curve (Infrastructure)

If you connect those three coordinates, you would have a new supply curve. In other words, if our government takes measures to improve our infrastructure, supply (or output) would increase. That would shift the Aggregate Supply Curve to the right from Point X to Point Y as illustrated in Figure 4-51. Once again, that is good news for consumers and workers.

The opposite is also true. If roads, highways, computer networks, internet access, buildings, and power supplies are not maintained in our country and/or if they fall into disrepair or if they are damaged by bad weather or any other means, supply will likely be reduced, and the Aggregate Supply Curve will shift to the left as shown in Figure 4-52.

That is bad news for both businesses and, therefore, workers could lose their jobs when production/supply is reduced. It is also bad for consumers who may see shortages and, therefore, high prices again.

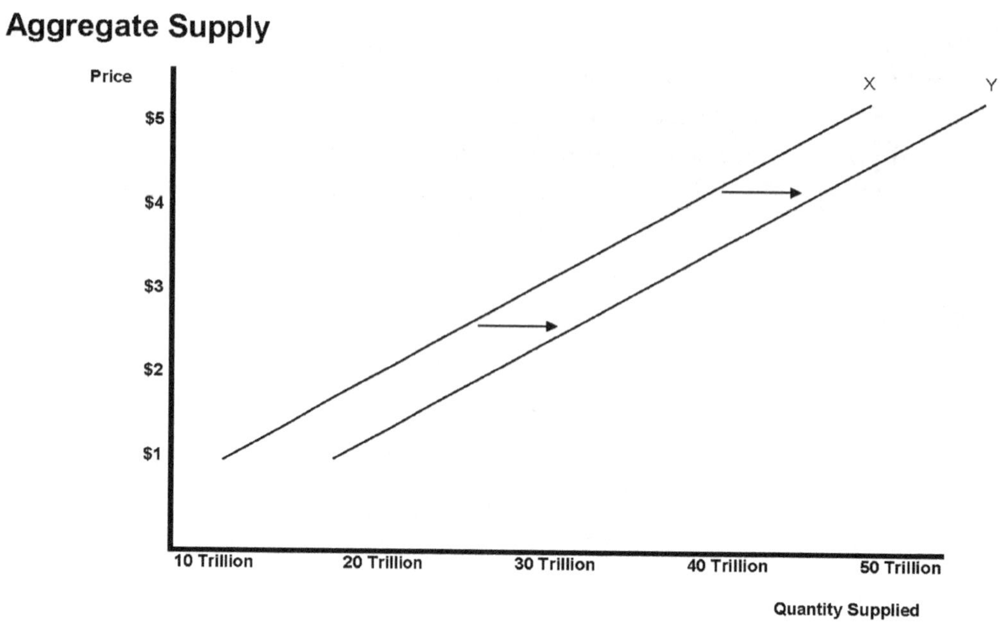

FIGURE 4.51 Aggregate Supply Curve Shift Right (Infrastructure)

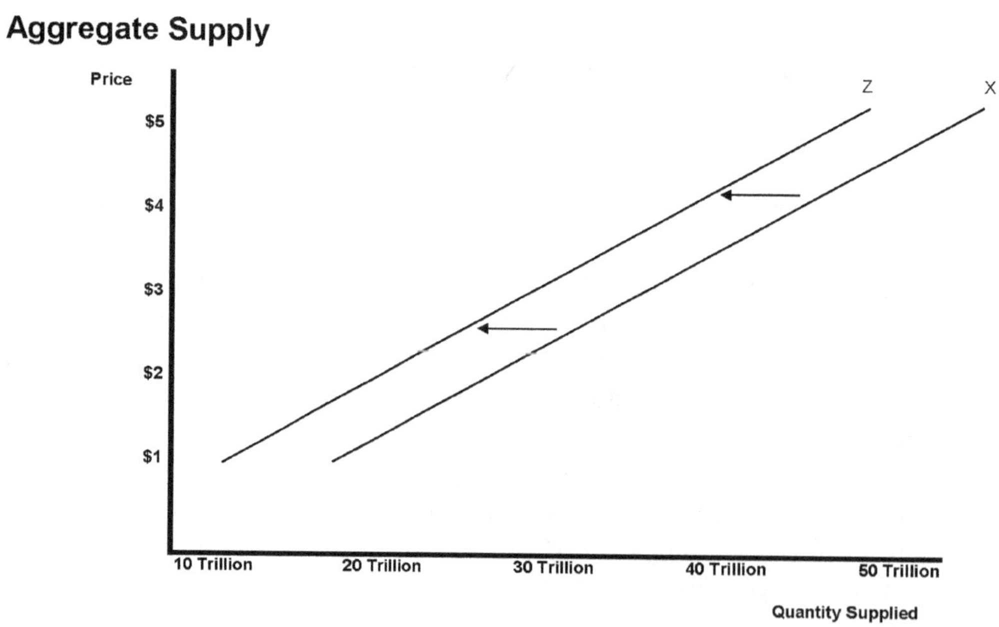

FIGURE 4.52 Aggregate Supply Curve Shift Left (Infrastructure)

NUMBER OF SELLERS

As the population increases, more people are available to offer their services and goods. This can increase supply.

If the average price paid for our goods and services is approximately $4, then supply could possibly increase to Point G or somewhere in that vicinity. Please observe Figure 4-53. If the average price paid for goods and services is approximately $3, then supply could possibly increase to point H or somewhere in that vicinity. If the average price paid for goods and services is approximately $2, then supply could possibly increase to Point I or somewhere in that vicinity.

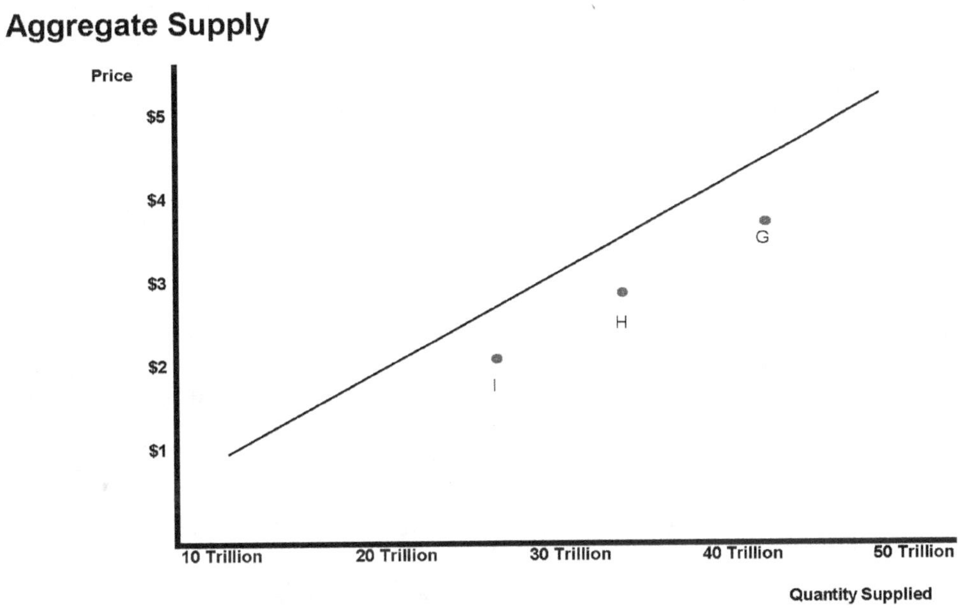

FIGURE 4.53 Aggregate Supply Curve (Number of Sellers)

If you connect those three coordinates, you would have a new supply curve. In other words, if the population in our country increases on a regular basis, supply (or output) would increase, and the Aggregate Supply Curve will shift out from Point X to Point Y as you can see in Figure 4-54. Indeed, that is good news for consumers and workers.

The opposite is also true. When population declines, there are fewer producers and, therefore, less supply/output and more bad news for both consumers as it means that there will be fewer goods available and higher prices. As you can see in Figure 4-55, aggregate supply would shift from Point X to Point Z.

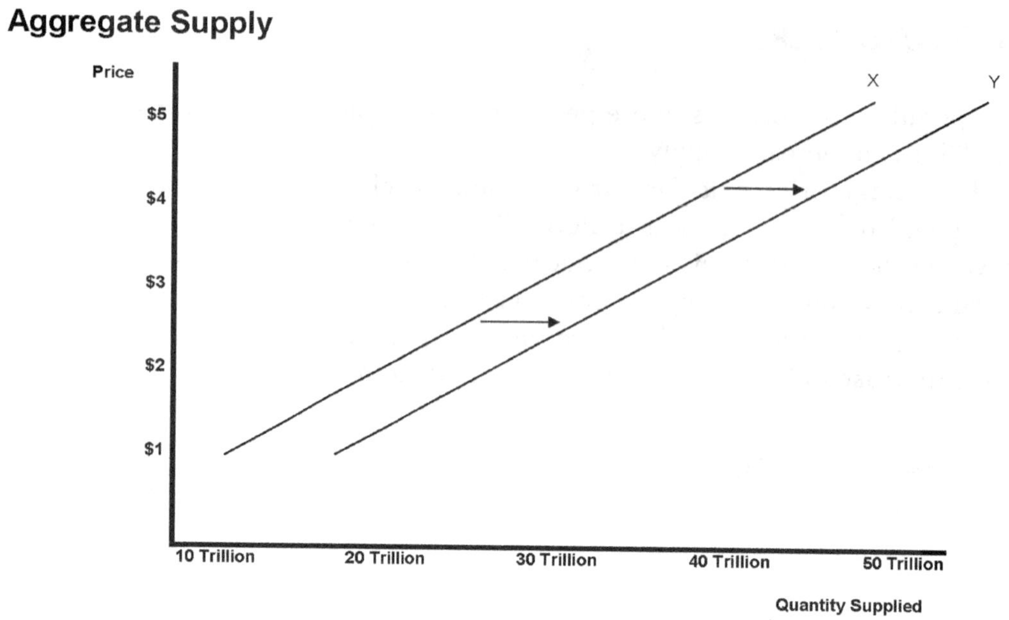

FIGURE 4.54 Aggregate Supply Curve Shift Right (Number of Sellers)

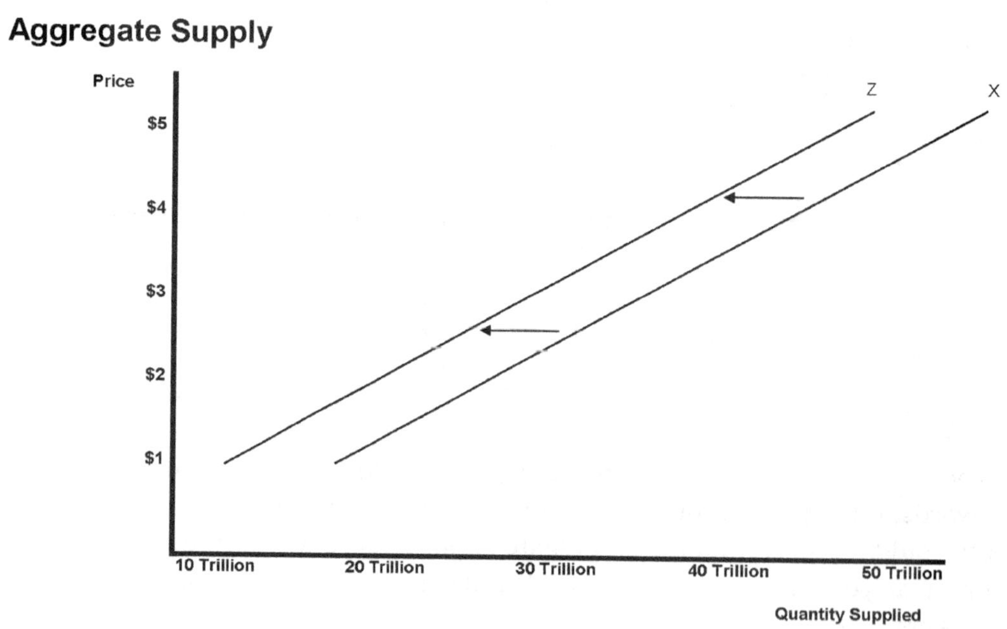

FIGURE 4.55 Aggregate Supply Curve Shift Left (Number of Sellers)

SUMMARY OF DETERMINANTS OF SUPPLY

- Price changes move supply along the supply curve.
- Other determinants of overall supply will shift the supply curve. They are as follows:
  - Technology
  - Factor Costs
  - Taxes
  - Regulation
  - Skills/Knowledge and Maximization of Use of Human Capital
  - Subsidies
  - Expectations
  - Infrastructure
  - Number of Sellers

Below is a summary of the effect of the effects of the determinants of demand and supply shown in Figure 4-56.

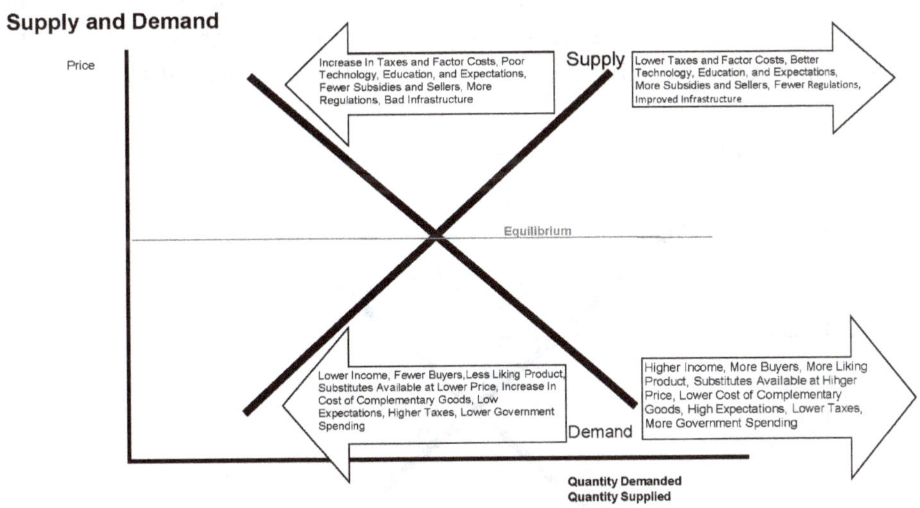

FIGURE 4.56 Summary of Supply and Demand

The chart in Figure 4-56 displays a new term that is important to understand: ***Equilibrium***.

Equilibrium exists where the supply and demand curves intersect. The price level at that point would be called the ***clearing price***. It is that which will set aggregate demand equal to the aggregate supply.

This is good news for both consumers and business, but it can be bad news for those who are unemployed.

If aggregate demand is equal to aggregate supply, that creates what is referred to as ***macro equilibrium***. Producers are able to find buyers of everything they make, and there are enough goods and services to go around for all buyers. Buyers experience no shortages, and sellers experience no surpluses. A ***surplus*** exists when sellers have more goods than they can sell. Surpluses are not good for producers as they either have to reduce their price to sell their surplus goods, or, in some cases, they can only dispose of them if they are the type of goods, such as food products, that won't last longer than a few days.

Shortages usually cause higher prices, and they require consumers to somehow manage without the things they want or need.

Macro equilibrium is only good news for the economy when it puts aggregate demand or GDP at the point where we have full employment. If it doesn't, those who are currently unemployed have little hope to find work. That's because at equilibrium, suppliers/producers are happy to keep output at that level. If they increase output to create more jobs, there is a chance that many of the goods they produce will go unsold or that a surplus may occur. Therefore, producers often stay at equilibrium, and it forces the unemployed to remain unemployed.

It is at this point that Adam Smith believed that our economy can self-correct. If, for example, producers have large surpluses as shown at the surplus level in Figure 4-57, where QD (quantity demanded) is less than QS (quantity supplied), they

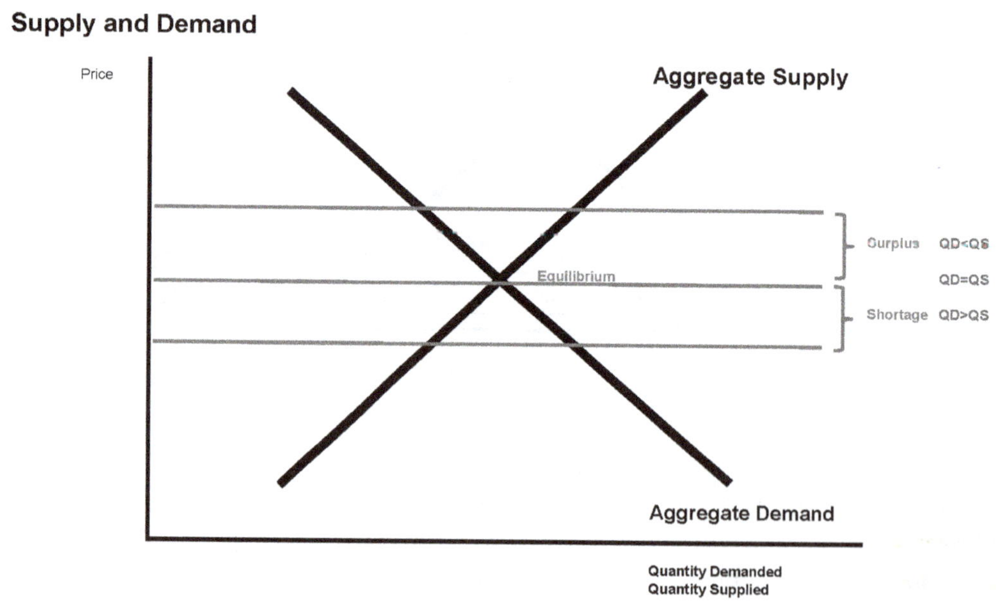

FIGURE 4.57 Shortages and Surpluses of Supply and Demand

will lower their prices, albeit reluctantly, to get people back into their stores, restaurants, and showrooms.

As the prices are lowered, they do not land exactly at equilibrium. It takes time for the demand to change or respond to a price change. Some people don't even know that prices have fallen and even if they do, they don't just run out and immediately buy things unless they need them.

Therefore, as prices fall below equilibrium, a shortage ensues as shown at the shortage level in Figure 4-57 where QD (quantity demanded) is greater than QS (quantity supplied). Shortages cause prices to rise, and, thus, demand will bring the price levels back up toward equilibrium.

TABLE 4.6 Surplus/shortage

Surpluses create full warehouses, thus, lower prices.
Shortages create empty warehouses, thus, higher prices.

This back-and-forth, up-and-down process will continue naturally, in many cases. Sometimes it takes a few weeks or months while, in other cases, it could take years to go through one complete cycle.

Therefore, macro equilibrium is only desired if it happens at full employment GDP. That is the point of GDP that puts everyone to work. It is also only desired if it is accompanied by stable prices. That is the status shown in Figure 4-58.

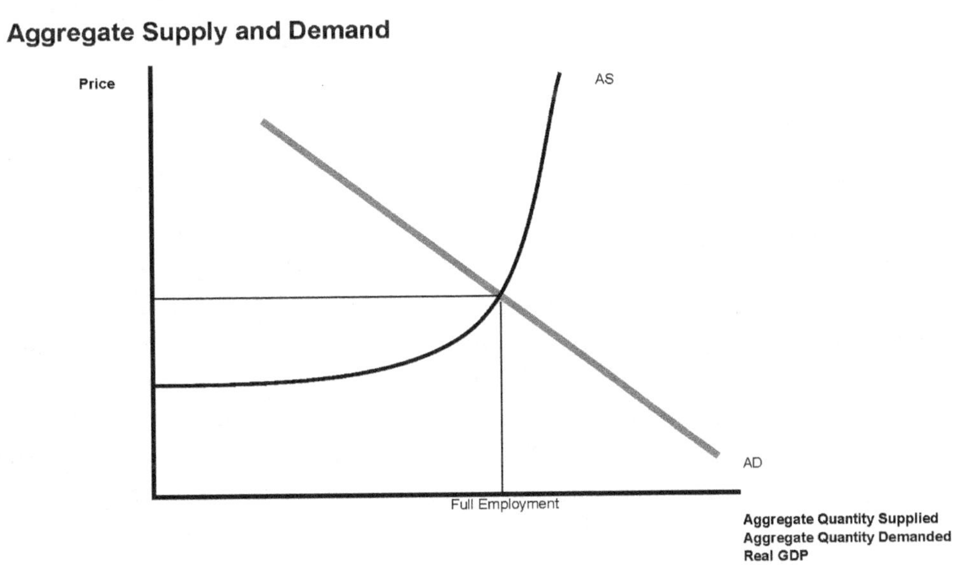

FIGURE 4.58 Macro Equilibrium (At Full Employment)

Please recall that Macro Equilibrium exists when producers and suppliers have an equal exchange of exactly the same quantity, but it is not necessarily the ultimate objective.

When we reach ***macro equilibrium GDP***, and if that point is not at ***full employment GDP*** (the GDP required in order to have full employment), we will experience either ***recessionary gap*** or ***inflationary gap***. Recessionary gap exists when the price-output relationship puts us short of full employment; thus, the jobs objective is not met. Recessionary gap is equal to the difference between ***macro equilibrium real GDP*** and ***full employment GDP*** when full employment GDP is greater than ***macro equilibrium GDP*** and is illustrated in Figure 4-59.

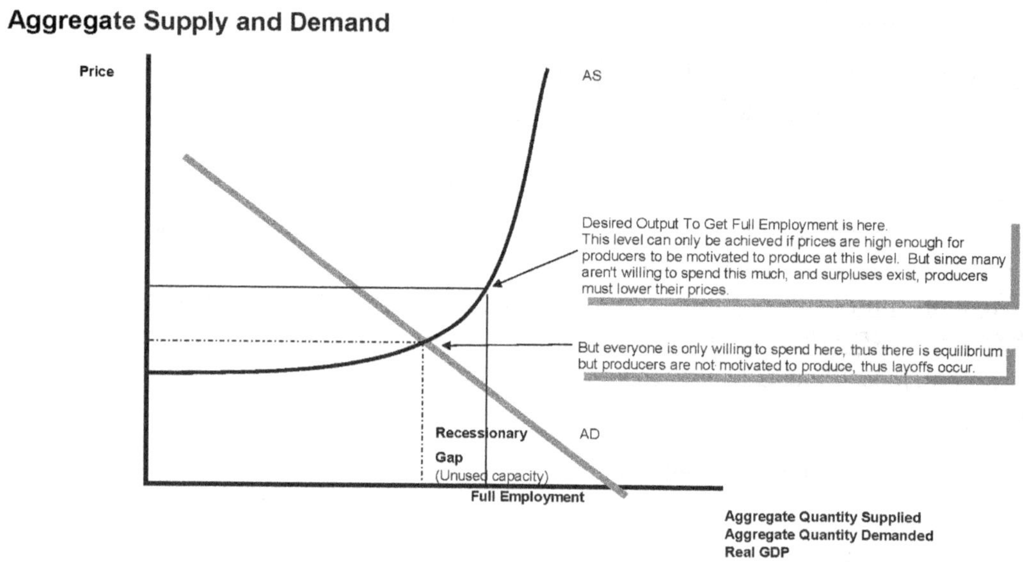

FIGURE 4.59 Macro Equilibrium (Recessionary Gap)

Inflationary gap exists if macro equilibrium is above the level of full employment GDP. Even if the equilibrium DOES create full employment, it won't last if prices are going to be too high. People will not be able to afford things with prices being so high, and aggregate demand would, thus, fall. Therefore, the objective of price stability is not met. Inflationary gap is equal to the difference between ***macro equilibrium real GDP*** and ***full employment GDP*** when full employment GDP is less than ***macro equilibrium GDP*** and is illustrated in Figure 4-60.

Another potential problem with macro equilibrium is that the price-output relationship at that point doesn't always mean we have and acceptable level of equality of the distribution of wealth.

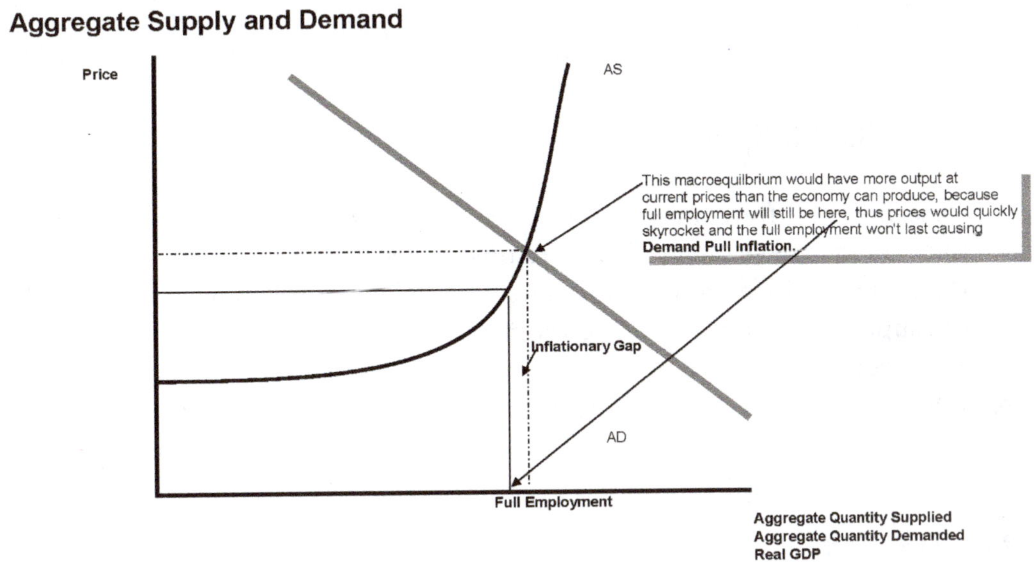

FIGURE 4.60 Macro Equilibrium (Inflationary Gap)

Also, we must consider whether or not we have stability at that point. Even if the equilibrium DOES create full employment and price stability, it could still be displaced by disturbances such as a change in consumer behavior, poor government policy and others. Also, both curves have been known to move rapidly and in different directions when the determinants discussed earlier have sudden changes.

Market participants make independent spending decisions, thus, no one can expect that their total will add up exactly to the right amount of aggregate demand to have full employment and/or price stability (or acceptable inflation).

Macro Failure exists when aggregate demand/GDP is too little, too much, or too unstable. When one or more of these exist, the goal of full employment and price stability cannot be reached.

Can we self-adjust from inflationary gap or recessionary gap? Some say yes. That is something that will be discussed later in this textbook in the theories chapter.

Chapter 4 Review

QUESTIONS TO THINK ABOUT

1. Describe the different determinants of demand and which way they will shift the demand curve under given circumstances.
2. Describe the different determinants of supply and which way they will shift the supply curve under given circumstances.
3. What determinant of demand does not shift the curve?
4. What determinant of supply does not shift the curve?

TERMS TO KNOW

Aggregate Demand
Aggregate Demand Curve
Aggregate Supply
Aggregate Supply Curve
Clearing Price
Demand
Disposable Income
Equilibrium
Factor Costs
Firm's Demand
Firm's Supply
Full Employment GDP
Income Effect
Individual Consumer's Demand
Inflation
Inflationary Gap
Law of Demand
Law of Supply
Macro Equilibrium
Macro Equilibrium GDP
Macro Failure
Market Demand
Market Supply
Personal Income
Recessionary Gap
Shortages
Subsidy
Substitute Goods
Substitution Effect
Supply
Surplus

CHAPTER FIVE

How Does Government Try to Remedy Social Problems?

IN CHAPTER 1, we discussed some basic concepts regarding the role played by government in macroeconomics as it impacts our society. In Chapter 5, we will discuss what government often does to remedy social problems with macroeconomics and the need for people to voice their feelings about what government is doing or should do. We will also show how the government's role is sometimes very effective but how, in other cases, it is not. In fact, some government intervention, while intended to help society, has actually made things worse. We will discuss what its actions were and why they were good or bad.

INFORMING THE GOVERNMENT ABOUT YOUR FEELINGS

Whether you like or dislike the way the government is managing the economy of our country, you may want to tell your members of Congress. If you inform representatives of the government what specific actions you feel they should take, believe it or not, you may often get a response. Many politicians engage in what is called ***ballot box economics***. This is what occurs when politicians ask the public if it wants a specific action taken toward economic policy whether it be taxation, government spending, foreign trade, or whatever social problems you would like to address.

Some believe, however, in what is called ***public-choice theory***. It suggests that politicians make "self-interest" decisions for recognition, assurance of reelection, prestige, power, or whatever their agenda may be. Many argue that politicians make decisions that may be good politics but bad economics. Tax increases imposed on the rich are very popular to some but have often been found to be bad economics as will be seen in the discussion that follows.

MAKING SURE WE ALL HAVE WHAT WE NEED

There are a few things, among many others, that make our government and politicians nervous.

As mentioned before, one of them is high prices for things we need. If prices for necessities like rent or food become too high, constituents complain to their political leaders. Therefore, the politicians will try to resolve these problems by imposing things such as ***rent ceilings*** to keep rents low and affordable.

Low prices for things we need can also become a problem if no company can make any profit at those low prices. When that happens, with no profits to be made, the product or service becomes unavailable as firms refuse to provide them. When this happens, they government may impose a ***price floor*** to keep prices artificially high so that the products will be produced. No producers is permitted to charge for their goods at a level below that price floor.

In the past, however, these measures usually backfire. Understanding the laws of supply and demand and their determinants will help you to understand why they backfire.

Let's look at rent ceilings first.

In big cities, there is usually a reduction in the number of housing units each year due to fires, demolition (when apartment buildings are purchased for parking and economic development), and for many other reasons. Fortunately, there is usually always out there someone who will build new housing units somewhere else to replace the lost units.

When the government imposes rent ceilings, however, many of the lost units are never replaced because housing suppliers are less motivated to create new units. If they can't charge the rate they need, units simply won't be built. Therefore, the supply of housing units declines (or shifts to the left). The government will usually set the rent ceiling at the equilibrium price, but when it does, the supply curve shifts left, and we instantly have a shortage as seen in Figure 5-1. How does a market take care of itself when there is a shortage? As mentioned earlier, prices will rise, thus, lowering demand and removing the shortage. But the price ceiling forbids housing owners to raise prices when there is a price ceiling! Therefore, the rent ceiling (meant to make housing more available to people by making it more affordable) actually makes things worse by creating a housing shortage.

Now let's look at price floors for milk.

When a price floor is imposed, the price will likely be set by the government, again, at equilibrium. Many who were once discouraged by the low market prices are now encouraged to get back into the business and to supply them again. That will shift the supply curve to the right. In doing so, the government has now created a surplus as seen in Figure 5-2. As mentioned before, producers will often lower prices to remove surpluses, but they aren't legally allowed to with a price floor. Suppliers/producers are

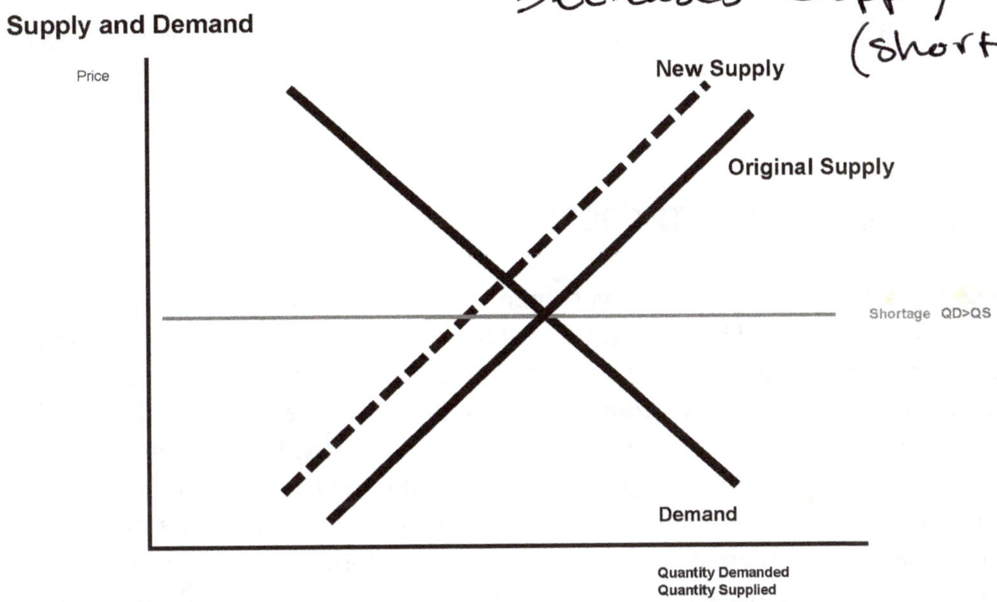

FIGURE 5.1 Supply and Demand (Price Ceilings)

Source: United Nations Development Programme, http://hdr.undp.org/en/content/income-gini-coefficient.

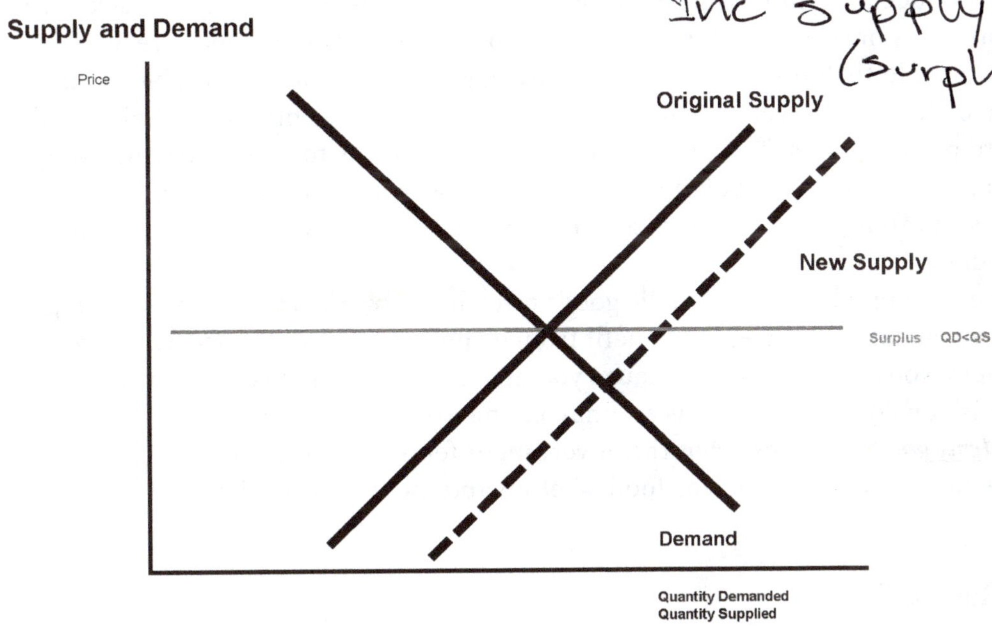

FIGURE 5.2 Supply and Demand (Price Floors)

Source: U.S. Census Bureau.

once again discouraged now because they cannot continue to be profitable when there is always a surplus. Government's action, even though with good intentions, actually makes the problem worse.

PUBLIC GOODS VS. PRIVATE GOODS

Public goods are those that the government often provides for us if the free market cannot feasibly do so. They are goods it feels we need and that no one should be denied. They include such things as emergency medical services, police protection, fire protection, military protection, highways, and, in some cases, medical facilities and mass transit. If I am a taxpaying citizen, theoretically, I should never be denied access to those goods although people are often denied them when there is a spike in demand for them without available staffs or resources to meet that demand. This often happens when there are budget cuts in a city, forcing it to reduce its staffs in these areas. It also happens when there is a local disaster, making it almost impossible for public servants to take care of all of the victims at one time.

On the other hand, ***private goods*** are provided by the ***private sector*** or by businesses at a profit. As we mentioned earlier, if a business has used all of its resources and produced the most that it can with those resources, I am out of luck if I need its products or services once they are sold out. Private goods, therefore, can, in fact, force people to "do without" when there are no more goods available. That is the main difference between public and public goods: you are entitled to public goods but not to private goods. This is why the government seeks to make sure that all goods, private and public, are available. Because the government doesn't provide the private goods, it often sets down rules and requirements to ensure their availability, often without success.

Another problem is that public goods often have ***free riders***. If you are visiting a city where you don't pay taxes but benefit from its police, firefighters, roads, and whatever it offers, you are a free rider because you get use and access to those services for free. This is considered by many as an unavoidable social injustice.

Merit goods are those that the government feels everyone is entitled to at least at some minimum level, such as food, shelter, and medical attention.

EXTERNALITIES

Externalities are costs that are experienced by a third party who does not benefit from those costs. Suppose, for example, that you experience illness or even death of family members because of pollution in the area in which you live. Suppose that pollution was caused by a business that does not employ you nor provides you with goods or services. You derive no benefit from the firm, but you wind up paying dearly from its conduct.

Pacific Gas and Electric was convicted of doing so back in 1993, and the government forced it to pay damages to the victims. This, therefore, is another thing that the government tries to do to eliminate social disorders, specifically those that cause economic issues.

MARKET POWER

As mentioned earlier, if the free market in our country was left to operate on its own with no government intervention, many feel that we would be much like some of the countries around the world with a small percentage of the population owning all of the wealth, while the overwhelming majority live in total poverty. There is not even a middle class in such countries. They also have a free market. and yet only a small percentage of their people have enough food, shelter, housing, or medical supplies available. This often happens when only a few people have all of the ownership of the businesses in those free-market economies.

The Sherman Act of 1890 was created to prevent firms from conspiring to monopolize. It outlawed the buying up of competition or conspiring in any way to eliminate competition. The problem is that many firms continued to dominate markets back in the late 1880s without violating these laws. They could often crush small businesses by the use of different actions. One such action was predatory pricing. ***Predatory pricing*** is a practice used by businesses where they their set prices very low enough (often below their costs) in a given market area to put a competitor out of business. Once the competitor is crushed, the firm would then raise prices much higher than before. A firm could become a monopoly without buying the competitor. Activities such as these were outlawed by the use of amendments to plug the loopholes of the Sherman Act. They include the ***Clayton Act of 1914***, the **Robinson Patman Act of 1936**, and the ***Celler-Kefauver Act of 1950***.

EQUITY

ECONOMIC MYTH #8	Only the rich people own stocks, so we need to tax those rich people as well as the big corporations and give that money to the poor.

ECONOMIC MYTH #9	Taxing the rich to give to the poor successfully created equality in wealth distribution in America.

ECONOMIC MYTH #10	The rich are getting much, much richer, and the poor in America are getting much, much poorer.

Equal distribution of wealth and income is seldom, and, perhaps, never, accomplished in any society. Even socialist societies such as the former Soviet Union, which was built on the idea of creating complete wealth equality, have been unable to keep wealth distribution perfectly equal. But if government can't accomplish it, they want, at least, to make the distribution of wealth acceptable to our citizens.

Many believe it is imperative to dramatically increase taxes levied against the rich (or the "Haves") and give that tax money to the poor (or the "Have Nots"). Transfer payments are already used to help create equity or minimize inequity. They include programs such as unemployment benefits, welfare, and Social Security. Many feel, however, that these programs need to be dramatically increased for the poor.

Taxing the rich to give to the poor may sound like a very good idea and one of compassion for the poor. It may also sound very easy. Historically, however, that strategy has failed here and in other societies for several reasons.

First of all, you need to define who is and who is not rich. A household that earns $100,000 per year may seem rich to some, but to others, especially those living on the East and West coasts, that income doesn't go very far. People living in some areas have much, much higher real estate and living expenses than those in the Midwest.

Another problem, as mentioned in a previous discussion, is that higher or excessive taxation of the rich, who are often employers, gives no incentive for them to increase employment, and, in fact, it usually gives them incentives to reduce employment. If employers feel that they are being overtaxed or disproportionately taxed, they will expand their operations abroad. Historically speaking, such action has created more unemployment and poverty, not less. Therefore, income and wealth distribution becomes even more unequal. The entrepreneurs who move their businesses abroad will maintain much of their income and wealth while the employees who lose their jobs fall deeper into poverty. In addition, the government's tax revenue actually decreases with higher taxes. With fewer people working, less taxable income is available, thus, there is less taxe revenue collected bygovernment. As a result, there is less money to help the poor as was originally intended. Other proof that higher tax rates bring the government less revenue is discussed in Chapter 6.

When people are urging the government to raise taxes on corporations, there is still another idea that we need to consider. In recent decades, a large percentage of the people in America owning a huge amount of corporate stock are not a bunch of rich fat cats. They are actually the middle class, and, in many cases, they are retirees. According to ***Business Insider:***

> Households directly own 38 percent of the U.S. equity [stock] market, however, the total effective household ownership is closer to 80 percent when combined with indirect ownership in the form of mutual funds (20 percent), pension funds (16 percent), and insurance policy holdings (7 percent). Kostin, quoted in Ro 2013

Stock ownership is no longer a "rich-person problem." If you study the data, it will show that, in fact, it's very common for middle-income families to own stocks. They own it either directly or indirectly through investments such as their 401ks and retirement accounts.

It has also been known that among the middle 20% of families, with incomes of approximately $50,000, nearly half own some stocks.

When politicians or the average person insist that we tax the rich corporations more, they are often taking steps to reduce the wealth and increase the taxes for the retirees and the vast majority of our middle class. Higher taxes on corporations also bring in lower dividends to the shareholders. Dividends are paid to shareholders out of the funds called ***net profit after taxes (NPAT)***. If taxes are higher, the dividends paid out to the shareholders will be lower. This not only gives lower income to retirees and our middle class, but it also reduces the value of their stocks because lower returns on a stock make it worth a lot less. Therefore, stock prices and the wealth of their owners are significantly affected by the dividends they pay.

So how does a country know if its distribution of wealth and income is acceptable. What is the report card on how much equality is obtained in a society?

First, it's important to understand that income is different that wealth. Income is usually what drives a person's wealth, but a person with a large income doesn't necessarily have large wealth (or net worth). Net worth is equal to the value the possessions a person owns minus what he or she owes on those possessions. If you own a $200,000 home but owe $195,000 on it and if you have no other assets, your net worth is only $5,000. Many people have a large income but often spend it faster than they receive it. It is very possible, therefore, to have a negative net worth as there are some who have more debt than wealth.

One way that we can tell if we are even close to some level of acceptable equity is by using what is known as the ***Lorenz Curve***. It was developed by ***Maxwell O. Lorenz (1880–1962)*** in 1905. It measures what percent of the wealth is owned by various percentages of the population. For example, if 1% of the population owns 1% of the wealth, if 2% of the population owns 2% of the wealth, if 3% of the population owns

3% of the wealth, if 4% of the population owns 4% of the wealth, if 5% of the population owns 5% of the wealth, and so on, distribution of wealth would be perfectly even.

The graph of those numbers would show a 45-degree line as shown in the Lorenz Curve in Figure 5-3. That 45-degree line would represent ***perfect equality in wealth distribution***.

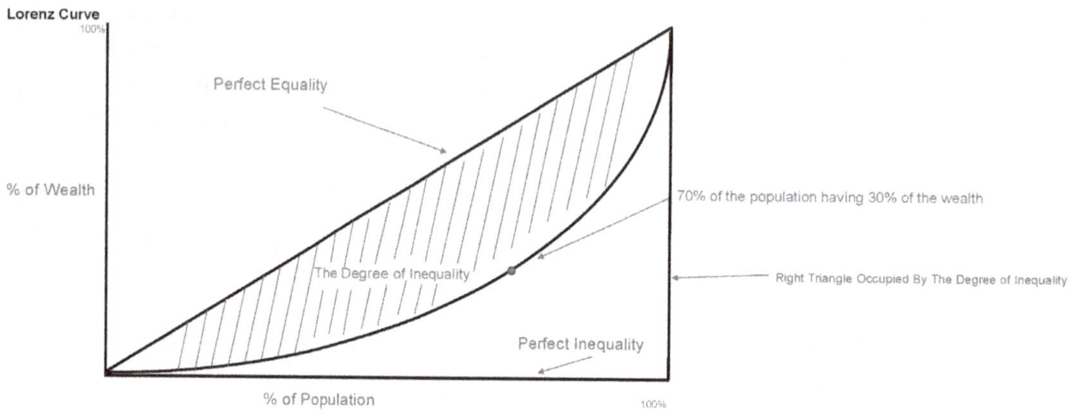

FIGURE 5.3 Lorenz Curve

There are no countries that have perfect wealth equality. Also, there are many who feel that it isn't the best scenario. If everyone had the same income or wealth regardless of how much he or she works or how skilled he or she is, there would be very little incentive for anyone to excel in his or her work or education. If the government forced such a circumstance, many would likely consider it to be unfair and may even flee that society.

Unfortunately, many societies have a very large percent of the population with a very small amount of the wealth. If 99.999% of the population had 0% of the wealth, your society's wealth distribution would be experiencing nearly ***perfect inequality in wealth distribution***. There are some societies that actually have circumstances such as that, in which less than 1% of the population has all of the wealth. That is not good or acceptable, and, in time, the people of those countries could revolt.

If, for example, 70% of the population had only 30% of the wealth, the distribution would not be at all equal. If each of those coordinates with those population/wealth relationships were graphed, you would have the curve (the Lorenz Curve) that would form a parabola. The parabola is shaded in the chart which is shown in Figure 5-3. If that parabola gets larger, and, hence, if the curve gets farther and farther away from the line of perfect equality in wealth distribution, then the distribution is getting less and less equal.

TABLE 5.1 Gini Coefficients (World Wide)

COUNTRY	GINI COEFFIC.	COUNTRY	GINI COEFFIC.
Sweden	25.0	India	33.9
Ukraine	25.6	Ireland	34.3
Norway	25.8	Greece	34.3
Slovakia	26.0	Albania	34.5
Belarus	26.5	Niger	34.6
Finland	26.9	Spain	34.7
Romania	27.4	Latvia	34.8
Afghanistan	27.8	Sudan	35.3
Bulgaria	28.2	Jordan	35.4
Germany	28.3	Sierra Leone	35.4
Montenegro	28.6	Palestine, State of	35.5
Kazakhstan	29.0	Guinea-Bissau	35.5
Austria	29.2	Viet Nam	35.6
Serbia	29.6	Syrian Arab Republic	35.8
Pakistan	30.0	United Kingdom	36.0
Luxembourg	30.8	Italy	36.0
Egypt	30.8	Estonia	36.0
Tajikistan	30.8	Cambodia	36.0
Netherlands	30.9	Tunisia	36.1
Iraq	30.9	Bosnia and Herzegovina	36.2
Slovenia	31.2	Sri Lanka	36.4
Hungary	31.2	Mongolia	36.5
Armenia	31.3	Uzbekistan	36.7
Bangladesh	32.1	Lao People's Democratic Republic	36.7
Canada	32.6	Maldives	37.4
Poland	32.7	Lithuania	37.6
Nepal	32.8	Tanzania (United Republic of)	37.6
Belgium	33.0	Yemen	37.7
Moldova (Republic of)	33.0	Indonesia	38.1
Mali	33.0	Bhutan	38.1
Burundi	33.3	Liberia	38.2
Kyrgyzstan	33.4	Iran (Islamic Republic of)	38.3
Ethiopia	33.6	Benin	38.6
Switzerland	33.7	Cameroon	38.9
Croatia	33.7	Israel	39.2
Azerbaijan	33.7	Togo	39.3

(continue)

TABLE 5.1 Gini Coefficients (World Wide) (*continued*)

COUNTRY	GINI COEFFIC.	COUNTRY	GINI COEFFIC.
Thailand	39.4	Mexico	47.2
Guinea	39.4	Dominican Republic	47.2
Burkina Faso	39.8	Congo	47.3
Chad	39.8	Gambia	47.3
Turkey	40.0	Kenya	47.7
Djibouti	40.0	Peru	48.1
Russian Federation	40.1	El Salvador	48.3
Senegal	40.3	Nigeria	48.8
Nicaragua	40.5	Ecuador	49.3
Mauritania	40.5	Cape Verde	50.5
United States	40.8	Costa Rica	50.7
Morocco	40.9	Sao Tome and Principe	50.8
Qatar	41.1	Rwanda	50.8
Gabon	41.5	Swaziland	51.5
Cote d'Ivoire	41.5	Panama	51.9
Georgia	42.1	Chile	52.1
China	42.1	Paraguay	52.4
Angola	42.7	Lesotho	52.5
Fiji	42.8	Suriname	52.9
Ghana	42.8	Belize	53.1
Philippines	43.0	Brazil	54.7
The former Yugoslav Republic of Macedonia	43.6	Colombia	55.9
Malawi	43.9	Guatemala	55.9
Madagascar	44.1	Bolivia (Plurinational State of)	56.3
Uganda	44.3	Central African Republic	56.3
Congo (Democratic Republic of the)	44.4	Honduras	57.0
Argentina	44.5	Zambia	57.5
Venezuela (Bolivarian Republic of)	44.8	Haiti	59.2
Uruguay	45.3	Micronesia (Federated States of)	61.1
Jamaica	45.5	South Africa	63.1
South Sudan	45.5	Namibia	63.9
Mozambique	45.7	Comoros	64.3
Malaysia	46.2	Seychelles	65.8

Sources: United Nations Development Programme
Human Development Reports
Source: World Bank (2013). "World Development Indicators 2013." Washington, D.C.: World Bank, http://data.worldbank.org. Accessed October, 2013, http://hdr.undp.org/en/content/income-gini-coefficient

So, to what degree does the equality or inequality exist? To figure it out mathematically, statisticians will take the area of that parabola and divide it by the area of the right triangle that it occupies. If that number is a large number, that bigger percent indicates a larger parabola and, hence, a larger degree of inequality and a greater likelihood of unacceptable inequality. This ratio is called the ***Gini Coefficient***, created in 1912 by ***Corrado Gini (1884–1965)***. In Table 5-1, you can see the Gini Coefficients of many countries as of 2013, with Sweden having the greater level of wealth distribution equality while Nambia and the Seychelles have the world's greatest level of inequality.

Here in the United States, we have had the Gini Coefficient rise only slightly over the years. In Table 5-2, you can see that between decades it only changed by a few percentage points.

TABLE 5.2 Gini Coefficients (United States—History)

YEAR	U.S. GINI COEFFICIENT	PERIOD CHANGE	CUMULATIVE CHANGE
1970	0.350		
1980	0.365	0.02	0.02
1990	0.390	0.03	0.04
2000	0.430	0.04	0.08
2012	0.450	0.02	0.10

Source: U.S. Census Bureau

The Gini Coefficient has been able to dispel two myths. The first myth is that taxing the rich to give to the poor has been thought to be effective to reduce our Gini Coefficient. In 1967, President ***Lyndon Johnson (1908–1973)*** introduced legislation for what he referred to as ***The Great Society***. It was in this effort that he launched his ***War on Poverty***. It shows, however, that the Gini Coefficient has always been on the increase rather than going down. Another myth that the rich in America are getting much, much richer, and the poor are getting much, much poorer has also been disproven. As one can see, for over forty years, the ratio has moved by only ten percentage points. Some may consider that significant, but it certainly is not to the severe degree that many people claim.

GOVERNMENT OPPORTUNITY COSTS

Whenever the government tries to manage social problems, as with everything government does, it involves opportunity costs; thus, a cost-benefit analysis is needed to see the effectiveness of its programs. If a taxpayer pays taxes, he or she can't spend that money to boost the economy by buying private goods or services, so the tax dollars must be spent properly. One cost of government spending is measured by the private-sector output sacrificed when the government employs scarce factors of production. Taxes transfer command over resources, and when this is done, government needs to make sure that it is better for society in the long run.

Unfortunately, it is often difficult to measure the cost and/or the benefit in programs that the government implements because it is hard to place a "market value" on many of their outcomes. It's hard to measure, in some cases, if the quality of life improved as a result of the given programs that the government funded.

In some cases, when it was found that the government was effective with our money, those programs were still killed for political reasons.

For example, many years ago, there were programs out there that were aimed at educating inmates who were institutionalized in our state and federal prisons. Studies showed that those programs dramatically reduced the chances that the inmates would commit another crime once they were released. Therefore, the return rate of those inmates going back to prison also dropped significantly. It costs a lot of money each year to keep a prisoner locked up. Therefore, it was found that educating them reduced prison costs. The program also actually made our society a little safer. There was no question that the costs of funding the program were far outweighed by the savings in costs, and by the benefits of less crime. It cost much less to educate the inmates than it did to lock them up each year.

Sadly, the programs were dramatically cut because many citizens did not want their tax dollars helping convicted criminals.

Chapter 5 Review

QUESTIONS TO THINK ABOUT

1. What are some of the economic myths of this chapter?
2. How effective are price floors and rent ceilings and why?
3. What does a large Gini Coefficient mean?
4. Has American society been experiencing a huge problem with the rich getting richer and the poor getting poorer?
5. Has any government regulation been good for the country? Has any been bad for the country?

TERMS/PEOPLE TO KNOW

Ballot Box Economics

Celler-Kefauver Act of 1950

Clayton Act of 1914

Corrado Gini (1884–1965)

Externalities

Free Riders

Gini Coefficient

The Great Society

Lyndon Johnson (1908–1973)

The Lorenz Curve

Maxwell O. Lorenz (1880–1962)

Merit Goods

Net Profit After Taxes (NPAT)

Perfect Equality in Wealth Distribution

Perfect Inequality in Wealth Distribution

Predatory Pricing

Price Floor

Private Goods

Private Sector

Public Goods

Public-Choice Theory

Rent Ceilings

Robinson Patman of 1936

The Sherman Act of 1890

War on Poverty

CHAPTER SIX

Where Does Government Get the Money?

ONCE AGAIN, AS mentioned in Chapter 1, government plays a major role in managing the economy. One of the major ways that it does that is by spending much of the money that makes up our gross national product. The question is: Where does government get the money that it spends? There are many sources it uses, and that is the focus of Chapter 6.

TAXES

Income taxes are taxes levied against citizens by charging them a percent of their income to raise revenue by the government. We use what is known as a ***progressive tax system*** where tax rates levied against Americans will increase as their income increases. This is different than a flat tax. With a ***flat tax*** rate (also known as the proportional tax system), where everyone pays the same income tax rate regardless of income, the rich will still pay more in taxes because they have more income to tax. There are no flat taxes on income taxes levied by the U.S. federal government. Taxes are collected at all levels of government. They are charged by small townships, villages, cities, state governments, and the federal government in Washington D.C.

Income taxes come in the form of ***corporate taxes*** and ***personal taxes***. Corporate taxes are those based upon corporations' ordinary income or ordinary profits (money earned in their day-to-day operations). They are also taxed on ***capital gains***. Capital gains come from the profit of selling one of their assets (such as old machinery) at a price higher than their book value or from the sale of stocks at a price higher than what was paid for the stock. They are also taxed on investment income they receive as many corporations buy stocks in other companies as well as bonds and other investments.

Personal taxes are those paid based upon citizens' ordinary income from their jobs. They are also taxed on capital gains if they too were to sell one of their assets, such as a car or home, at a price higher than its book value. They,

TABLE 6.1 Tax Structure

	FROM	TO	BUCKET RATE	BASE TAX	ADDED TAX	NET PROFIT EXAMPLE	TAX	WEEKLY INCOME	AVERAGE
CORPORATE	$0	$50,000	15.0%	$0		$40,000	$6,000	$ 961.54	15%
	$50,000	$75,000	25.0%	$7,500	+ 0.25 × Income Exceeding 50000	$60,000	$10,000	$1,442.31	17%
	$75,000	$100,000	34.0%	$13,750	+ 0.34 × Income Exceeding 75000	$85,000	$17,150	$1,923.08	20%
	$100,000	$335,000	39.0%	$22,250	+ 0.39 × Income Exceeding 100000	$110,000	$26,150	$6,442.31	24%
	$335,000	$10,000,000	34.0%	$113,900	+ 0.34 × Income Exceeding 335000	$400,000	$136,000	$192,307.69	34%
	$10,000,000	$15,000,000	35.0%	$3,400,000	+ 0.35 × Income Exceeding 10000000	$10,200,000	$3,470,000	$288,461.54	34%
	$15,000,000	$18,333,333	38.0%	$5,150,000	+ 0.38 × Income Exceeding 15000000				
	$18,333,333	Infinity	35.0%	$6,416,667	+ 0.35 × Income Exceeding 18333333				
SINGLE	$0	$2,650	0.0%	$0			$0	$50.96	
	$2,650	$9,800	10.0%	$0	+ 0.1 × Income Exceeding 2650	$5,000	$235	$188.46	
	$9,800	$31,500	15.0%	$715	+0.15 × Income Exceeding 9800	$10,000	$745	$605.77	
	$31,500	$69,750	25.0%	$3,970	+ 0.25 × Income Exceeding 31500	$35,000	$4,845	$1,341.35	
	$69,750	$151,950	28.0%	$13,533	+ 0.28 × Income Exceeding 69750	$75,000	$15,003	$2,922.12	
	$151,950	$328,250	33.0%	$36,549	+ 0.33 × Income Exceeding 151950	$170,000	$42,505	$6,312.50	
	$328,250	$999,999	35.0%	$94,728	+ 0.35 × Income Exceeding 328250	$350,000	$102,340	$19,230.75	
MARRIED	$0	$6,450	0.0%	$0		$0	$0	$124.04	
	$6,450	$18,450	10.0%	$0	+ 0.1 × Income Exceeding 6450	$9,000	$255	$354.81	
	$18,450	$51,550	15.0%	$1,200	+0.15 × Income Exceeding 18450	$25,000	$2,183	$991.35	
	$51,550	$109,700	27.0%	$6,165	+ 0.27 × Income Exceeding 51550	$75,000	$12,497	$2,109.62	
	$109,700	$176,800	30.0%	$21,866	+ 0.3 × Income Exceeding 109700	$150,000	$33,956	$3,400.00	
	$176,800	$311,900	35.0%	$41,996	+ 0.35 × Income Exceeding 176800	$200,000	$50,116	$5,998.08	
	$311,900	$999,999	38.6%	$89,281	+ 0.386 × Income Exceeding 311900	$350,000	$103,987	$19,230.75	

too, have capital gains from the sale of stocks at a price higher than what was paid for the stock. They are also taxed on investment income they receive when they buy stocks, bonds, and/or other investments.

An example of the rates charged by the federal government for corporate and personal income is shown in Table 6-1.

Social Security is another means by which our government collects money from us. Each paycheck an American receives will deduct 6.2% of those earned dollars for your Social Security Retirement and for disability payments to minors in your household should you become deceased or unable to work before they reach adulthood. An additional 1.65% is also deducted from your earnings to put aside for your medical benefits when you retire. This adds up to 7.85% of your earnings that goes to the government. Your employer will also match what is deducted from your paycheck; thus, they, too, will send an additional 7.85% to Washington for your retirement income and retirement medical benefits. What is different here is that the government hopes to give that money back to you and then some, assuming that you live long enough to reach retirement age to be able to receive it back. The only income on which you and your employer do not pay a Social Security tax is on the income you make that is above $90,000. It is for that reason that Social Security is the only tax in our country that is a ***regressive tax*** where the rate you pay goes down when your income rises. Table 6-2 shows how your rate goes down (or regresses) when your income goes above $90,000.

TABLE. 6.2 Social Security As a Regressive Tax

INCOME	PAID TO SOCIAL SECURITY	% PAID
$ 50,000	$ 3,925	7.85%
$ 60,000	$ 4,710	7.85%
$ 70,000	$ 5,495	7.85%
$ 80,000	$ 6,280	7.85%
$ 90,000	$ 7,065	7.85%
$100,000	$ 7,065	7.07%
$110,000	$ 7,065	6.42%
$120,000	$ 7,065	5.89%
$130,000	$ 7,065	5.43%

Excise taxes (often called usage taxes) are paid by Americans only if they use certain products. They include gasoline taxes, whiskey taxes, cigarette taxes. Whiskey and cigarette taxes are often called the ***sin tax*** as many feel that you don't pay those taxes unless you utilize these "vices." You don't pay those taxes unless you buy the items that have excise taxes levied on them. ***Sales taxes*** are taxes charged at the state and local levels for transactions on merchandise and on some services and their rates will vary. Most vendors will add the sales tax to your purchase, thus making your purchase costs rise. ***Property taxes***, also charged at the local level, are levied to owners of homes and personal possessions. The taxes they pay are based upon the value of the properties. Businesses are also charged property taxes for the inventories they hold

When compiling GDP, approximately two thirds of government spending (G) is comprised of state and local taxes.

TAX STRATEGIES

ECONOMIC MYTH #11	Higher taxes always bring the government more revenue.

ECONOMIC MYTH #12	Lower taxes always bring the government less revenue.

The average American pays nearly 40% of his or her income in taxes to the government when you factor in federal, state, local, social security, sales, property, and excise taxes.

Obviously if the income tax rate is at 0%, there will be no income tax revenue collected by the government. Once income taxes begin to be levied against the people, however, the income revenue collected by government will significantly increase.

Suppose the government raises income taxes to a rate of 100%. In other words, suppose it required you to pay all of the money you earn to the government in taxes. Sometimes it may seem like that. But if that were to happen, economists believe that there would be no taxes collected. Why? Because no one would have the incentive or motivation to get a job if he or she knew that all of the money they earned would go to the government. If taxes rise, people often refrain from working those extra hours or those second jobs at night or on weekends because they know that they are not likely to be able to enjoy much of the financial fruits from that added work. Some may also hide their income to avoid taxes. Of course, it is never acceptable to hide income from the Internal Revenue Service (IRS)! Never!

Another reason that higher tax rates can also reduce the amount of money collected by the IRS is that higher taxes usually reduce jobs. It compels businesses to move to places where tax rates are lower, and it also gives many people of the middle class less disposable income to spend. Remember, many people feel that those earning more than $100,000 in a given household are rich, but in different parts of the country, that is below the average income of many middle-class families. Therefore, when their taxes go up, they have less money to spend; thus, retail sales, and ultimately jobs decline. When layoffs begin, the government will always collect fewer taxes. The opposite is also true. Lower tax rates have generated jobs, often creating more taxable income and ultimately more tax revenue.

Therefore, we have then proven that at some point higher income tax rates will eventually take government revenue to zero. The question becomes: At what point does that happen? To what level would we have to raise taxes when government revenue would start to decline? Government should never set their rates above that level, because in doing so, they would bring in less tax revenue in spite of the fact that they are charging a higher rate.

Economist ***Arthur Laffer*** was prominent as an economist in the 1980s. He created what is referred to as the ***Laffer Curve*** (sometimes called the ***Laffer-Khaldun Curve***) which is shown in Figure 6-1. It depicts graphically what has just been stated. According to the curve, the government should not raise its rates above the level where the arrow is pointing in Figure 6-1. If tax rates go above it, tax revenue will fall. If rates are below it, the government could raise taxes to get the revenue to that point where its collection of tax revenue is maximized.

"Wait a minute!" some will say. If a person pays $2,000 less in taxes this year, that money can't create a job of $20,000. Actually, it can. Later in this book, we discuss

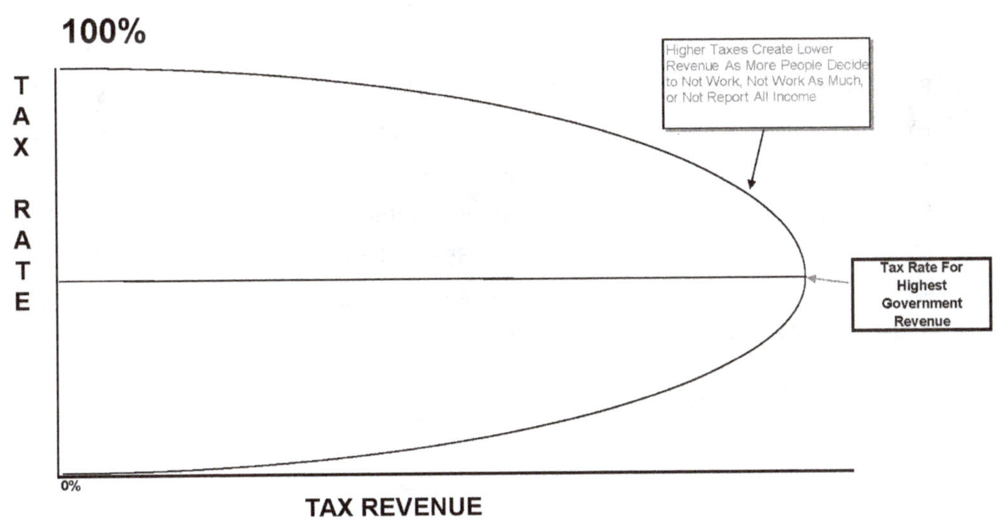

FIGURE 6.1 Arthur Laffer Curve

what economists call the ***multiplier effect***. If you spend $2,000, it becomes someone else's income. When that "someone else" spends it, it becomes yet another person's income. By the time that money stops changing hands, it can create many times itself in added, taxable income. It has been proven mathematically.

What tax rate, therefore, would cause tax revenues to begin to decline? It's hard to say because it depends on the mood of the country. Some of the biggest tax increases in our country have generated fewer rather than more dollars while some tax cuts have actually given the U.S. Treasury more revenue for reasons we have just stated.

Table 6-3 shows the tax revenues of only the federal government by year.

TABLE 6.3 Revenue Collected by the Federal Government by Year

YEAR/REVENUE	YEAR/REVENUE	YEAR/REVENUE
FY 2016 - $3.268 trillion.	FY 1997 - $1.58 trillion.	FY 1978 - $399 billion.
FY 2015 - $3.250 trillion.	FY 1996 - $1.45 trillion.	FY 1977 - $356 billion.
FY 2014 - $3.021 trillion.	FY 1995 - $1.35 trillion.	FY 1976 - $298 billion.
FY 2013 - $2.775 trillion.	FY 1994 - $1.26 trillion.	FY 1975 - $279 billion.
FY 2012 - $2.45 trillion.	FY 1993 - $1.15 trillion.	FY 1974 - $263 billion.
FY 2011 - $2.3 trillion.	FY 1992 - $1.09 trillion.	FY 1973 - $231 billion.
FY 2010 - $2.16 trillion.	FY 1991 - $1.05 trillion.	FY 1972 - $207 billion.
FY 2009 - $2.1 trillion.	FY 1990 - $1.03 trillion.	FY 1971 - $187 billion.
FY 2008 - $2.52 trillion.	FY 1989 - $991 billion.	FY 1970 - $193 billion.
FY 2007 - $2.57 trillion.	FY 1988 - $909 billion.	FY 1969 - $187 billion.
FY 2006 - $2.4 trillion.	FY 1987 - $854 billion.	FY 1968 - $153 billion.
FY 2005 - $2.15 trillion.	FY 1986 - $769 billion.	FY 1967 - $149 billion.
FY 2004 - $1.88 trillion.	FY 1985 - $734 billion.	FY 1966 - $131 billion.
FY 2003 - $1.72 trillion.	FY 1984 - $666 billion.	FY 1965 - $117 billion.
FY 2002 - $1.85 trillion.	FY 1983 - $601 billion.	FY 1964 - $113 billion.
FY2001 - $1.99 trillion.	FY 1982 - $618 billion.	FY 1963 - $107 billion.
FY 2000 - $2.03 trillion.	FY1981 - $599 billion.	FY 1962 - $100 billion.
FY 1999 - $1.82 trillion.	FY 1980 - $517 billion.	FY 1961 - $94 billion.
FY 1998 - $1.72 trillion.	FY 1979 - $463 billion.	FY 1960 - $93 billion.

Source: https://www.thebalance.com/current-u-s-federal-government-tax-revenue-3305762.

Chapter 6 Review

QUESTIONS TO THINK ABOUT

1. Does a tax increase always increase government revenue? Why or why not?
2. Does a tax decrease always reduce government revenue? Why or why not?
3. Explain the circumstances under which an American citizen can experience regressive taxation.

TERMS/PEOPLE TO KNOW

Arthur Laffer

Corporate Taxes

Excise Taxes

Flat Tax

Income Taxes

Laffer Curve

Laffer-Khaldun Curve

Multiplier Effect

Personal Taxes

Progressive Tax System

Property Taxes

Regressive Tax

Sales Taxes

Social Security

CHAPTER SEVEN

Revisiting GDP and Inflation

IN CHAPTER 2, we discussed gross domestic product. Now in Chapter 7, we will discuss how the numbers given to us by government statistics are not always a good representation of how the economy is doing. Additionally we will address some of the measurement problems of our economic performance, and talk about how GDP is used to tell us how much our production capacity has been changed over a given period of time. There is also a second approach to computing GDP, that will be discussed as well.

GDP = C + I + G + X_N

The uses of output are the four major elements of GDP: C + G + I + X_N, where C is equal to consumer spending, G is government spending, I is investment by business in the purchase of capital expenditures, and X_N is equal to net exports.

Remember, one definition of gross domestic product is that it is the measure of all purchases in our country that created jobs and income here during a given period of time.

MEASUREMENT PROBLEMS

In finding out what GDP is during a given calendar quarter, there are measurement problems that can impede its accuracy.

Non-market activities are services for which there is no record available. It can include illegal financial gains, unrecorded transactions by those illegally hiding income, and activities for which there is no charge. For example, if you have had a relative babysit your children for you without paying him or her, that relative gave you a valuable service for which there was no charge. In a sense, there was a form of productivity going on there. That productivity did not get counted in GDP because no money was exchanged.

You must also remember that no counting of intermediate goods takes place. No sale is counted if there is no "added value" to that product for resale. The problem is that it is often difficult to determine whether or not that has happened.

REAL GDP VS. NOMINAL

Sometimes a rise in GDP implies that the economy is getting better when it actually is not. Remember, a growth of GDP doesn't help the economy unless it creates more jobs. If it rises only because prices go up, then we really are kidding ourselves if we say the economy is getting better. That's why it needs to be adjusted downward for inflation. ***Inflation*** is the increase in the *average* level of prices of goods and services.

Nominal GDP is GDP with no adjustments for inflation while ***real GDP*** does take inflation into consideration.

In order to adjust GDP, the actual inflation rate is subtracted from 100%. That number is then multiplied times the nominal GDP to create real GDP. For example, the IMF (International Monetary Fund) estimates that our nominal GDP in 2018 will be $20.199960 trillion and that in 2019 it will jump to $21.024421 trillion. If the current inflation rate were to be at about 2%, then the real GDP for 2019 would be adjusted downward to $20.199960 trillion.

Table 7-1 shows an example from several years ago when inflation was 1.50% between 2001 and 2002. That 1.5% was subtracted from one, giving us a multiplier of 98.5% that is multiplied times nominal GDP. That will give us a better picture of what real GDP would be.

TABLE 7.1 Nominal GDP Converted to Real GDP 2001 and 2018

	2001	2002
NOMINAL GDP	$10,101,000,000,000	$ 10,481,000,000,000
	Actual Inflation 2001-2002	1.50%
	GDP For Which 2002 Should Be	=100% - 1.5% = .985
	Real GDP 2002	$10,323,785,000,000
	2018	2019
NOMINAL GDP ESTIMATES BY THE IMF	$20,199,960,000,000	$ 21,024,421,000,000
	Actual Inflation Estimate 2018-2019	2.00%
	GDP For Which 2019 Should Be	=100% - 2% = .980
	Real GDP Estimate for 2019	$ 20,603,932,580,000

NET DOMESTIC PRODUCT

Gross domestic product is more than just a measurement of how we are doing in the creation of jobs. Particularly, the investment (I) portion of GDP measures how much more in production possibilities we have. Remember, investment here is what businesses have in the way of costs for capital equipment. Capital equipment drives how productive we are and thus what are output capacity is. If businesses are buying more of it, it implies that our Production Possibilities Curve on a national scale is being pushed outward and that there is economic growth. However, sometimes businesses buy more equipment, not to expand, but to improve or replace existing equipment that is worn out. When that happens, production possibilities are mostly unchanged.

So how much does a country spend to replace existing equipment or expand production possibilities? When you calculate ***net domestic product*** you are taking these things into account. It is equal to GDP minus depreciation. Depreciation is the estimated decline in the value of an asset. For example, if I have a pizza parlor that makes deliveries, I can expand my production possibilities by buying more cars for delivery. Cars depreciate (or lose value) by driving them more miles and by how long you own them. The IRS estimates that vehicles lose their value as much as 20% the first calendar year you own them and 32% the second year you own them. That's more than half of its value in two years. Therefore, if I buy more cars to replace the ones I have, my production and delivery of pizzas is unchanged.

Another way of looking at net domestic product is that it is the amount of output we could consume without reducing our stock of capital equipment and, therefore, without reducing our production possibilities.

Thus, the main difference between GDP (gross domestic product) and NDP (net domestic product) is the difference between ***gross investment*** and ***net investment***. Net investment is positive as long as the dollar value of business purchases of plants and equipment (gross investment) exceeds depreciation. If not, our possibilities of added output are simply not happening. If net investment actually declines, we have an even more serious problem. That would indicate that the economy is not only failing to grow but that is contracting.

GDP FROM THE INCOME APPROACH

Another approach to looking at GDP is to look at what people are being paid to produce goods and services, rather than how much people are paying for the goods. In other words, one side of computing GDP adds up *expenditures of those who demand them* (the demand side) while the other adds up the *income* of those who supply them (the supply side).

The total value of market *income* should equal the total value of final output. One person's expenditure represents another's income. If we add up everyone's income, however, it will not equal our existing GDP without making a few adjustments.

What makes the equation out of balance?

First, as mentioned earlier, a major diversion of sales revenues occurs as a result of depreciation costs incurred by businesses. Our capital resources are used up in the process of production in their wear and tear and obsolescence. Thus, they consider some of the sales revenue to be compensation for that, and they will subtract depreciation from gross revenues while calculating their income. Depreciation expense is tax deductible.

Second, you must consider the foreign factor. Income that is earned here is often diverted out of the country as some income is generated in U.S. Markets that belong to people who live in foreign countries. That sends an outflow of money out of the country.

Third, the reverse is also true. U.S. citizens also own businesses in other countries, thus, they receive inflows of income back into the United States from sales not generated here.

Fourth, we have ***indirect business taxes***, such as sales taxes, which must also be deducted from GDP for it to be correct as this money disappears before any factor of production gets a chance to claim it. If you own a business, a part of your sales includes sales tax even though that money doesn't belong to you. It needs to be sent directly to the government.

Fifth, many corporate profits are kept in retained earnings and not given as dividends to stockholders. Many shareholders prefer not to receive dividends from corporations in which they have invested, because they are afraid of those dividends being taxed. They would rather receive the dividends when they retire when they will be in a lower tax bracket. Until they, the want the corporations to take those dividends and grow the business to make their stock values higher, creating more wealth for the shareholder. Therefore, if firms don't pay out profits in dividends, stockholders can't spend them. It becomes the income of a nonhuman entity. On top of that, income for corporations is also taxed at the corporate level. That's why we say that the same corporate profits are taxed the first time when the corporation earns them and a second time when you receive it as a dividend.

Therefore, to make the income approach in calculating national income GDP equal to the expenditure approach of calculating GDP, you must use the following formula:

National Income = Total Income received by current Factors of Production:

a. *Less*, indirect taxes, corporate taxes, retained earnings, Social Security taxes, foreign factors.
b. *Plus*, transfer payments from government, net interest, income from outside the U.S. from U.S.-owned factors.

National income, therefore, also equals personal income. ***Personal income*** is the income of all American households before it is taxed. ***Disposable income*** is the income you can actually spend. You can't spend the money owed or paid to the government in taxes. Some call it ***after-tax income*** of households. That is something that will be important to remember later. Another term that is income related is discretionary income. ***Discretionary income*** is what households can spend at their own discretion. It is equal to disposable income minus any expenses you must pay, many of which you have been committed to before you even earn the income. For example, you can't spend your disposable income at your own discretion until you first pay for food, shelter, clothing, or medical expenses. In some cases, you may have monthly payments on home and auto purchases that you were committed to long before you received your paycheck.

Disposable income is either spent or saved. Therefore, ***savings*** are equal to disposable income minus what you actually spend. Disposable income that is not spent becomes savings. You can either put it in a shoe box, in your attic, in a bank, or into some investments. That is going to be talking about in great detail later in this textbook.

Chapter 7 Review

QUESTIONS TO THINK ABOUT

1. What are some of the flaws in the current methods used for calculating gross domestic product?
2. How is net domestic product calculated, and why is it relevant?
3. Describe why the income method and the expenditure method of calculating GDP are initially out of balance. What can make the two methods balance and be reconciled?

TERMS TO KNOW

After-Tax Income
Discretionary Income
Disposable Income
Gross Investment
Indirect Business Taxes
Inflation
National Income
Net Domestic Product
Net Investment
Nominal GDP
Non-Market Activities
Personal Income
Real GDP
Savings

CHAPTER EIGHT

Inflation

SO FAR, INFLATION, and how it has impacted different aspects of the macro economy, has been discussed quite frequently in this text. In Chapter 8, we will discuss it in more depth, with a look at the different types of inflation, how it is measured, additional ways that it impacts our society, and what some of its sources can be.

WHAT IS INFLATION?

Please recall that ***inflation*** is the increase in the *average* level of prices of goods and services. The ***inflation rate*** is the rate at which it is rising. When prices are actually falling or if the inflation rate is negative, we are experiencing ***deflation***. Some even call it reverse inflation.

The initial assumption is that nobody wants inflation. But, as mentioned earlier, we really don't want inflation to be zero or below zero. Why? Wouldn't it be great if prices stayed put? Wouldn't it even be better if the price of goods and services would actually go down so we could buy more with our money? The answer is no. Sure, buying things at a lower price is great for consumers, but it is not good for producers. When inflation becomes zero or less than zero, producers lose their motivation to produce as mentioned earlier in the law of supply (Chapter 4). Declining prices cause lower profits and less desire to produce. When producers don't produce as much, there are layoffs.

Cheaper goods are of no use if employers cut jobs. You can't buy anything, cheap or expensive, if you are out of work.

Deflation has not occurred often. Below is a list of years when it existed in the United States.

1939, 1940, 1949, 1950, 1954, 1955, 2009

In order to know the ***inflation rate*** each month, the ***Bureau of Labor Statistics (BLS)*** swings into action. It surveys thousands of households and businesses to see what is happening to costs both from the consumer's perspective as well as from the producer's vantage point.

To understand what is happening to costs, the BLS will make three major calculations. First, it calculates what we know as the ***Producers' Price Index (PPI)***. If these prices are rising, it may sometimes signal that the price increases experienced by producers will be passed on to their customers, thus, causing a rise in the ***Consumer Price Index (CPI)***. The CPI measures, thus, the cost of living to general population of consumers. Let's not forget about the middleperson. The wholesalers and distributors of products will also likely have to pay more if producers' costs rise. Therefore, the ***Wholesalers' Price Index (WPI)*** will also be calculated. In the same way, the wholesalers sometimes raise their prices when producers do.

A CLOSER LOOK AT THE CONSUMER PRICE INDEX (CPI)

The BLS has created what we call the basket of goods in order to see and study what is happening to the cost of living. This basket of goods is a list of the different types of goods and services people typically need and purchase during a given time period. They include things such as housing, transportation, food, medical, clothing, and others. In a sense, the BLS goes shopping in 85 cities for such goods and services, visiting approximately 19,000 stores and 60,000 renters, landlords, and homeowners to see what's happening to their prices. These statistics are posted regularly at http://www.bls.gov/.

This basket of goods changes over time. There are things we need and buy now that didn't exist years ago when the CPI was first developed, such as internet service, cell phone service, and more. These things, subsequently, have been added. Other items have been included in the CPI for many decades, but their impact on our family budget has changed, such as in telecommunications. Telecommunications is now a much bigger percentage of the average monthly budget for a family because it now plays a bigger role. An example of the breakdown of these items in the ***market basket of goods*** is shown in Figure 8-1.

As these things change, so too does the weight that is given to each category.

The CPI will often come out with a simple number. That number is compared to prices that existed during what is known as the ***base year***. Generally, the government tries to pick a year from the past where prices became relatively stable. Then, inflation for subsequent years is compared. Right now, that base year is 1984.

For example, as of October 2017, the CPI was 246.4, and that means that whatever had a cost of $100 in 1984 now costs $246.40. That is what is shown from the BLS in Table 8-1 (https://www.bankrate.com/rates/economic-indicators/reports.aspx, 2017).

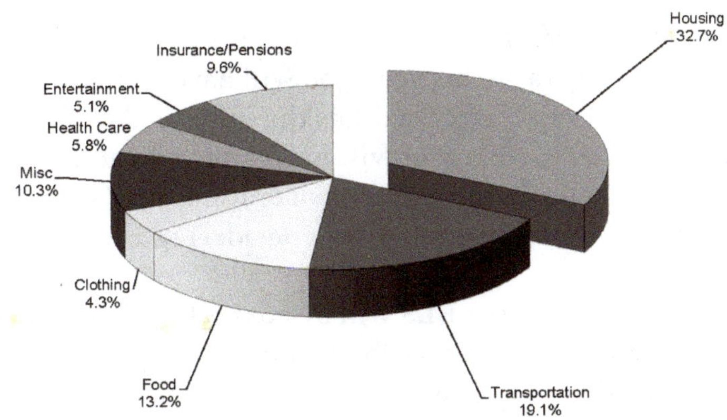

FIGURE 8.1 The Market Basket of Goods

The BLS would then compare that number to previous months to find the rate at which it is moving. Prices fall in some months and rise in others. That is why the annual rate is what is watched very closely.

The ***GDP deflator*** is similar to the CPI. It is a measure of the level of prices of all new, *domestically produced*, final goods in our economy during a certain period of time. Just like CPI, the GDP deflator measures price levels compared to a specific base year of 100. Please recall that the CPI uses a fixed basket of goods in its analysis while the GDP deflator's basket of goods and services is not fixed but is allowed to change from year to year as people's consumption and investment habits change (Gregory, *Essentials of Economics*, 2005)

Inflation is often an element of a *shifting of wealth* as it makes some poorer while making others richer.

One of the complexities of measuring inflation is that some prices go up while others don't, or others do not rise at the same rate. Some prices even fall while others are rising. On several occasions when gasoline prices were falling, they fell so much that they brought down the entire consumer price index to a negative number.

Chain-weighted indexes use a moving average of price levels in consecutive years. This is used as an inflation adjustment. Why? Because there is a flaw in the computation of real GDP. As mentioned earlier, sometimes prices drop, such as in the technology fields and energy while others may rise. If we use higher prices of a few years ago to compute *real* GDP growth, we *inflate the actual* output from those years. On the other hand, if we use today's lower prices for them, we underestimate the output of those things in the past.

TABLE 8.1 Consumer Price Index 10/31/07

	THIS WEEK	MONTH AGO	YEAR AGO
Consumer Price Index 10/31/17	246.4	245.0	241.0

Source: https://www.bankrate.com/rates/economic-indicators/reports.aspx.

Nominal income (discussed in an earlier chapter) is something that will be affected by inflation. If you get a pay raise this year, you will have no more spending power if the rate of increase of that raise, after taxes, is the same as the rate of inflation. ***Real income*** on the other hand, is what you will have after you adjust nominal income downward when you take inflation into consideration. The same process for this is used when nominal GDP is reduced after considering inflation, thus giving us real GDP.

Sometimes the reports from the BLS will discuss ***relative prices***. It is the price of a commodity (such as corn or soy beans, for example) or any other good or service in terms of another. A relative price is often expressed in terms of a ratio between any two prices. It can also be expressed in terms of the ratio between the price of one particular good and a weighted average of all other goods available in the market. For example, if the price of corn goes up at the same rate that other commodities do, that means that corn costs the same in comparison to other food items. If the price of a particular good goes up, for example, by 3%, it's possible that the prices of the other goods and services could go down enough that the overall price level is unchanged. Then, the relative price of the particular good has increased while purchasing power has been unaffected (Wikipedia, 2017).

The effect of a specific price change on the inflation rate depends on the product's relative importance to peoples' budgets known as the ***item weight***. In other words, if clothing is a very small percent of the average budget, clothing price changes are expected to have little effect on the CPI, whereas, if housing or transportation costs rise, their impact on the CPI will be much greater, because they represent a much larger percentage of the average budget.

EFFECTS OF INFLATION

Inflation, like unemployment, causes a great deal of social stress and uncertainty. It can impact our lives in various ways.

The first is the ***price effect of inflation***. This exists when people end up with fewer goods because higher prices make it so that they cannot afford them. The second is the ***income effect of inflation***, which affects people whose nominal incomes go up, but not always as high as the rate of inflation. They wind up with fewer goods as a result. In a sense, when your income cannot buy as much, it is the same as experiencing a drop in income. This often leads to ***money illusions*** where people think their income or wealth is increasing with each pay raise when, in fact, it is declining by not keeping up with the rise in inflation. Your pay increases, after taxes, must increase at a rate that is higher than the inflation rate for any of them to actually increase your income,

The ***interest rate effect of inflation*** is extremely important. People who charge interest for loaning money will almost always charge an ***inflation premium*** to compensate them for inflation. Suppose I put $1,000 in a savings account, and I get an annual interest rate of 3% return from the bank on that account. At the end of one year, I will have $1,030 in that account: the $1,000 I started with, and the 3% interest rate times $1,000 is added in. Let's also suppose that inflation during that period of time was also 3%. Will my spending power at the end of that first year be any greater than the spending power I had with my $1,000 one year earlier? No. My spending power is unchanged because my return in interest is the same as the inflation rate. I would only be breaking even. Therefore, if I want to do better than just break even, I have to make sure that I get an interest rate that is higher than the inflation rate. So, if I want to make at least, perhaps, 4% in interest or increase my spending power by 4%, and if inflation is also 3%, I would have to demand a return of 4% for what I want to net in interest plus a 3% inflation premium, making my required rate of return now at 7%. *This is why inflation is a huge determinant of interest rates*! Higher interest rates make monthly payments higher and thus home and auto loans less affordable.

If lenders don't raise their rates due to inflation, the U.S. Federal Reserve (also called the Fed) will. It will raise interest rates to slow down the growth of GDP when it feels that we are at full employment and that unacceptable inflation is imminent. More on that later.

THE FULL EMPLOYMENT, INFLATION, AND STOCK MARKET CHAIN REACTION

The ***stock market chain reaction effect*** is another factor to consider as a result of inflation. The stock market plays a major role in our economy and is very important.

One reason is that many people assume that when the stock market is doing well that the economy is also doing well. This isn't always true, but whether it is true or not, the public will often base its expectations of future economic health on the stock market's performance. When stock prices fall, expectations become full of pessimism, and, as mentioned earlier, the Aggregate Demand Curve may shift left and cause a recession.

Another reason that it is important is that businesses have trouble expanding if they can't issue stock as easily. When stock prices fall, companies can't get the price they want to expand much as they want. They would need to sell more shares of stock to raise a certain amount of money.

Also, many people, including our retirees, rely heavily on the stock market because their incomes are derived (in addition to any Social Security income they receive) from money they have invested over the years in 401k plans and the like. Any person or institution that relies on higher value in stocks and higher dividends is going to have a problem.

During the stock market plummet in the summer of 2008, many retirees had to dramatically reduce their consumer spending. In some cases, people who were more than eighty years old had to find jobs as their retirements weren't able to help them pay the bills.

All of these things spell trouble for the economy.

That's why it's also important to understand the effects of the stock market on full employment.

One thing that will often bring down stock prices is high interest rates, and high interest rates are commonly the result of higher inflation for reasons discussed earlier. *High interest rates, and, therefore, high inflation hurt stock prices*. Why? There are two major reasons.

First, businesses get less business when interest rates are high, particularly in the industries that rely on them. The big ones, i.e., housing, cars, and appliances, have a tough time selling their goods with high interest rates because people usually can't pay cash for these things, and, thus, they have to borrow to buy them. Higher interest rates make the monthly payments on those products less unaffordable (see Table 8-2).

TABLE 8.2 Interest Rates Impact on Loan Payments

LOAN AMOUNT	YEARS	INTEREST RATE	PAYMENT/MONTH
$100,000	25	3%	$448.62
$100,000	25	4%	$527.84
$100,000	25	5%	$584.59
$100,000	25	6%	$644.30
$100,000	25	7%	$706.78
$100,000	25	8%	$771.82
$100,000	25	9%	$839.20

Second, when interest rates are higher, people will move their invested money from stocks to other investments where they can charge interest, such as certificates of deposit in banks or corporate bonds. In 1980, for example, certificates of deposit (CDs) were paying depositors 10% of their deposit to them in interest. Why would someone take a much higher risk to own a stock that might be paying a return that is almost the same as the low-risk CDs?

In Figure 8-2, the obvious thing to observe is that stock prices will usually rise as income and employment rise. Obviously, as the unemployment rate declines, the employment rate increases. This means more spending by consumers, which will likely create more spending by business, so they can expand in order to cash in on the consumption boom. All of that will bring up profits, and profits will bring up stock prices.

Notice, however, that as we get near full employment, stock prices start to fall. Many wonder why a booming economy would hurt the stock market.

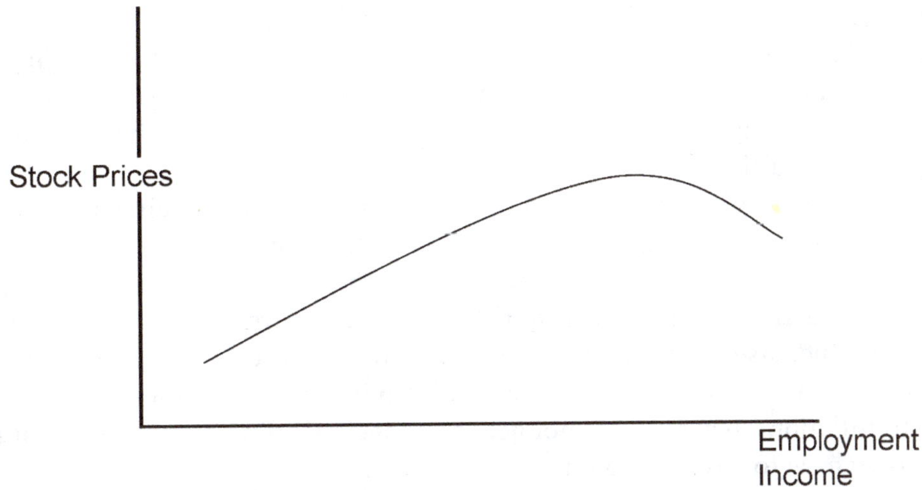

FIGURE 8.2 Employment and Income Impact on Stock Prices

This is the chain reaction that causes the stock market to fall as we near full employment. First, as we near full employment, inflation is believed to be imminent by many shareholders because everyone is working, and aggregate demand is sky-high. Remember, higher demand can bring higher prices. At full employment, demand could possibly get ahead of supply. If inflation does, in fact, become the result of it, shareholders know that the economy will slow. Many times, they will begin to sell off their stocks even before all of these things happen. They dump their stocks today for something that could take months or even a year to occur.

Some argue that there is a short-term tradeoff between unemployment and inflation, but many argue that it doesn't have to be that way. ***Full employment*** is not zero unemployment but the rate of unemployment consistent with price stability, ranging approximately from 4 to 6% in years past. If government can take measures to make sure that supply can keep up with demand by the use of capital equipment (because nearly all employable human capital is already employed at full employment), then GDP can still rise without inflation. Government would not likely set out to reduce GDP to avoid inflation because such a measure could put people out of work. It is more inclined to slow the growth of GDP in order to maintain full employment and stable prices.

The ***bond effect*** is another thing to consider. *High interest rates and, therefore, high inflation hurt bond prices*! Why? Bonds exist when you loan money to various organizations. Neither party normally can change the interest rate on a bond as rates change. I don't want to buy a bond from you (or loan you money) if that bond is going to pay me a low interest rate for it if, in fact, the going interest rates are expected to rise. If I am getting, for example, a 4% return on the bond, while the going rates have now risen to 8%, nobody will be willing to buy that bond from me unless I lower the price. Therefore, the stock effect and the bond effect lead to the ***wealth effects of inflation***. It impacts people who own assets (such as stocks or bonds) because, as mentioned earlier, their value is going down with an increase in inflation; thus, if you own these assets you lose wealth.

Bracket creep is a phenomenon that can confound the average citizen even more. Inflation can cause a taxpayer to be cheated if inflation increases his or her income into a higher tax bracket. As mentioned earlier, those with higher incomes pay a higher rate on that income in our progressive tax structure. If their rate of income (before taxes) increases at a rate that is less than the inflation rate, once again, their spending power is not what it would appear. Even if their rate of increase in income is equal to inflation, they still will not get the added spending power with that raise because they have to pay taxes on it.

Hyperinflation is inflation in excess of 200% lasting one year or more. Fortunately, we have not experienced that here in recent memory, but some foreign countries have.

Let's take another look at the relationship between full employment and inflation.

When we talk about full employment, it is considered by many to be the lowest rate of unemployment consistent with stable prices. Why? Because as we get close to full employment, or when we get there, it is more difficult for firms to hire new people in order to meet their added demand. When we are at full employment, the economy booms, leaving businesses the desire to cash in. They can't, however, if they don't have enough workers to help them produce. They can't hire more people because everybody who is employable is working.

When this happens, I, as a business person, can either hire people from another firm who are already working, or I can simply not increase output but just charge more due to the ensuing shortage of my product. If I hire someone from another firm, I will have to pay him or her more to quit where he or she is now working to motivate my future new hire to come to work for me. Seldom does one leave a given job to go to another voluntarily unless there is more money to be made. If I pay these added workers more than the going wage, or more than what they were paid at their previous job, I have to raise my prices to make up for that cost increase. In either of those two options, I am likely to raise prices. *That's why full employment can cause inflation*.

WHY DO PEOPLE ACCEPT A RATE OF 3% INFLATION OR LESS?

There are three reasons why a 3% inflation rate is acceptable.

First, as mentioned earlier, declining inflation often spells increased unemployment because low or declining prices give no incentive for producers to maintain or increase their output.

Second, products are improving, and we should expect to pay more for higher quality goods. In addition, the CPI does not adjust for quality improvements. Telephone service, for example, is much more expensive than it was twenty years ago, but that is to be expected because telephones can do hundreds of more things than they could back then.

Third, new products have been added to our budgets since the base years of the CPI. There are things we purchase now that didn't even exist then, such as cell phones, personal computers, and GPS trackers.

CAUSES OF INFLATION

Demand-pull inflation exists when demand exceeds supply, causing shortages. It is the result of too much money chasing too few goods. ***Cost-push inflation*** exists when factor costs, or the costs of goods sold, increase for vendors. When that happens, they must raise their prices to maintain their given level of profits per sale.

PROTECTION AGAINST INFLATION

There are some things that are used to reduce the ill effects of inflation.

First, many people simply choose to work extra hours to keep up with inflation, or they seek raises from their employers. As hinted at before, if you increase your income, either by more work or an employer's wage, it is not going to help you if your income, for example, rises by 5% while inflation does. Why? Because you are going to be taxed on that added income. You can't keep up with inflation or beat it unless your income increase meets or beats the inflation rate *after taxes*.

Some employees seek what is called a ***Cost of Living Allowance (COLA)*** from their employers. This is an automatic pay increase that is tied to the inflation rate and given to workers often regardless of performance. It's simply a means for employees to stay ahead of inflation. Again, however, it's no good unless it factors in a person's income after taxes. It is also the reason that the calculation of the CPI is so important to people because their paychecks are directly affected by it.

The ***banking effect of inflation*** is one that has hurt many financial institutions.

These institutions have taken a financial hit over the years with inflation because of the way inflation raises interest rates. Why?

For example, suppose my bank loans you money to buy a home, and I put it on a thirty-year mortgage. That means you have thirty years to pay it back to my bank, in full. Suppose also that I loan it to you at a rate of 4%.

After time passes, if inflation kicks in and pushes interest rates to perhaps 8%, I then have a problem. Some say that interest rates can't change very quickly, but the economic events between 1978 and 1983 proved that wrong. Inflation drove interest rates to well over 12% within eighteen months in that period. How is it that I can continue to afford to keep your loan intact? By having depositors put money in my bank. Over the years, depositors put money in and take it out over and over again, but each time they do so, I have to pay them the going rate of interest, or they simply will not keep putting money into my bank. However, when interest rates I have to pay depositors go above what I am charging you, I'm losing money on you. This is what happened to many banks during those dark days between 1978 and 1983. As a result, many banks failed and had to be bought out by bigger banks.

To avoid this in the future, banks have since offered ***Adjustable Rate Mortgages (ARMs)***, which allow creditors to get more interest when inflation increases and pushes up interest rates. In the example I have here, if the loan I gave you allows me to raise your rate to current levels, I would no longer lose money on your loan.

THE CORE CPI

So how is the government doing when it tries to keep prices stable? Sometimes, the CPI can be misleading. If prices of food and energy rise, it may not be the government's fault because there are things outside the scope of the government's powers to control them. Food relies heavily on weather while energy prices rely on the volatility of stability of other countries that produce oil, which directly impacts energy prices.

Therefore, the ***core CPI*** was created. It is a special index published by the Bureau of Labor Statistics (BLS) which removes the volatile prices of food and energy. By excluding these components, the BLS realizes that prices that swing dramatically in response to unusual shifts in weather and other unforeseen events could skew calculations of inflation trends. In August 1995, the Congressional Budget Office upgraded its analysis of inflation by adopting a separate definition of core inflation. At that time, it began to exclude used cars in addition to food and energy from the overall CPI. Again, it was done to reduce the potentially distorting effects of unusually volatile prices. The CPI is a kind of report card on how well economic policy is managing prices, and if things beyond the control of policymakers are pushing prices up, the core CPI will minimize such distortions (*Current Issues in Economics and Finance*, 2017).

Chapter 8 Review

QUESTIONS TO THINK ABOUT

1. What are some of the major effects of inflation?
2. How does inflation affect interest rates and stock prices?
3. Why does the stock market not like inflation?
4. Why does the stock market not like high interest rates?
5. What are the things that society can do to cope with inflation?

TERMS TO KNOW

Adjustable Rate Mortgages (ARMs)

Banking Effect of Inflation

Base Year

Bond Effect

Bracket Creep

Bureau of Labor Statistics (BLS)

Chain-Weighted Indexes

Consumer Price Index (CPI)

Core CPI

Cost of Living Allowance (COLA)

Cost-Push Inflation

Deflation

Demand-Pull Inflation

GDP Deflator

Hyperinflation

Income Effect of Inflation

Inflation

Inflation Premium

Inflation Rate

Interest Rate Effect of Inflation

Item Weight

Market Basket of Goods

Money Illusions

Nominal Income

Price Effect of Inflation

Producers' Price Index (PPI)

Real Income

Relative Prices

Stock Market Chain Reaction Effect

Wealth Effects of Inflation

Wholesalers' Price Index (WPI)

CHAPTER NINE

Employment and Unemployment

PREVIOUSLY, WE HAVE discussed the idea of unemployment, but in Chapter 9, you will have a better understanding as to how the unemployment rate is calculated and the different types of unemployment.

CALCULATING UNEMPLOYMENT

ECONOMIC MYTH #13	The monthly unemployment figures come from unemployment benefit records.

Each month, the United States Labor Department, using the Bureau of Labor Statistics (BLS), does a survey to see how many people are unemployed. It cannot use unemployment information for those receiving unemployment benefits because there are those who are unemployed who are not receiving unemployment benefits either because the benefits have run out or because they have simply chosen not to apply for them. Still others are unemployed but not eligible for unemployment benefits because they may have quit their jobs voluntarily or for other reasons.

So how does it do it? According to the Bureau of Labor Statistics, it does a survey. Any survey must be done properly in order to remove any bias or inaccuracies.

There are approximately 60,000 eligible households in the sample for this survey. Due to the fact that there is an average of two people in each household, there are approximately 110,000 individuals each month who are surveyed. That's a lot of surveying when you consider that many presidential election surveys only use 1,000 voters in their surveys. The sample is selected so that it will be a good representation of the entire population of the United States.

The sample is a state-based design and reflects urban and rural areas, different types of industrial and farming areas, and the major geographic divisions of each state (Bureau of Labor Statistics, 2017).

ECONOMIC MYTH #14	If you are out of work, you are considered to be among the unemployed when the unemployment rate is calculated.

If you are not working, you may still not be considered as unemployed by the BLS for several reasons. First, suppose, for example, that someone for the BLS calls your home to interview you. If your 12-year-old child answers and says that he or she is not working, obviously your child is not counted among the unemployed because a person must be at least sixteen years old to be considered as a part of the American labor force.

Also, if you are not working, it may be your choice not to work. You may be a stay-at-home parent, or you may be retired. Therefore, you are not considered to be unemployed unless you are jobless and actively seeking work.

You're also not counted among the jobless if you're out of work because of vacation, sickness, labor dispute, and/or bad weather. These reasons are only temporary and are not factors by which the government feels that it needs to fix.

There are those who are excluded from the survey, such as unpaid family workers in family businesses (such as farms), active members of the military, and/or if you're institutionalized, such as those in a prison or nursing home.

SUMMARY FOR UNEMPLOYMENT CALCULATION

You are NOT considered to be among the American workforce and, thus, NOT unemployed (if jobless) while calculating unemployment if:

1. You're under 16 years old.
2. You're not actively seeking work.
3. You're out of work because of vacation, sickness, labor dispute, and/ or bad weather.

Once it has been determined as to how many are legitimately out of work, that number is then divided by the number of people in the American labor force.

If you are any one of the above, even though you are not working, you are not considered a member of the American workforce. (**See latest month's stats at http://www.bls.gov/**)

PROBLEMS CAUSED BY UNEMPLOYMENT

As the unemployment rate climbs, it not only creates problems in the obvious ways of stress and social upheaval from financial woes for many Americans but it also hurts our production possibilities growth (mentioned in Chapter 1), which relies on the availability of factors of production and our technological know-how. If many of these people are jobless, those resources are going to waste.

According to ***Arthur Okun (1928–1980)***, each additional 1% of unemployment reduces real output by 3%. In recent times, that number is now determined to be between 1% and 2%. This, in part, is due to the chain reaction of less people working means there is less work or output performed. Less output means less sold. Lower sales can then raise unemployment even further. It has become to be known as ***Okun's law***. Arthur Okun was an American economist, serving as the chairman of ***The Council of Economic Advisers (CEA)*** between 1968 and 1969, The Council of Economic Advisers (CEA) is a federal government agency within the Executive Office of the President. It was established in 1946 during the administration of President Harry Truman. It advises the president on economic policy The CEA provides much of the nonpartisan research for the White House and prepares an annual economic report for the president (Wikipedia, 2017).

One silver lining that statistics have shown us over the years is that most of the unemployed (more than ¾) find work within six months. However, when workers find new jobs, the jobs don't often pay as much as what the worker was getting before he or she became unemployed.

FLAWS IN THE SYSTEM

Should we consider the monthly statistics for unemployment to be completely accurate? Actually, many economists feel that those numbers need major adjustments for various reasons.

For one thing, the survey relies on the truthfulness of the respondent. There are many who are working but say they are not because they are trying to avoid taxes. Truthfulness from a respondent is hard to assume. Second, the unemployment rate doesn't factor in discouraged workers. Many who are out of work are not actively seeking work because they have tried for so long to get work but have given up. In recent years, our unemployment rate went down, not because there were more jobs but because a record number of people exited the American workforce, largely because they were tired of looking for work to no avail. If those people *could* find work, they would take it in a heartbeat.

Third, there are many who get new jobs, but the new job they get to replace the one they lost pays a much lower wage or salary and in many cases they are only part-time jobs replacing full-time jobs While they are considered employed, they are often referred to as ***underemployed*** or victims of underemployment. Fourth, others say they are looking for jobs but are not making a true effort, thus, they are counted as unemployed when they shouldn't be. Finally, there are the ***phantom unemployed***. They report that they are seeking work when they're not. Quite often they are riding out unemployment benefits and fearing that if it is known that they are not looking for work, there will be consequences, perhaps the loss of their unemployment benefits which often requires that recipients make good faith efforts to find work.

Some say that the ***real unemployment rate*** is often nearly double the rate that is reported by the federal government after factoring in the underemployed and the discouraged workers. In April of 2009, when unemployment hit 8.5%, the real unemployment rate was calculated to be more like 15.6%.

These problems are addressed by the BLS as it digs deeper into the nature of the unemployment circumstances that people are facing. For example, U1 is the percentage of the labor force that have been unemployed for 15 weeks or more. U2 is the percentage of the labor force who have lost jobs or have had their temporary jobs completed. U3 is the official unemployment rate that uses the definition defined by the International Labor Organization (ILO). This occurs when people are without jobs, and they have been actively seeking work within the past four weeks.

U4 is the same as U3 except that it adds discouraged workers who want very much to work but are no longer seeking work because they believe that there are no jobs out there due to the current status of the economy. U5 is the same as U3 and U4 but also adds workers who are able to work but have not been seeking it. Finally, you have U6. These include all of U3, U4, and U5 but are currently working. They simply need more hours, but they can only find part-time jobs. Their income is often dramatically lower than what they were paid in the jobs they lost. They are among the underemployed mentioned earlier (Springer, 2017).

OTHER WAYS TO CATEGORIZE UNEMPLOYMENT

ECONOMIC MYTH #15	Unemployment is only caused by a bad economy.

Unemployment can come in several forms, and it is not always the result of a drop in GDP or a bad economy. The types of unemployment are named after the nature of their causes.

Seasonal unemployment exists when there is a change of season, for example, between cold to warm and warm to cold. There is also the Christmas season that changes into the end of Christmas season. As the Christmas holiday retail boom business begins to slow down, many retailers begin to let workers go. Because of times such as these, there is a spike in unemployment.

For example, in the spring, many of the places whose business relies on cold weather in the North, such as ski resorts, and tourist spots in the South will see a decline in business, and, thus, they will lay workers off. In some situations, even some school teachers will lose their jobs at the end of an academic school year.

In the same way, summer jobs are lost when school starts again, and weather begins to turn cooler. During such times, construction workers, lifeguards, and other workers who are in greater demand during warmer months lose their jobs.

Frictional employment exists when people are found to be in between jobs. Some people don't begin a new job right away after leaving another one. It can happen for several reasons. Some may quit a job voluntarily if they are not happy with their jobs and then take time looking for another, often turning down job offers when they think there is something better out there. Sometimes they want to take a job quickly, but employers who could employ them don't advertise the position openings because they assume, falsely, that there would not be anyone qualified to apply for them.

Frictional unemployment is not considered to be the fault of government policy because the jobs have been created and are, in fact, out there. Government is considered to have done its part by creating the jobs, but employers and workers are just not taking the action to connect. Sometimes workers who are qualified for given employers don't know about those employers who are able and willing to hire them. At same time, those employers don't know that those qualified workers are available either.

Structural employment exists when a worker's skills are, in fact, obsolete. This can happen when technology changes while workers don't upgrade their skills to keep up with those changes. Sometimes older workers are reluctant to learn new skills, especially if they are nearing retirement. Once again, even if the economy is teeming with job openings, many of these people will remain unemployed long after a recession until they can upgrade their skills.

Cyclical unemployment is the most common. It exists when there is a bad economy due to the decline or slow growth in aggregate demand or GDP. In order to understand why it is called cyclical unemployment, you must understand the concept of an ***economic cycle*** or ***business cycle***. An economic cycle is what takes place after an economy has gone full circle (or cycle) between prosperity and recession and then back again.

In Figure 9-1, you can see what happened between the start of the Great Depression and its full recovery by the middle of World War II. The blue line represents GDP and shows how it plummeted during the times of the Depression. When World War II came along, the country was at full employment as everyone was working in the factories to make sure that our soldiers had all they needed for the war effort.

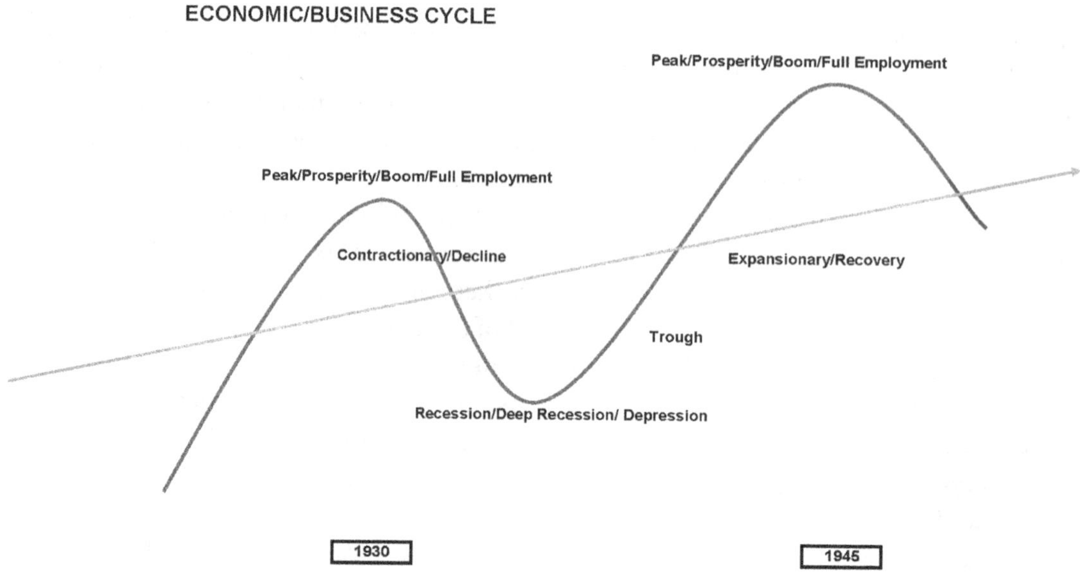

FIGURE 9.1 Economic/Business Cycle

When the blue line is at its highest, the economy is considered to be at its peak or in prosperity, whereby, there is a boom in the economy that is accompanied by full employment. But as the economy begins to contract or decline, it moves into the ***contractionary/decline*** sector of the cycle, and GDP falls into the ***trough***. When that happens, a large number of Americans will experience cyclical unemployment. How deep is the "trough"? That all depends upon the things that begin to happen to correct decline. It could become no more than a mild recession, but it could become a deep recession. Heaven forbid, that it could get bad enough to become a depression.

Many economists do not agree on what level unemployment would have to reach in order to have a depression. In the Great Depression of the 1930s, unemployment reached close to 25% with no safety nets available from the federal government, such as unemployment benefits and welfare programs. The closest that we have come to that point since then was in 1982 and in 2009 when unemployment reached nearly 11%, but safety nets were well in place at those times. Therefore, many economists don't feel that those circumstances compared to those that existed during the Great Depression and thus were only deep recessions.

As recovery begins to take place, GDP begins to go into the ***expansionary/recovery*** sector of the cycle and, once again, reaching the level of prosperity.

Over the years, we have often seen structural and frictional unemployment increase. There have been several theories of the causes.

One theory is that years ago, in the late 1960s and early 1970s, more youth and women entered the workforce during that time, and most of them lacked skills needed during that period. As they were all taking their time to find the right job and without matching skills, many argue that frictional and structural unemployment was the result. Rapid change in demand and technology reduced jobs in unskilled positions and increased them in skilled positions.

Also, during those same times, many more people were eligible to receive welfare and unemployment benefits, which increased prolonged frictional unemployment.

If you lose your job because the economy is somewhere below the boom, you are experiencing cyclical unemployment. Of all of the different types of unemployment, that is the only one that the government feels that it can really take action to correct by applying economic policy.

Some economists do not agree as to what rate of unemployment might start serious inflation. Some economists no longer believe that a rise in inflation should be a sign of full employment. Later, we will discuss an economic philosophy called the ***Monetarist Theory***, which was endorsed by economist Milton Friedman (who will be discussed later). The ***Monetarists*** prefer to use the term ***natural unemployment*** that doesn't depend on inflation trends. It contains structural and frictional unemployment only. Natural unemployment is the "rate of unemployment that will exist when there is no one experiencing cyclical unemployment" (Schiller, *The Macro Economy Today*, 2016).

Over the years, the ***structural determinants*** of unemployment, (such as age and composition of the labor force) change. When these forces change, natural unemployment will likely change. (Schiller, *The Macro Economy Today*, 2016) For example, during the 1970s, there were few teens in the workforce, thus, lowering unemployment without a change in inflation. Why? Because teens in the 1970s experienced a lot of structural unemployment as technology was on the rise. As they lacked some of the skills needed, when their entrance into the workforce slowed down, there was not much of a shortage of workers because their skill level was not needed as much anyway.

The level of aggregate supply depends mostly upon the production capacity of our businesses in the way of machinery, the efficiency and effectiveness of our labor market who work in those factories, and other "structural" forces, such as education and skill level of our workers, which create natural unemployment. These structural forces are often driven by demographics, such as age and income levels. Those demographics often determine the level of skills that some people have. For example, low-income families may not have the opportunity to afford college or some other form of technical training of skills that are required by employers. Age can also be a problem for those who attended college during a time when such technological information was not available. That natural unemployment rate is not likely to be affected by any short-run government policies. Why? Because you can have a booming economy but still be unable to get work for the people who lack the skills that are needed in that labor market (Schiller, *The Macro Economy Today*, 2016).

The Aggregate Supply Curve tells us that as we near full employment, or the level of output where we have reached our limits of production capacity, the risk of inflation is higher.

FULL EMPLOYMENT

Understanding cyclical unemployment helps you to understand why we say that ***full employment*** doesn't have to be zero unemployment. Many economists feel that full employment has been reached under various circumstances.

Some say it has been achieved when unemployment dips below 5%, but that has been found to be untrue. When unemployment was at 4.9%, many said full employment had been reached, but soon after that it continued to go down. On several occasions, it has gone down below 4%.

Full employment has often been declared to have been reached when we still see unemployment in existence while there are still many, many jobs going unfilled. As the unemployment rate is compiled each month, among the questions asked on the survey concerns the reason for the unemployment. In many cases, it is found that those who comprise the unemployment rate are experiencing frictional or structural unemployment which the government feels there is little they can do to correct.

The government has taken measures to sponsor programs to help people get the skills they need to compete in the job market. They often have programs that help workers to find employers and for employers to find workers while trying to match workers and their skills with open job positions. But those programs are different from the policies that government sets up to end cyclical unemployment.

Many say that rising prices are a signal of nearing full capacity and full employment. However, this thinking was criticized when the late 70s and early 80s' saw rampant inflation and high unemployment (also known as stagflation).

Chapter 9 Review

QUESTIONS TO THINK ABOUT

1. Explain why a person who is not working may not be considered unemployed.
2. Describe what happens during an economic cycle.
3. Under what circumstances does a society experience full employment?
4. What are the flaws in the system of calculation of unemployment?
5. Why doesn't the government just use its own records of those who receive unemployment benefits when calculating unemployment?

TERMS/PEOPLE TO KNOW

Arthur Okun (1928–1980)

Contractionary/Decline Sector

Cyclical Unemployment

Economic Cycle

Expansionary/Recovery

Frictional Employment

Full Employment

Monetarist Theory

Monetarists

Natural Unemployment

Okun's Law

Phantom Unemployed

Real Unemployment Rate

Seasonal Unemployment

Structural Determinants

Structural Employment

The Council of Economic Advisers

Trough

Underemployed

CHAPTER TEN

Economic Theories

SO FAR, THE idea of economic theories has been discussed in a rather abstract manner. In Chapter 10, we will now begin to get deep into the heart of those theories that are typically applied in one fashion or another in our society. Sometimes policy makers of government apply them in a deliberate manner with full understanding of them, while other policy makers apply them without really knowing them. Some have endorsed one theory over another without really understanding them. By the end of this chapter, you should have a firm grasp on what the macroeconomic theorists feel is the best for our economy under given circumstances and why they feel that way. You will also learn how government has changed its views over the centuries when it comes to getting involved with the economy.

You will also learn what the major causes were of the Great Depression of 1929 and how the theorists felt about it.

THE EVOLUTION OF GOVERNMENT INVOLVEMENT IN THE ECONOMY

The way for our government to reach its goals in managing the economy is by understanding macroeconomics, which helps us to know how stable the economy is, what causes the instabilities, and what can be done about it, if anything.

Before the Great Depression of the 1930s, bad economies were called ***panics***. Aside from those mild downturns in the economy, it was believed a depression could never happen and that no need for government intervention was necessary. This thinking embraced the ***laissez-faire philosophy***, which basically prescribed that government should practice a "hands-off" mentality.

When the Great Depression hit, the opinions of many began to rethink things, believing that government intervention was now necessary. It was soon after that, that the task of managing the economy was put squarely on the shoulders of the federal government by law.

It taught us that there are things that government did that may have caused the Great Depression or failed to prevent it. Many wanted to make sure that this would never happen again.

We need to briefly look at the main factors contributing to the severity of the Great Depression of the 1930s.

ECONOMIC MYTH #16	The Great Depression was caused only by the stock market crash of 1929.

Many always think that the stock market crash caused the Great Depression, but there were actually many things in addition to the crash that converged to make it more of a perfect storm. In some ways, the stock market crash of 1929 was a symptom of other things going wrong in the economy at that time. Once it happened, we could have gotten through it with fewer problems, as we did in 2008, but there were other things that happened or that the government did, or failed to do, that made the Great Depression worse and last longer.

First, there was the *overstimulated economic euphoria of the 1920s*, causing more people to buy with credit and to buy stocks that were not worth what people were paying for them. When people realized that the economy wasn't so good and that stocks were overpriced, everything came crashing down. Something similar to that happened in the summer of 2008.

Euphoria and optimism about the economy are good as long as it is realistic. If people buy stock and borrow with the false assumption that we can never have bad economic times again, credit becomes over used and stocks become overpriced. Both of these can do major damage to the economy. When people borrow too much with credit and then can't pay the money back, the institutions who loaned to those borrowers could collapse. If people pay more for stocks than their true worth, a day will come when those stockholders will take huge losses as those prices fall.

Second, *wealth distribution inequities led to the overuse of credit*. Many people who weren't rich wanted to live a better life, thus, they began to borrow to get things they could not afford. When the credit was extended to them, the economy was greatly damaged when these people couldn't pay. When banks and financial institutions began to collapse, the economy began to collapse, as well. Later, we will discuss why banks and financial institutions are vital to an economy.

Third, *common people were investing in stocks and bonds with no experience*. Many had purchased war bonds during World War I; before then, few people did any kind of investing. It was almost a stigma to invest as it was considered to be similar to gambling by many people. When war bonds gave many people nice financial rewards, after the war they naturally began to move up to stocks, not knowing what they were doing. Many of those who were pros at stock trading took advantage of the inexperienced, building a powder keg ready to explode, which the market finally did in the fall of 1929.

Fourth, *many people's life savings and wealth were gone*. They have what they call ***margin call***, which means that if you borrow to buy stock (which many did in those days due to the over optimism people had), when those stocks plummet in value, the lenders for the purchases of those stocks foreclose on them. In 1929 if stockholders didn't have enough in their savings to pay the debt (which was the case for many), they had to sell their homes and cars to pay it back.

Fifth, obviously a major decline in spending took place *because consumer confidence was destroyed*.

Sixth, *the United States Federal Reserve began a very harsh monetary policy from 1930 through 1933* because of lenders previously giving too much credit. Many economists feel, however, that the federal reserve went too far in that policy, thus, few people could get loans. This caused an even further drop in purchases of appliances, cars, and homes.

Seventh, as businesses began to fail, it was assumed that it was due, in large part, to the loss of business obtained by American firms, because Americans did a lot of importing. Therefore, the Smoot-Hawley Tariff was passed in 1930 to help protect these American companies. It charged a high tax for imports. Those import taxes caused less trade between the United States and several countries abroad, and those countries retaliated with their own taxes levied against American goods that they would otherwise have imported from us. Trade wars such as these did serious damage to our export market (Beacon Historical Society, 2018). To this day, there are those who still insist that we impose tariffs and import taxes again while forgetting that such policies hurt our export markets in the past. Many people fear that international trade wars have few victors.

Eighth, instead of lowering taxes to give Americans more disposable income to spend, taxes were raised. With the government collecting fewer dollars as a result of the Great Depression, there was a dramatic increase in income taxe rates in 1932 that many believe prolonged the downturn.

Ninth, there was also *a sharp reduction in the money supply* in banks available to those who wished to buy cars, homes, and appliances due to inadequate bail-out procedures for banks and no depositors' insurance in those days.

Tenth, there were *no safety nets for those who were out of work*, with the exception of a few bread lines and soup kitchens. There was no such thing as unemployment benefits, Social Security, Medicare, or welfare programs. These programs were mostly created in response to the Great Depression. They were designed to act as ***automatic economic stabilizers*** ever since. They were given that name because they have now automatically come into play whenever people are eligible for such financial help toward the stabilizing of their economic situations.

Table 10-1 and Figure 10-1 show the actual numbers during those dark economic times compared to unemployment before and since.

TABLE 10.1 Unemployment/Inflation Rates Since 1929

1929	3.2%	NA	0.6%	Market crash
1930	8.7%	-8.5%	-6.4%	Smoot-Hawley
1931	15.9%	-6.4%	-9.3%	Dust Bowl
1932	23.6%	-12.9%	-10.3%	Hoover's tax hikes
1933	24.9%	-1.3%	0.8%	FDR's New Deal
1934	21.7%	10.8%	1.5%	New Deal
1935	20.1%	8.9%	3.0%	New Deal
1936	16.9%	12.9%	1.4%	New Deal
1937	14.3%	5.1%	2.9%	Spending cuts
1938	19.0%	-3.3%	-2.8%	FLSA starts min wage
1939	17.2%	8.0%	0%	Drought ended
1940	14.6%	8.8%	0.7%	U.S. draft
1941	9.9%	17.7%	9.9%	Pearl Harbor
1942	4.7%	18.9%	9.0%	Defense tripled
1943	1.9%	17.0%	3.0%	World War II persists
1944	1.2%	8.0%	2.3%	Bretton Woods
1945	1.9%	-1.0%	2.2%	War ends. Min wage $.40.
1946	3.9%	-11.6%	18.1%	Employment Act
1947	3.9%	-1.1%	8.8%	Marshall Plan
1948	4%	4.1%	3.0%	Truman reelected
1949	6.6%	-0.5%	-2.1%	Fair Deal. NATO
1950	4.3%	8.7%	5.9%	Korean War. Min wage $.75.
1951	3.1%	8.1%	6.0%	Expansion
1952	2.7%	4.1%	0.8%	Expansion
1953	4.5%	4.7%	0.7%	Korean War ended
1954	5%	-0.6%	-0.7%	Dow returned to 1929 level
1955	4.2%	7.1%	0.4%	Unemployment fell
1956	4.2%	2.1%	3.0%	Min wage $1.00
1957	5.2%	2.1%	2.9%	Recession
1958	6.2%	-0.7%	1.8%	
1959	5.3%	6.9%	1.7%	Expansion.
1960	6.6%	2.6%	1.4%	Recession.
1961	6%	2.6%	0.7%	JFK. Min wage $1.15.
1962	5.5%	6.1%	1.3%	Cuban Missile Crisis
1963	5.5%	4.4%	1.6%	LBJ. Min wage $1.25.

TABLE 10.1 Unemployment/Inflation Rates Since 1929 (*continued*)

YEAR	UNEMPLOYMENT RATE (DECEMBER)	GDP GROWTH	INFLATION (DECEMBER YEAR-OVER-YEAR)	WHAT HAPPENED
1964	5%	5.8%	1.0%	Tax cut
1965	4%	6.5%	1.9%	Vietnam War
1966	3.8%	6.6%	3.5%	Expansion
1967	3.8%	2.7%	3.0%	Min wage $1.40
1968	3.4%	4.9%	4.7%	Min wage $1.60
1969	3.5%	3.1%	6.2%	Nixon took office
1970	6.1%	0.2%	5.6%	Recession
1971	6%	3.3%	3.3%	Emergency Employment Act. Wage-price controls.
1972	5.2%	5.2%	3.4%	Stagflation
1973	4.9%	5.6%	8.7%	CETA. Gold standard. Vietnam War ended.
1974	7.2%	-0.5%	12.3%	Watergate. Min wage $2.00.
1975	8.2%	-0.2%	6.9%	Recession ended
1976	7.8%	5.4%	4.9%	Expansion
1977	6.4%	4.6%	6.7%	Carter took office.
1978	6%	5.6%	9.0%	Fed raised rate to 20% to stop inflation
1979	6%	3.2%	13.3%	
1980	7.2%	-0.2%	12.5%	Recession
1981	8.5%	2.6%	8.9%	Reagan tax cuts. Min wage $3.35.
1982	10.8%	-1.9%	3.8%	Job Act. Garn-St.Germain Act.
1983	8.3%	4.6%	3.8%	Reagan increased military spending
1984	7.3%	7.3%	3.9%	
1985	7%	4.2%	3.8%	Expansion
1986	6.6%	3.5%	1.1%	Tax cuts
1987	5.7%	3.5%	4.4%	Black Monday
1988	5.3%	4.2%	4.4%	Fed raised rate
1989	5.4%	3.7%	4.6%	S&L Crisis
1990	6.3%	1.9%	6.1%	Recession
1991	7.3%	-0.1%	3.1%	Desert Storm. Min wage $4.25.
1992	7.4%	3.6%	2.9%	NAFTA drafted
1993	6.5%	2.7%	2.7%	Balanced Budget Act

(*continue*)

TABLE 10.1 Unemployment/Inflation Rates Since 1929 (*continued*)

YEAR	UNEMPLOYMENT RATE (DECEMBER)	GDP GROWTH	INFLATION (DECEMBER YEAR-OVER-YEAR)	WHAT HAPPENED
1994	5.5%	4.0%	2.7%	School to Work Act
1995	5.6%	2.7%	2.5%	Expansion
1996	5.4%	3.8%	3.3%	Welfare reform
1997	4.7%	4.5%	1.7%	Min wage $5.85
1998	4.4%	4.5%	1.6%	LTCM crisis
1999	4%	4.7%	2.7%	Euro. Serbian airstrike.
2000	3.9%	4.1%	3.4%	NASDAQ hit record high.
2001	5.7%	1.0%	1.6%	Bush tax cuts. 9/11 attacks.
2002	6%	1.8%	2.4%	War on Terror
2003	5.7%	2.8%	1.9%	JGTRRA
2004	5.4%	3.8%	3.3%	Expansion.
2005	4.9%	3.3%	3.4%	Bankruptcy Act. Katrina.
2006	4.4%	2.7%	2.5%	Expansion.
2007	5.0%	1.8%	4.1%	EU became #1 economy.
2008	7.3%	-0.3%	0.1%	Min. wage = $6.55/ hour. Financial crisis.
2009	9.9%	-2.8%	2.7%	ARRA. Min wage $7.25. Jobless benefits extended.
2010	9.3%	2.5%	1.5%	Obama tax cuts. Iraq War ended.
2011	8.5%	1.6%	3.0%	26 months of job losses by July. Debt ceiling crisis.
2012	7.9%	2.2%	1.7%	QE. 10-year rate at 200-year low. Fiscal cliff.
2013	6.7%	1.7%	1.5%	Stocks up 30%. Long term = 50% of unemployed.
2014	5.6%	2.6%	0.8%	Unemployment at 2007 levels.
2015	5.0%	2.9%	0.7%	Natural rate
2016	4.7%	1.5%	2.1%	Presidential race

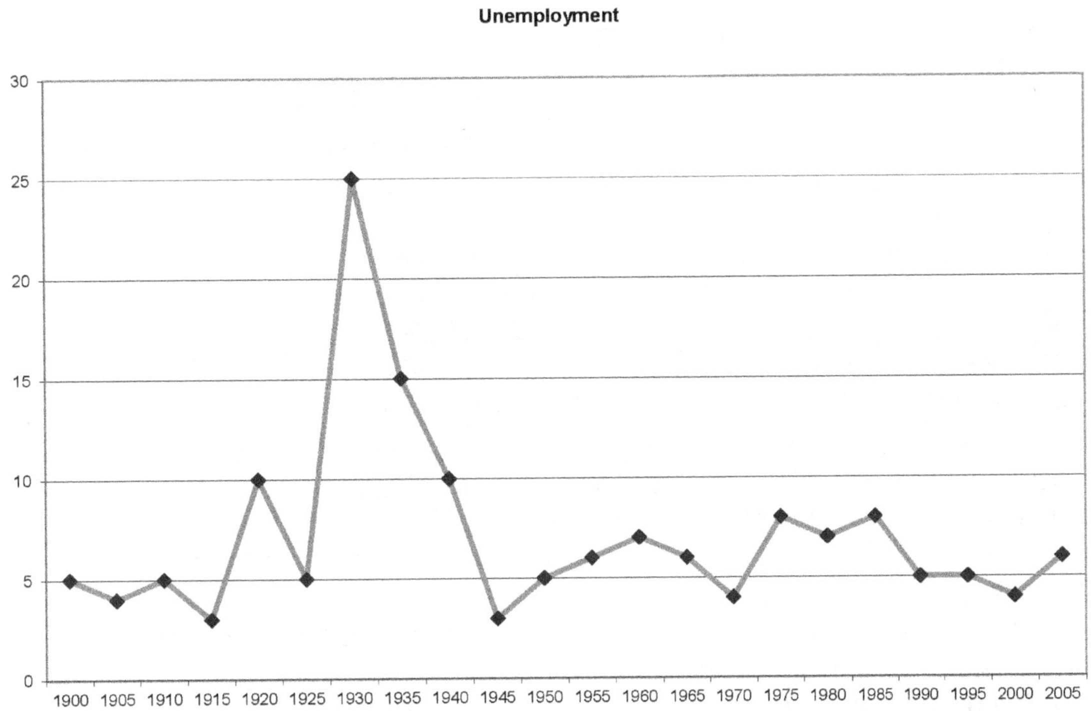

FIGURE 10.1 Unemployment/Inflation Rates Since 1929 (Graph)

SO HOW DO WE MAKE SURE IT WILL NEVER HAPPEN AGAIN?

There are four major economic theories that prescribe how government should manage the economy. As stated earlier, both liberal and conservative economists have come to believe that none of the theories is right or wrong. Theories simply should be applied at the right time and not at the wrong time. They are like medication for the economy. They should be used or avoided at the appropriate time.

First, the ***Classical Theory*** embraces the "hands off" mentality of government intervention with the economy in that it proposes that it self-regulates (as did Adam Smith). It embraces the proverb developed by French economist ***Jean Baptiste Say (1767–1832)*** known as ***Say's Law***: Supply creates its own demand. The logic of the law implies that if all markets except one are balanced, then the last one also must balance. This conclusion from Say's Law was named after ***Leon Walras (1834–1910)*** and has become known as ***Walras's Law***.

When Franklin D. Roosevelt was president, he believed in using ***Keynesian Economics***, (or the Keynesian Theory), which is the second theory we will discuss. It is the complete opposite of the Classical Theory. Keynesian Theory (also called Demand-Side Economics) was developed by economist ***John Maynard Keynes (1883–1946)***, who wrote ***The General Theory of Employment, Interest and Money***. He was a British economist whose philosophies dramatically changed the theories, practices, and policies of different governments.

The Keynesian Theory actually began to be applied by Herbert Hoover in the later years of his presidency, but he was criticized by FDR in the election of 1932. Ironically, FDR embraced and implemented it more than any other administration prior or since he became president.

John Maynard Keynes developed it and prescribed that government should pull out all the stops to increase GDP by lowering taxes, increasing government spending, and increasing the money supply available to buyers and borrowers. He strongly believed that the government must buy its way back into prosperity. After all, GDP is the sum of $C + I + G + X_n$. He felt that we needed to just make G (government spending) rise to put everyone back to work. *It is important to note that Keynes believed that the money spent should be for programs that would fulfill legitimate social needs*. He did not endorse paying someone to dig a hole and to then fill it back in. He prescribed the idea of spending the money on things such as improvement of our roads and infrastructure..

What Keynes prescribed, therefore, was to *shift the Aggregate Demand Curve outward, or to the right*, using whatever means possible as shown in Figure 10-2. That is why his theory is often referred to as ***Demand-Side Economics***.

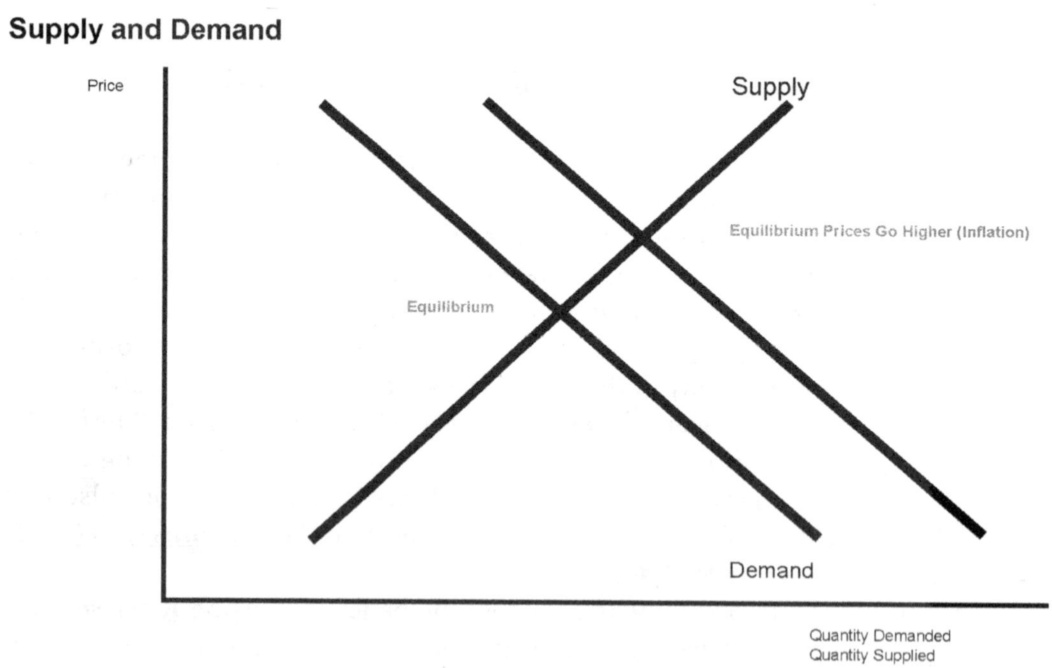

FIGURE 10.2 Demand-Side Economics

Classical theorists believe that when FDR spent money to stimulate the economy in this way, it would cost jobs because they believed that such a plan required higher tax dollars from American businesses and consumers. If Roosevelt were to raise taxes to do this kind of spending, the theorists felt that disposable income would then be lower as would be the amount of money spent in the economy for consumption and investment by business. Therefore, they felt that higher taxes would offset any increases in spending by government and that GDP would remain low.

Keynes argued that the government didn't have to raise taxes to pay for the government's added spending, thus, no jobs would be lost. He felt that the government could spend more than it brought in, in the way of tax revenue (known as ***deficit spending***). He felt that the government could borrow to pay for the deficit and then, when the economy boomed again, the government would collect more in taxes from the added taxable income created by the boom. At that point he felt that that they could use the added tax revenue they collected during such boom times to pay off that loan. He also prescribed that all people, rich people, middle-class people, and poor people should all be given a tax break. Taxes would not go up as predicted by the classical theorist, but, rather, they would go down. This, he said, would increase consumer spending (C), and and spending by business as they invested in more capital equipment (I). He believed that his policies would not decrease C and I, but would in fact increase them. This he felt would thus push the Aggregate Demand Curve out.

Figure 10-3 shows a summary of what Keynes and the Monetarists (the fourth theory, to be discussed later in this chapter) believed would happen with an increase in government spending.

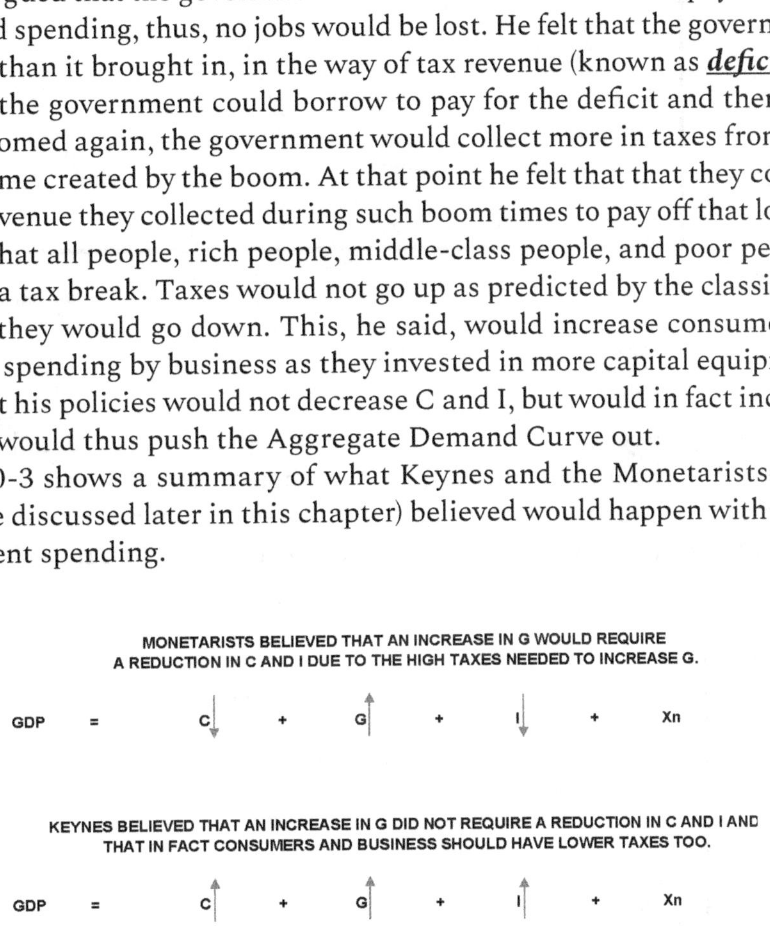

FIGURE 10.3 $C + G + I + X_n$ Changes Predicted by Keynes and Classical Economists

Another criticism of Keynes's thinking was that shifting the Aggregate Demand Curve outward would raise equilibrium prices, causing significant inflation as is also shown in Figure 10-2.

Keynes's response to that was that during bad times, when aggregate demand is needed to be shifted out, the *Aggregate Supply Curve would be flat* as shown in

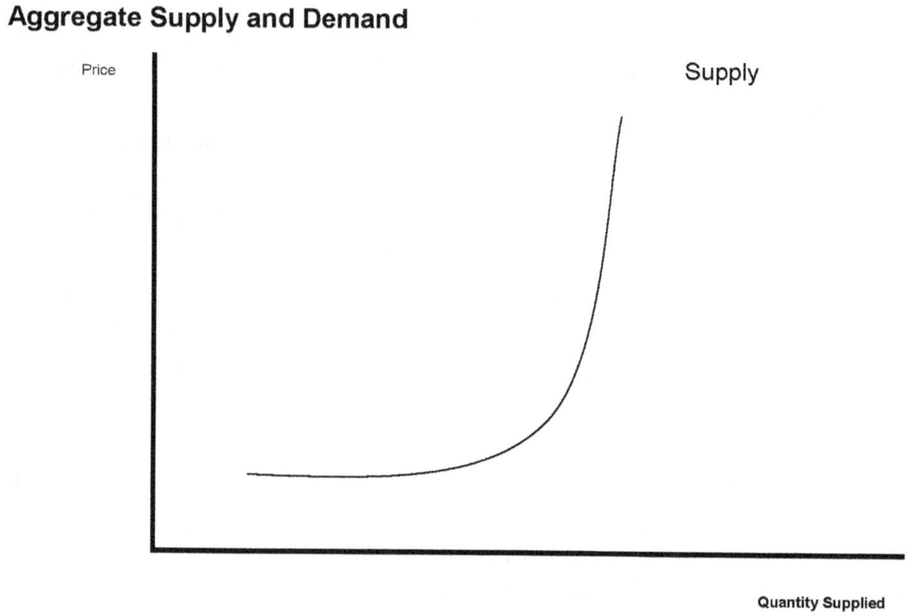

FIGURE 10.4 Long Run Aggregate Supply

Figure 10-4. Why? Because during bad times, people will be more than happy to supply more and without requiring more pay per hour or unit produced. During deep recessions, factories are just happy to get work. They usually have a great deal of idle areas in their factories, and idle factories are costly to own when there is no business

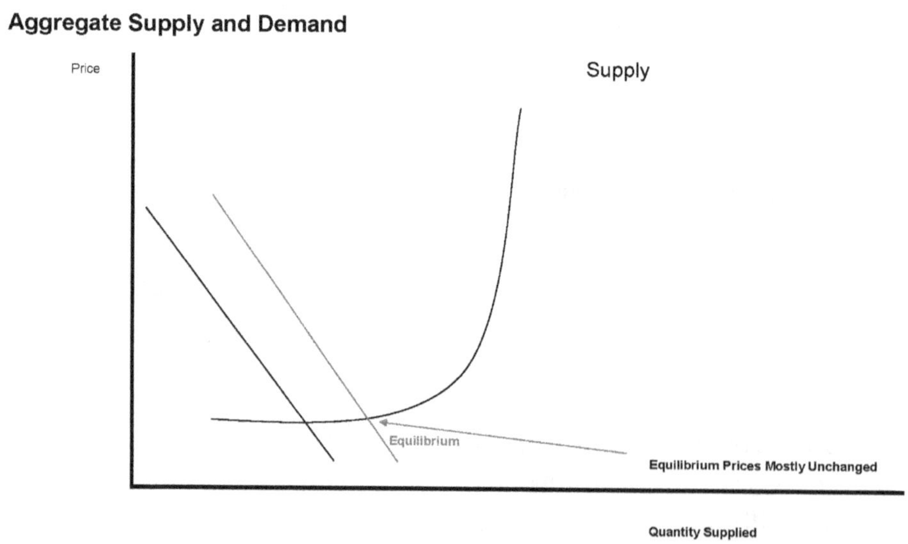

FIGURE 10.5 The Effect of Keynesian AD Curve Shift on the Long Run Aggregate Supply

to keep them active. Workers are the same way. They are just happy to get back to work, and they will not demand a larger wage as more of their time is needed. Thus, they will supply more labor at the same wage.

Another reason that the Aggregate Supply Curve is flat during recessions is that suppliers of resources to factories and businesses often lower their prices to get business volume back to where it was before the bad times set in. If suppliers lower their prices, as a producer, I can actually make more money per unit produced, motivating me to increase supply.

If Keynes is correct, then shifting the Aggregate Demand Curve outward will not cause inflation during those times as equilibrium would remain mostly unchanged as illustrated in Figure 10-5.

Even if higher prices did ensue, Keynes argued that price levels don't have as much of an impact on aggregate demand (AD) as their income does. He feels that people will spend money if they have it regardless of price levels.

Classical view: The economy will turn around in the long run, and to let it self-correct is better for the economy in the long run.

Keynesian View: People don't eat in the long run.

Herbert Hoover was president when the Great Depression hit us, but he also embraced the Classical view; thus, he did little to intervene with government action during the Depression. He asked people to be patient and that the economy would soon turn around on its own. Many Classical economists believe to this day that the Depression would have been solved, but that FDR's programs slowed down the process (all of which are still subject to debate).

The third theory, ***Supply-Side Economics***, postulates that it isn't the Aggregate Demand Curve that needs to be shifted to the right but, rather, that the *Aggregate Supply Curve should be shifted out*, and when you do so, you get the better of both worlds. *GDP and, therefore, aggregate demand will still increase and with stable prices*. Please note in Figure 10-6 how equilibrium prices actually decline while GDP is still growing when the Aggregate Supply Curve is shifted to the right. That is the main objective of the government: to have full employment through higher GDP and with stable prices. It's like a dream come true.

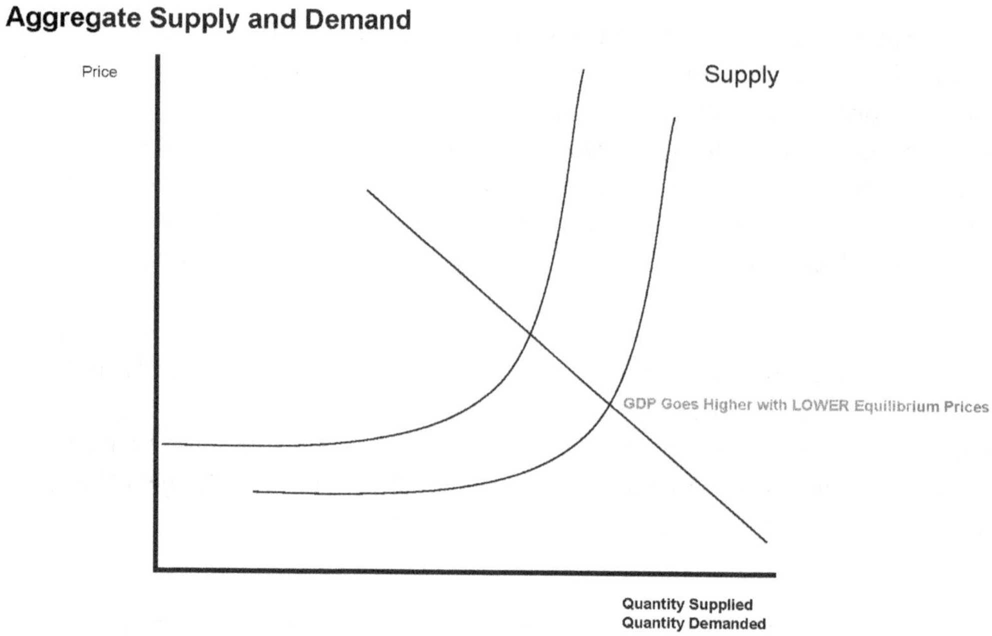

FIGURE 10.6 The Effect of Supply-Side Economics AS Curve Shift on the Long Run Aggregate Supply

On the other hand, a leftward shift of the Aggregate Supply Curve is a nightmare, bringing us to stagflation with higher unemployment and higher prices. Such action would increase what many have called the ***Misery Index***. The Misery Index (also called ***the tragic number*** by President ***Jimmy Carter*** in 1976), is equal to the inflation rate plus the unemployment rate. A leftward shift it is believed, therefore, should be avoided in any way possible. Higher unemployment and inflation combined are a bad combination. It's bad enough to be out of work but much worse when prices for necessities are also rising. Leftward shifts can be caused by a natural disaster or an abrupt price increase of necessary commodities, such as oil. Oil shocks also create circular flow leakages as we become more dependent upon foreign oil. Supply-Side theorists also argue that government policies can and have already shifted the supply curve left over the years, with the rise of taxes and unnecessary government regulations.

Supply-Side Economics was originally tagged nationally as ***Reaganomics*** because President ***Ronald Reagan (1911–2004)*** was a firm believer in its thinking. However, the theory came from a group led by economists ***Robert Mundell*** and ***Arthur Laffer***. Many believe that the term "Supply-Side Economics" was the brain child of journalist ***Jude Wanniski*** in 1975. Others say that the term was first used by ***Herbert Stein*** in 1976. He was an economic advisor to President ***Richard Nixon (1913–1994)***.

Supply-Side Economics is also often compared to ***trickle-down economics***, which is the belief that when there are economic benefits provided to the rich, it will help society as a whole because the rich can create more jobs with their wealth. It is thought that they will be motivated to increase output, and when their extra wealth is spent into the economy, it provides wealth for lower income earners and creates jobs. This wealth, in turn, is turned back into the economy. Thus, the wealth of the rich trickles down to those who need jobs.

Supply can be shifted out in the ways described earlier. Supply-Side theorists believe that anything that creates bottlenecks in production or whatever impedes a firm's ability to get the product or service completed and into the hands of customers must be removed. Bottlenecks can include, but are not limited to, inadequate workers skill, bad highways, bridges, and out-of-date computers.

Another of the many ways that Supply-Side theorists believe you can increase supply is that, they insist, society must eliminate discrimination. There should be a zero tolerance of it. <u>***Discrimination***</u> prevents good, qualified people to be hired for jobs based upon their demographics rather than their skills, knowledge, and experience. They feel it is immoral and unethical. It is also illegal. Supply-Side theorists also feel that it leads to waste of the valuable resources that all people have to offer to enhance productivity.

Supply-Side theorists also feel that qualified people who are offered a living by not working can become another bottleneck in an economy. Many of them feel that assistance should only be given to the truly needy, compelling good workers to be willing to supply their labor. Many believe that the <u>***Welfare Reform Act of 1995***</u>, signed by President Bill Clinton, truly put this kind of thinking of Supply-Side Economics to work. It put a limit on the length of time a person could accept welfare benefits, and it created a <u>***welfare-to-work program***</u> in which a great deal of training and skill enhancement was performed to bring people out of welfare and into paying jobs. Welfare reform encouraged people to work rather than live off the government. Between 1996 and 2001, it managed to get over 2.5 million Americans to work and off welfare. Soon after its passage, the U.S. reached full employment and without a threat of rampant inflation. Unemployment dropped significantly after its implementation, many feel, because the Welfare Reform Act encouraged people to supply their services and boost productivity and supply, which increased GDP and kept prices in check.

Other ways to shift the Aggregate Supply Curve to the right include, as mentioned earlier, tax breaks. Please note that <u>*both Keynesian Economics and Supply-Side Economics endorse tax cuts*</u> but for different reasons. Keynes believed in them because it made more money available for both consumers and business to spend in the economy. Supply-Side theorists endorsed them because they felt that tax breaks would motivate businesses and workers to increase output, to create jobs, and to lower prices.

<u>***Tax incentives***</u>, as prescribed by Supply-Side theorists, would also encourage people to put more money into their bank savings and to invest more in stocks. This would, in turn, give banks more money to lend, and businesses would be able to sell more stock. These two things would help people to start new businesses, and it would help existing businesses to expand their production capabilities. The tax breaks could also

compel businesses to buy more capital equipment, which will increase the investment (I) in GDP. It also encourages people to work. All of these things will encourage greater output.

Tax incentives include a reduction in the ***capital gains tax***. ***President George H. W. Bush*** pushed for the Congress to implement such reductions. President ***Bill Clinton*** also advocated tax incentives to people when they invested in more plant and equipment up to about 10% of their investment. This was a huge tax break for corporate America and one that many feel was very effective toward getting to full employment on President Clinton's watch.

The effectiveness of those tax reductions, however depends heavily upon the ***tax elasticity of supply***. It is the level of sensitivity to supply by a change in tax reductions. It will also provide a better understanding of how much production will be reduced if taxes go up.

It is equal to the absolute value of the percent change in quantity supplied divided by the percent change in the tax rate.

▲ % Quantity Supplied / % ▲ Tax Rate

If the percent change in quantity supplied divided by the percent change in the tax rate equals a number greater than one, then there is a good chance that tax breaks will work in giving productivity a boost. For example, if the percent change in quantity supplied during a given period of time was 1.50%, and the change in taxes during that same period was 1.00%, then your calculation of 1.50% / −1.00% would then = −1.5. Remember, we are only interested in the absolute value of that calculation. This result is basically saying that the percent change in output is greater than the percent change in tax rates, thus, the supply is indeed elastic or sensitive to tax rate changes, and the government would, indeed, be wise to lower the tax rate if increases in supply are needed.

Another way of looking at it, therefore, is that if there is a tax cut of 10%, there would be an *increase in the supply of goods and services* of 10% × 1.5 = 15%.

Supply-Side theorists feel that other ways of shifting supply to the right is by a better use of workers, or what we refer to as a ***human capital investment***. As mentioned before, an increase of skills and knowledge in the workforce by training and by using tax credits to do so improves labor productivity and, ultimately, the utility of each worker, giving them more skills and more income.

Some of the ways to do that is by the government's increased funding for local schools. President George H. W. Bush advocated getting more money into classrooms and better preparing students for the workforce. President Bill Clinton put into effect more than $30 billion in new tax credits for higher education. This made the first two years of college a middle-class entitlement. By the end of 1999, more than 70% of Americans eligible for the program took advantage it.

As stated earlier, ***deregulation*** is an attempt to remove any and all of the unreasonable and costly regulations that are imposed by governments that are not effective. In many cases, many small businesses suffered and, in fact, were run out of business by some of those regulations while the bigger firms had more resources to help them to comply with them.

There will always be a debate, however, as to which laws are unreasonable, ineffective, or too costly.

One of the hotly contested debates about regulations is the minimum wage. Supply-Side economists argue that there should be a reduction of the minimum wage and mandatory benefits and that government should allow wages and benefits to be driven by the market. Many claim that workers have lost jobs as the minimum wages rise, because the higher price or wage reduces the the demand for. Therefore, they believe that opposition to minimum wage is not by those who are opposed to workers' rights and well-being. They feel that it is better for workers to have a slightly lower wage in their jobs rather than no job at all. Many firms are in states that set their own minimum wages, and it is argued that those firms have begun automating more of their tasks to remove the cost of the higher minimum wages. The jury on those claims is still out.

Some politicians and economists feel that there are unreasonable occupational safety and health standards. They feel that many of them are costly and difficult to fulfill, and they don't make for a safer workplace. Again, they are not opposed to worker safety, but just like minimum wage, they believe *there needs to be a balance*. They feel that government should not raise these standards to the point of encouraging producers to move their operations to another country. Job security must not be lost. There is a significant level of safe working conditions that must maintained and many economists and people in government say that it can be maintained without adding exorbitant costs. When costs such as these go up, it doesn't only shrink profits, but, in some cases, it has put firms out of business and, therefore, the workers on the unemployment line. We are living in a global economy where prices are extremely competitive.

Some industries are said to need deregulation. Typically, it is those that are in direct competition with foreign firms who have far less regulation. Removal of unreasonable food and drug standards and unreasonable environmental protection have also been endorsed.

Trade liberalization of the factor markets is also strongly urged by Supply-Side economists. As mentioned earlier, global protectionism is one of the factors that was a preamble to the Great Depression of 1929. Supply-Side Economists feel that easing of trade barriers here would eliminate tariffs on out goods that we try to sell to foreign customers. Some politicians and economists argue that those tariffs and import restrictions are needed to keep the low-priced goods out of our country that cost us our jobs. The flipside of that thinking, however, is that when we impose restrictions and tariffs on countries, they retaliate. It also causes prices in our country to go up. For example, imported sugar costs producers and, ultimately, consumers $2 billion each year. By reducing tariffs on imports, prices on our products and factors of production drop and also might lower tariffs that are charged to us by foreign countries. Thus, doing so could help us sell more of our goods. It is believed, therefore, that the free flowing of products between borders increases supply and GDP, and thus keeps prices stable.

The ***North American Free Trade Agreement (NAFTA)*** is a good example of the application of Supply-Side Economics. It was pushed, passed, and signed by President Bill Clinton in 1993. It was an agreement signed by Canada, Mexico, and the United States, creating what many call a trilateral trade bloc in North America. The main objective was to remove trade and investment barriers between them. The agreement took effect in January of 1994.

Immigration is also something that Supply-Side theorists encourage as they feel it gives more possibilities for increasing supply and lowering costs. As with discrimination, if we limit those whom we permit into this country and, ultimately, who we hire, the opportunity for more output is lost.

Infrastructure development is also instrumental. Improving roads, transportation, communication, and our judicial systems, binding the pieces of the economy into a coherent organism, is vital if we are serious about increasing productivity and the supply of goods and services. Funding for these projects must be maintained to keep our roads and bridges in good repair and our communication systems state of the art. The judicial system must also work swiftly to resolve all legal issues so that resources can be put into production rather than into litigation.

Expectations in our country must always remain optimistic. Government should take all measures to create optimism in our economy. Anything it can do will likely compel business to buy more capital equipment and invest in the future. Supply Side theorists feel that optimism encourages people to buy stocks and bonds in firms, thus, betting on a good future. Higher taxes and more regulations tend to impede optimism and expectations.

The fourth economic theory to consider is that of the ***Monetary (or the Monetarist) Theory***. It was promoted by ***Milton Friedman (1912–2006)*** during the 1960s. Friedman was also a very influential advisor to President Ronald Reagan and British Prime Minister ***Margaret Thatcher (1925–2013)***. His political philosophy praised the ideas of a free market economic system with very little intervention.

Monetarism was embraced as an alternative macroeconomic policy. Friedman's ideas were similar to Classical Economics in that they propose that Keynes's intervention would not help and, in some cases, would hurt the economy in the long run. Two major differences between the Classical Theory and the Monetarist Theory is that the Monetarists do believe that there is some minimal need for government intervention. They feel that the government should increase the money supply in order to increase demand only on a limited, predicted pace or level. They believed in what is now known as the ***equation of exchange***: the money supply (M) times the velocity of money (V) is equal to the average price of goods and services (P) in our economy times the Quantity (Q) of individual items sold in our economy. In other words:

$$MV = PQ$$

All of the theories concede that the equation is correct. Both Keynes and the Monetarists concede that increased demand can result in increased inflation.

The velocity of money is basically the number of times it changes hands. If I buy something from you and then you take the money I paid you and then you buy something and if the person you buy something from spends that money, that is an example of the velocity of money. Money must change hands, or a larger money supply is of little use. If the money supply grows, it only helps if people get it and spend it many times over.

The Monetarists basically feel, therefore, that money will not change hands many times over if there is nothing to buy. They feel that the quantity supplied and, therefore, the quantity sold is fixed because producers can't just wake up one morning and decide to sky-rocket their output that day after seeing a spike in demand. Thus, if there is more money but nothing more to buy, Q remains the same and, thus, V stays the same. If that happens, increasing the money supply (or M) will only cause inflation. Why? Because if V and Q are stable and the money supply increases, as with all other equations, both sides must be equal. Therefore, the only thing left to change is P or price, and it will only go up. So, the Monetarists feel that increasing M won't create jobs; it will only cause inflation.

If you increase the money supply or demand too quickly, they feel, it will not likely increase output or employment. They believe it takes time to adapt to increases of money and demand and if producers can't adapt quickly enough, they will only raise prices. Hence, they feel that the Aggregate Supply Curve is vertical, preaching that no quick-fix action should be taken.

Those who endorse Keynesian theories argue that there is a flaw in the Monetarists thinking. Monetarists are correct that V and Q are fixed or stable during boom times when expansion is very difficult, with full employment making it difficult to hire people for expansion. But during bad times, Q can easily be increased. Keynes' followers say that during such times, there are a lot of idle factories that could be activated quickly to accommodate the demand that would come from an increased money supply.

SUMMARY OF ECONOMIC THEORIES

a. **Demand-Side/Keynesian**: Shift the AD curve to the right.
b. **Supply-Side**: Shift the AS curve to the right.
c. **Monetarists**: Do very little. Increase the money supply at a predictable, gradual rate and with notice.

d. **Classical**: Do nothing. Use the laissez faire concept, allowing the economy to self-correct and to self-maintain.

DETERMINANTS OF OUR ECONOMY'S PERFORMANCE

In order to get a better idea of how the economy needs to be managed, if at all, it's important to understand the various things that drive it.

First and foremost are the ***internal market forces***. They include such factors as population growth and spending behavior of business and consumers. When these things change, so, too, does the economy. When our population gets into a pattern of spending, the economy booms. As population grows, there are more people who can spend, thus, helping the economy further.

Sometimes things can happen that alter these behaviors outside the scope of our people's behavior and government control. They are known as ***external shocks***. They include events such as war, disaster (including but not limited to droughts, fires, floods, earthquakes, tornadoes, and terrorism), or any major event that can cause significant trade disruptions.

Policy levers by the government usually have a huge impact on the economy. These can either be increased or restrained depending upon the current status of our economy. These policy levers are usually implemented in order to manage the other two determinants of the economy, (internal market forces and external shocks) when they destabilize things.

There are two types of policy levers: ***Fiscal Policy*** and ***Monetary Policy***.

Fiscal Policy

Fiscal policies are those that the government implements by making changes to a fiscal budget. They include either changing tax rates or changing government spending during a fiscal cycle.

Raising taxes lowers disposable income (how much money is available for purchases in the economy). This is done to restrain the economy's growth in order make sure that supply will be able to keep up with demand in order to prevent inflation.

Lowering taxes is done to increase the disposable income when the economy is in a slump.

Spending is increased to raise the G of the GDP to stimulate the economy.

Spending can be reduced to lower the G to slow down the economy's growth.

Monetary Policy

The government can regulate the money supply (the amount of money available to the public with which it can buy more things). There are several options with which it can do this.

Raising interest rates, specifically the overnight or federal funds and the prime lending rates (discussed in more depth later), would lower the money supply because when these rates for consumer and business loans rise, fewer people can afford the monthly payments for them, thus, they will buy fewer homes, cars, appliances, and capital equipment

Lowering of interest rates increases the money supply as more people will now have access to it as payments are more affordable.

The Minimum Reserve Requirement is imposed on banks. When you make a deposit, banks must put some of those deposits into a reserve, NOT for keeping a backup of money in case funds run dry by too many depositors withdrawing their funds, but purely to manage the money supply. The Federal Reserve will determine the rate. If it raises it, fewer loans can be made because a larger percent of the deposits banks receive must go to the Fed rather than to be loaned out for purchases. If it lowers the reserve required, more loans will be possible, and more purchases would be the result.

If *credit standards become more stringent*, that lowers the money supply because fewer people qualify for loans, thus, there will be fewer loans.

Relaxing credit standards on the other hand is a tool used to increase the money supply. Even if rates are low and the banks have lots of money to lend, it doesn't help unless more people are eligible for a loan. Relaxing the standards can do that.

The United States Treasury, can *create money* (through the United States Mint, for coinage, and the Bureau of Engraving and Printing, for paper money) when ordered to do so by the Federal Reserve if the economy is needing more money or a larger money supply. When this happnes, the money is circulated through the Federal Reserve banks around the country, which will be discussed later. That means more loans available in those Federal Reserve banks or in member banks. The Fed also loans some of that money to other banks. All money that is printed is backed up by our gold reserves in the United States.

Many years ago, people traded with gold as it is very valuable due to its appearance and its durability when used as the substance of durable products. However, carrying the gold around became too cumbersome for people back then, therefore, our government made coins and currency for the use of making transactions. These items, as mentioned, are backed up by our gold reserves. Paper money wasn't used until the Civil War in the early 1860s. They were then called ***greenbacks***. Using paper for currency was cheaper than using precious metals, so its use helped cut federal costs in order to fund the Civil War. When the war was over, the greenbacks were still seen as a good way to save government money and they are therefore used to this day.

For many years, the Fed used to only put enough money into circulation to match the gold reserves we had, but as time wore on, it became obvious that it was no longer needed to match each ounce of gold with each dollar. On June 5, 1933, President Franklin Roosevelt signed a resolution so that Americans could not convert currency into gold while still allowing foreign governments to make such conversions to maintain stability and confidence in the dollar (http://www.history.com/this-day-in-history/fdr-takes-united-states-off-gold-standard).

When the United States stopped selling gold to foreign officials in 1971, it was giving holders of dollars $35 an ounce.

The government must be cautious to not print so too money. Doing so could cause the value of our money to drop. Like anything else, when there is a high supply of something its value diminishes.

Printing less money, therefore, creates less money in the Federal Reserve banks and in all banks, thus, lowering the money supply.

Bond sales by the federal government will lower the money supply. When this happens, people give money (by a loan) to the government, thus, tying up the money of those citizens and contracting (or lowering) the money supply. Normally these people would have their money in banks, but when they drain their bank accounts to loan it to the government, then the banks have fewer deposits, thus, fewer bank loans can be obtained.

Bond purchases by the Fed are a way of its granting loans, thus, doing so increases the money supply.

A summary of fiscal and monetary policies is shown in Table 10-2.

Please recall that ***aggregate demand*** is the total quantity of output (real GDP) demanded at various price levels at a given time (all things held equal). Also, recall that the ***Aggregate Demand Curve*** shows this aggregate demand, and it is downward sloping.

There are several explanations of the downward slope of the curve.

The real-balances effect is one way of explaining it. Cheaper prices make dollars more valuable and it gives them more buying power. It creates a better climate for the demand of goods and services. The reverse is also true. Also, the value of the dollar is measured by how many goods and services each dollar buys. Lower prices make your money in your pocket or your bank account worth more, and the opposite is also true. Therefore, lower prices increase aggregate demand.

It is also explained by ***the foreign-trade effect***. The impact on imports and exports is that if the average price of U.S. goods rises, imports are more desirable and Americans will go abroad to buy what they need. At the same time, people from other countries are less inclined to buy our high-priced goods, and thus exports are less desirable (and the reverse of this is also true). Therefore, net exports, and, consequently, aggregate demand will rise if our prices are lower.

The last explanation is from ***the interest-rate effect***. Price increases make more need to borrow, thus, driving up interest rates. As people demand more funds for borrowing, as with anything with large demand, the price goes up. In this case, the price is interest rates. Once again, The reverse is also true. Price increases, as stated earlier, will also directly increase interest rates making houses, cars, and appliances out of reach for some who can't afford the higher monthly payments that have been

TABLE. 10.2 Summary of Fiscal and Monetary Policy Levers

CURING A BAD ECONOMY (MILD RECESSION, DEEP RECESSION, DEPRESSION)	
1. Decrease Taxes	Fiscal Policies
2. Increase Government Spending (G of GDP)	
3. Increase Money Supply	
a. Lower Interest Rates	
b. Lower Lending Standards	Monetary Policies
c. Print More Money	
d. Lower Minimum Reserve Requirement	
e. Buy Bonds	
f. Lower Yields	
MAINTAINING A GOOD ECONOMY (FULL EMPLOYMENT WITH PRICE STABILITY AND ACCEPTABLE WEALTH DISTRIBUTION)	
1. Increase Taxes	Fiscal Policies
2. Decrease Government Spending (G of GDP)	
3. Decrease Money Supply	Monetary Policies
a. Raise Interest Rates	
b. Raise Lending Standards	
c. Print Less Money	
d. Raise Minimum Reserve Requirement	
e. Sell Bonds	
f. Raise Yields	

pushed up by higher prices. Price increases make interest rates rise because the inflation rate must be added to the desired rate of return. Also, the Fed will likely raise interest rates when it sees inflation here or imminent. It feels that higher interest rates will slow down the growth of GDP to make sure that there are no shortages and, hence, so that inflation doesn't kick in.

Please recall that ***Aggregate supply*** is the total quantity of output (real GDP) producers are willing and able to supply at various price levels, all things held equal. The ***Aggregate Supply Curve*** shows this and is therefore upward sloping.

As with aggregate demand, there are explanations for this, as well.

The ***profit effect*** exists as producers can make more profit with higher prices, and the reverse is also true. Hence, higher prices give incentives for higher output.

The ***cost effect*** also causes the upward slope because if prices of goods and services go up *as long as the cost of producing* those goods does not go up with them *at the same or greater rate, supply then will also increase*. Otherwise, the motivation to produce more will vanish.

The Aggregate Supply Curve is flat at low levels of output (recession) and then gets steeper as we get closer to full employment. This is because, as discussed earlier, cost pressures are minimal at low outputs because the factors of production have less demand if producers aren't using them. As output of those goods increases, so does the demand for the factors used to produce them, and their costs go up, requiring a producer to charge even more to make a profit; thus, the aggregate supply curve gets much steeper.

To have a perfectly vertical supply curve implies that no matter how much the market is willing to pay producers, it can't supply more. Full employment will cause that because producers can't hire more people to produce for them if every qualified person is working. They would then rely more on capital equipment to increase output, but it takes time to buy equipment, install it, test it, and get it working smoothly enough to help increase production. Many businesses would rather cash in on the higher prices rather than take the risk of buying more equipment to only have demand fall once the equipment is up and running.

Some economists believe that studies of short-run changes in aggregate demand and aggregate supply are pointless, and, rather, it is more useful to study the long-run self-adjustment trends of the economy.

Another important point to consider is that after having an understanding of what the major theories prescribe to have a healthy economy, some embrace different types of policy levers.

The Classical theorists believe, basically, in the use of no policy levers.

The Monetarists believe only in the use of Monetary policy by raising the money supply gradually with adequate notice.

Keynesian thinking uses every policy lever to stimulate the economy and every policy lever to restrain it when unstable prices begin to threaten the economy.

The Supply-Side theorists believe in using only fiscal policy but no monetary policy. Even when the fiscal policy is used by the Supply-Side theorists, spending is very specific, unlike that of Keynesian Theory. Keynesians will recommend that spending be done in every place needed to improve our way of life, but Supply-Side theorists prefer to only have added spending toward things that increase supply, such as better highways, better education, better infrastructure. and so on. There are policies that the Supply-Side theorists prescribe that are neither fiscal or monetary, such as free trade, and the elimination of discrimination. A summary of these policies can be found in Table 10-3.

So, what have the different presidential administrations embraced over the years?

Since the time of the Great Depression, presidents have been more vocal on their economic ideas. However, it has been found that while they preached a certain theory, they didn't always practice it. The reason for this is that the theories they held dear weren't always appropriate at the time that their administrations were in office. The status of the economy had to have the right theory applied.

TABLE 10.3 Summary of Fiscal and Montary Policy Levers Recommended by Monetarists, Supply-Side Theorists, and Keynesian Theorists

THEORY	FISCAL POLICY LEVERS PRESCRIBED	MONETARY POLICY LEVERS PRESCRIBED	NONFISCAL AND NONMONETARY POLICY PRESCRIBED
Classical	None	None	None
Monetarist	None	All of them, gradually increasing M with adequate notice to producers.	None
Keynesian	All of them	All of them	None
Supply-Side	All of them, but not to increase aggregate demand, but to increase supply. Tax cuts, plus specific spending in education, infrastructure, and welfare to work programs, etc.		Removal of Discrimination, trade barriers, ineffective regulations, and immigration barriers.

This is what is often descried as ***eclecticism***. It is an approach by different administrations that does not hold fast to a single argument but, instead draws upon multiple theories or applies different theories in particular cases.

Economists believe that various views for various ailments/statuses of the economy should be applied.

Most presidents have used various opposing theories within their own administrations. As mentioned earlier, Herbert Hoover preached Classical Economics, but when it didn't seem to be taking effect toward the end of his term, he caved in and began to apply Keynesian Economics. Franklin Roosevelt criticized him for it and yet Roosevelth later embraced Keynesian Economics when he took office.

In later years Ronald Reagan preached Supply-Side Economics but often applied Keynesian ideas. President Bill Clinton quite often criticized Supply-Side Economics, but during his term, it was applied quite often.

Chapter 10 Review

QUESTIONS TO THINK ABOUT

1. Describe the economic theories in depth.
2. What are the effects of the policy levers?

TERMS/PEOPLE TO KNOW

Aggregate Demand
Aggregate Demand Curve
Aggregate Supply
Aggregate Supply Curve
Arthur Laffer
Automatic Economic Stabilizers
Bill Clinton
Capital Gain Tax
Classical Theory
Cost Effect
Deficit Spending
Demand Side Economics
Deregulation
Discrimination
Equation of Exchange
External Shocks
Fiscal Policy
George H. W. Bush
Global Protectionism
Greenbacks
Herbert Stein
Human Capital Investment
Immigration
Infrastructure
Internal Market Forces
Jean Baptiste Say (1767–1832)
Jimmy Carter
John Maynard Keynes (1883–1946)
Keynesian Economics
Laissez-Faire Philosophy
Leon Walras (1834–1910)
Margaret Thatcher (1925–2013)
Milton Friedman (1912–2006)
Misery Index
Monetary (or Monetarist) Theory
Monetary Policy
North American Free Trade Agreement (NAFTA)
Panics
Policy Levers
Profit Effect
Reaganomics
Richard Nixon (1913–1994)
Robert Mundell
Ronald Reagan (1911–2004)
Say's Law
Supply-Side Economics

Tax Elasticity of Supply

Tax Incentives

The General Theory of Employment, Interest and Money

The Interest-Rate Effect

The Minimum Reserve Requirement

The Real-Balances Effect

Trade Liberalization

Tragic Number

Trickle-Down Economics

Jude Wanniski

Walras's Law

Welfare Reform Act of 1995

Welfare-To-Work Program

CHAPTER ELEVEN

A Closer Look at Gross Domestic Product (GDP)

IN EARLIER CHAPTERS, gross domestic product has been discussed at length. In Chapter 11, we will discuss how each of its components, Consumption (C), Investment (I), Government (G), and Next Exports (X_n) are what drives our economy. Now, let's look at them in more depth to see what drives *them*.

CONSUMPTION

It is important for economists and government to have an idea as to what consumers are likely to do in the near future. Business investment (I) is likely to be stagnant if business owners don't perceive that consumers are going to spend much. Income and consumption historically have had a close positive relationship, but there are some non-income determinants of demand, as well.

Please recall that income and output are equated here. But not all people are producing while they are consuming. There are many who are retired and living off their previously earned income. Many are unemployed and are either using their savings from previously earned income or collecting unemployment benefits, welfare, and Social Security. In any of these cases, they do not produce to get this income. They consume each day just like all others who are working. This is called ***autonomous consumption***. In other words, their consumption is independent of income; it is NOT driven by income.

What are the things that have an impact on autonomous consumption?

First, *expectations* of a pay raise, a tax refund, or a gift, any money they don't currently have may compel people to consume now and pay later when they receive the money they expect.

Wealth is used for consumption even if income has stopped, such as at retirement or when people have saved for given purchases. This is also called the ***Wealth Effect***. If people's wealth rises, so too may autonomous consumption.

Credit makes it possible to borrow today and pay back later when work is resumed or money is received. If credit becomes more available or with lower interest rates, autonomous consumption may increase.

Taxes going up reduces consumption, but when it goes down, it will increase it. Taxes have an impact, for example, on how much wealth I will wind up with and, thus how much I can draw from it.

Price levels going up will reduce autonomous consumption, because things are not as affordable, while lower price levels give more spending power.

Transfer payment increases from government will increase autonomous consumption while decreases will lower it. Obviously, if people have less government aid, they will have to find work to pay their bills and thus their autonomous consumption would fall. The drivers of transfer payments are primarily government policies and the eligibility of those who are in need.

Other things that drive autonomous consumption include the aid of friends, family members, or donors who give of their resources to help those who are unable to work or to find work.

Now think about what people do with their income. *All Disposable Income (Y_D) is either spent for Consumption (C) or put into Savings (S)*. We hope that money saved is not put into a mattress somewhere, but, rather, we hope it is put into a bank or into investments, perhaps, for retirement. In any case, disposable income is, therefore, equal to the sum of consumption plus savings. Therefore, we can state:

$$Y_D = C + S$$

How much is spent at various levels of income is measured by the ***Average Propensity To Consume (APC)***. A propensity is another way of saying an inclination or tendency. It is found by dividing Total Consumption (C) by Total Disposable Income (Y_D) or C/Y_D. Therefore, we can state:

$$APC = C/Y_D$$

In 2001, total consumption was $7,342 billion while total disposable income was $7,469 billion. Thus, in that year, Average Propensity To Consume was $7,342 billion/$7,469 billion or 98%.

The same thinking is applied to the idea of finding out how much is saved at various levels of income. It is measured by the ***Average Propensity To Save (APS)***. It is found by dividing Total Savings by Total Disposable Income or S/Y_D. It can also be found by subtracting average propensity to consume (APC) from 1 (or 1-APC) and dividing that by income. Therefore, we can state:

$$APS = S/Y_D \text{ or } APS = (1-APC)$$

As disposable income continues to rise, each _additional_ dollar may be spent at a different rate. If you know that you are getting a tax refund, for example, you may act differently toward it that you do on an average or regular basis. In that case, the percent that you likely spend of it is called the ***Marginal Propensity To Consume (MPC)***. It is found by dividing the change in Consumption (C) by the change in Disposable Income ($Y_{D)}$. Therefore, we can state:

$$MPC = \Delta C/\Delta\ Y_D$$

If Y_D Increases by $1, and you are inclined to spend 80 cents of that, then your own personal MPC would be 80%.

How much is _saved_ at _additional_ levels of income is measured by the ***Marginal Propensity To Save (MPS)***. As you would expect, it is the change in saving, divided by the overall change in income. It can also be found by subtracting the Marginal Propensity To Consume from 1 (or MPS = 1-MPC). Therefore, we can state:

$$MPS = \Delta S/\Delta\ Y_D \text{ or } MPS = (1\text{-}MPC)$$

It is this set of terms and concepts that we use to predict what the consumption (C) will be for a given period, especially if we expect to give the public a tax cut or some ***fiscal stimulus***. We need to know how much the public will spend of it in order to see if Consumption (C) will rise and to see if it's going to help or have no impact on the economy. Later, it will also tell us _how much_ of a stimulus or tax cut is needed.

One tool we can use to make the prediction in consumption is referred to as the ***consumption function***. It is a line that represents a formula. It provides a precise basis for predicting how changes in income (Y_D) will affect consumer spending. Each individual has his or her own consumption function as does all consumers in the overall consumer sector of the economy.

Economists feel that total consumption (C) will be equal to autonomous consumption (a) plus marginal propensity to consume (b) times disposable income (Y_D). In other words:

$$C = a + b(Y_D)$$

Therefore, the level of total consumption changes if any one of those variables changes.

Autonomous consumption could change by going up or down, and if it does, without a change in MPC, the Consumption Function Curve will have a parallel shift. It will shift upward from an increase of autonomous consumption, and it will shift downward from a decrease in autonomous consumption.

For a moment, we need to study the graph in Figure 11-1. Notice the ***45-degree line***. It represents what the level of consumption would be when it is exactly equal to income. The actual consumption function is graphed by the line that intersects the 45-degree line.

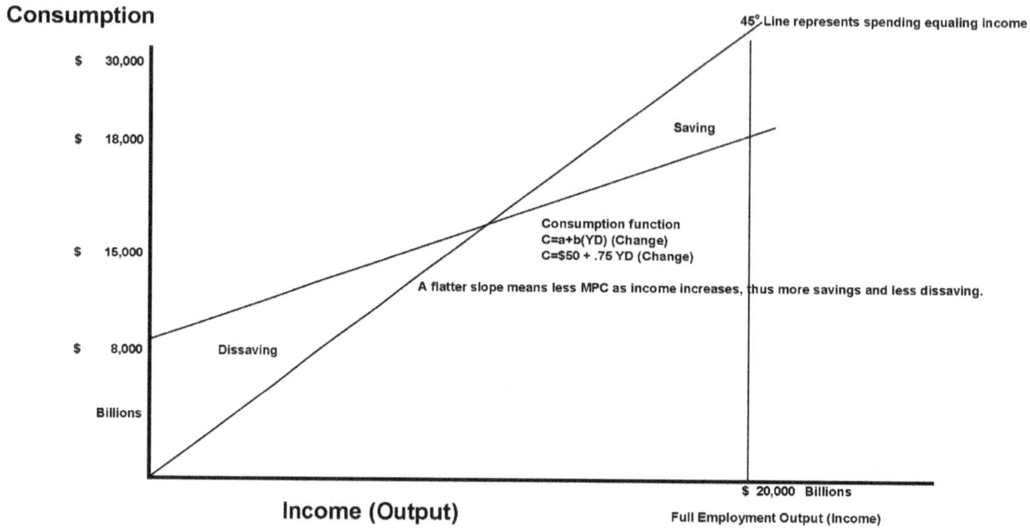

FIGURE 11.1 The Consumption Function

Dissaving represents the gap between the consumption function and the 45-degree line where consumption exceeds income. When you spend more than you earn, you have to dip into savings and/or your retirement accounts. ***Saving*** on the other hand, represents the gap between the consumption function and the 45-degree line where consumption is less than income. If you're not spending it, then you're putting aside into some form of savings.

When the marginal propensity to consume changes, the Consumption Function Curve does not shift, it rotates. For example, if the MPC declines, there would be less consumption, thus, the gap of saving would become larger while the gap showing dissaving would become smaller as illustrated in Figure 11-2.

The consumption function is useful in predicting consumer behavior, but its weakness is that people often change their behavior in both their autonomous consumption and their marginal propensity to consume. Sometimes they change them quickly and dramatically.

Shifts or rotations of the consumption function are reflected in shifts of the Aggregate Demand Curve as follows:

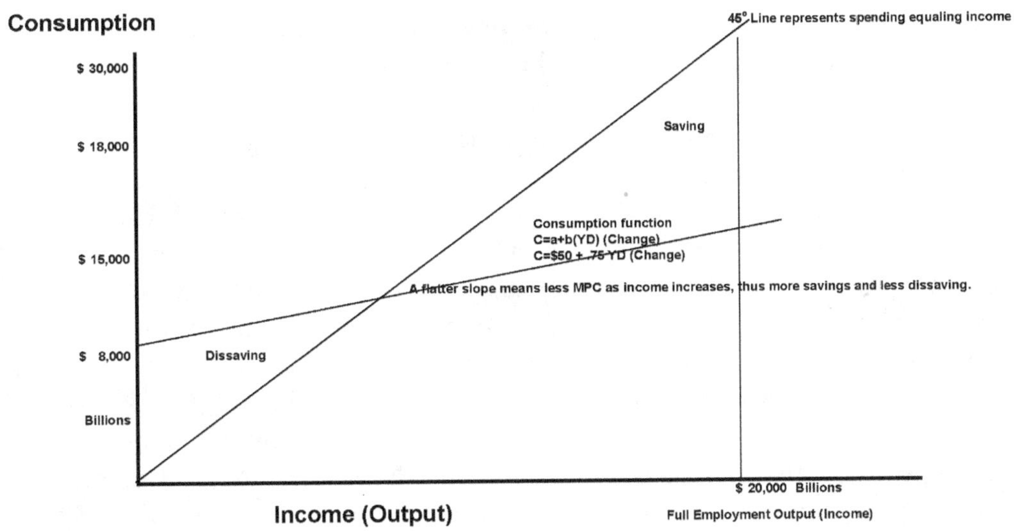

FIGURE 11.2 The Consumption Function (With a Smaller MPC)

- Downward shifts, or downward rotations of the curve, represent leftward shifts of the AD curve because the C (or consumption) of GDP is declining.
- Upward shifts, or upward rotations of the curve, represent rightward shifts of the AD curve.

Let's now take a look at Figure 11-3. To figure out how much output consumers will demand at full employment output, suppose full employment output (or the

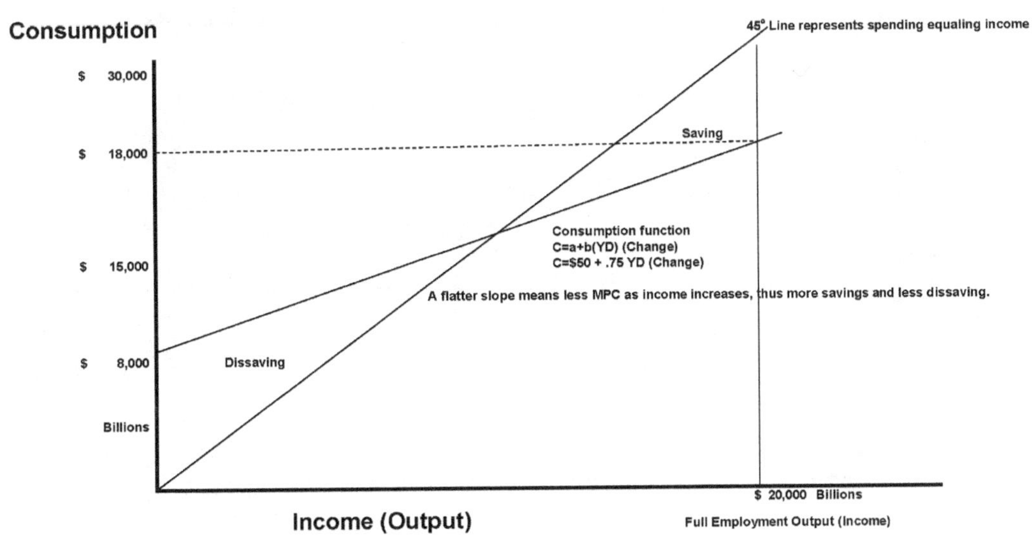

FIGURE 11.3 The Consumption Function (With Recessionary Gap)

output required in order to have full employment) is at $20,000 billion as seen on the X Axis. If you begin at that point and then trace the line upward to reach the consumption function line, you will see that the $20,000 billion income/output line intersects with the consumption function line. Looking straight across the dotted line, now look at where that point corresponds to the Y Axis. In this example, the consumption amount of $18,000 billion will be demanded at the point of full-employment output of $20,000 billion. That means that the remaining $2,000 billion ($20,000 billion – $18,000 billion) would not be purchased (or would be saved) by consumers. If the other players in GDP, such as government, investment by business, and net exports don't make up the difference, we will then experience recessionary gap. These unsold goods would create undesired surpluses for producers, which, as mentioned earlier, lead to layoffs and a spike in unemployment.

The opposite is also true. Now look at Figure 11-4. Suppose full-employment output (or the output required in order to have full employment) is still at $20,000 billion as seen on the X Axis. If you begin at that point and then trace the line upward to reach the consumption function line, again you will see that the $20,000 billion income/output line intersects with the consumption function line. Looking straight across the dotted line, now you will see that it corresponds to the Y Axis at the point of about $23,000 billion. Thus, the consumption amount of $23,000 billion will be demanded at the point of full-employment output of $20,000 billion. That means that the additional $3,000 billion ($23,000 billion – $20,000 billion) would be purchased by consumers. Once the other players in GDP, such as government, investment by business, and net exports, add to that in purchases, there would then be inflationary

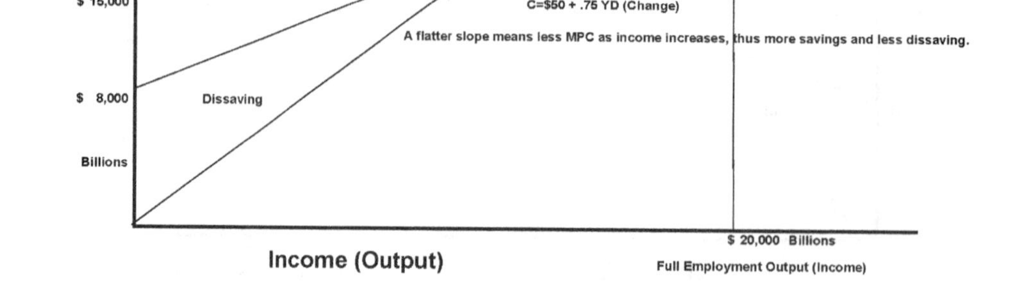

FIGURE 11.4 The Consumption Function (With Inflationary Gap)

gap. Why? Because demand will then exceed output, and the ensuing shortage would cause inflation.

INVESTMENT

Investment by business is a huge factor in GDP. Just like a demand curve, there is an ***investment curve***. The difference is that investment (I) goes up as interest rates fall as seen in Figure 11-5. The opposite is also true.

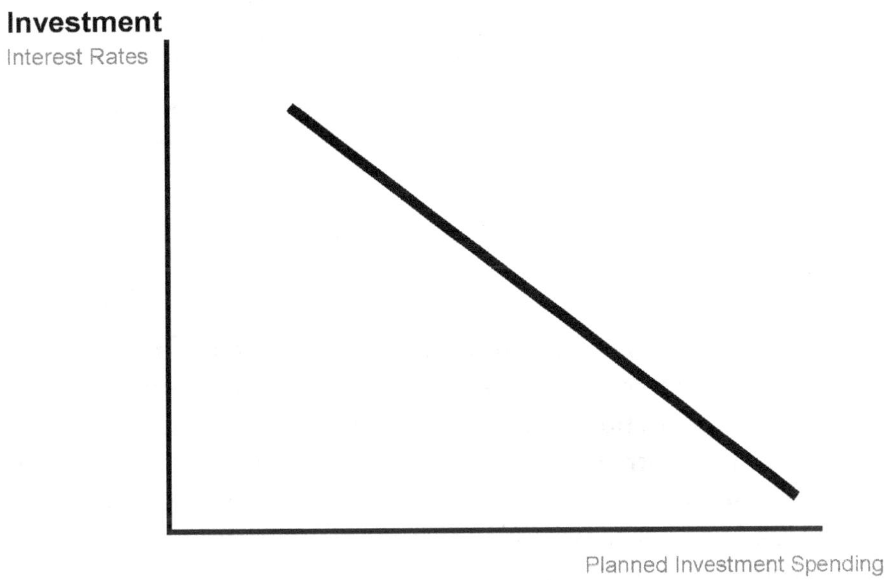

FIGURE 11.5 The Investment Curve

Why? Because the purchase of capital equipment is less affordable by businesses if interest rates are higher, but they are more affordable when interest rates are low.

The major determinants of investment are *interest rates* (which moves investment along the investment curve), *expectations of the future* of the economy, and, available or needed *technology and innovation*.

As expectations for better times exist, businesses may be more inclined to buy more capital equipment to accommodate the imminent rise in demand. The investment curve will then shift outward from Point A to Point B as shown in Figure 11-6. Bad outlooks shift it left from Point B to Point A.

Innovation will shift the curve outward, too, even if the expectations of the future don't look so good. Companies must have the latest in technology regardless of the future economic status to remain competitive. Thus, more innovation creates the

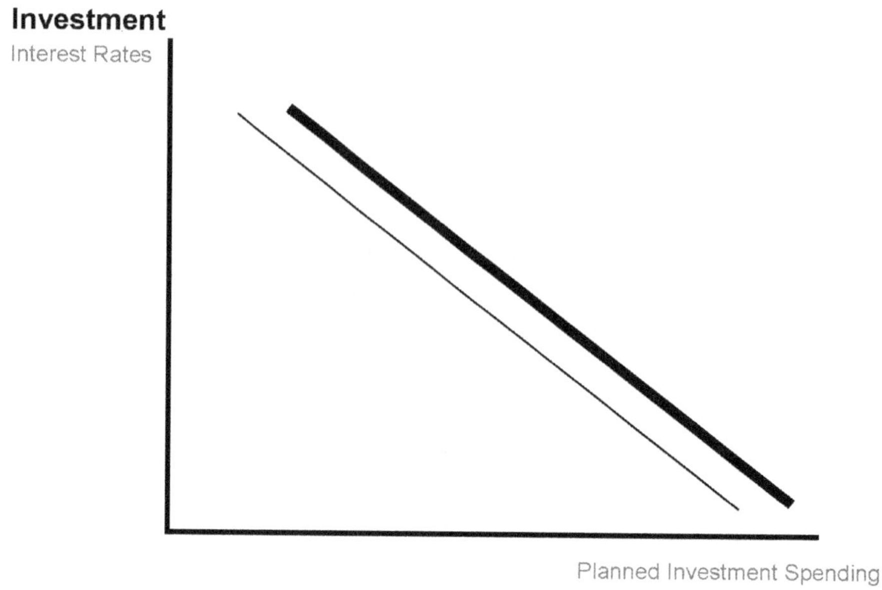

FIGURE 11.6 The Investment Curve With a Shift to the Right

need for firms to buy more of the latest innovations. Remember, technology is often obtained for survival to match that of the productivity of competitors.

The problem with prediction future investment is that investor expectations are unstable. Changes in investment are often more than proportional than that of consumption when consumption falls. In 2001, drops in consumption were only 7% while investment dropped by 13.3%. In a similar response, when consumer spending rises, investment will not rise as much. It takes a great deal to convince businesses to start buying capital equipment after a consumer spending drop has occurred. They will be very reluctant to purchase equipment to accommodate consumption increases until they are completely convinced that the consumer spending increases are here to stay.

A drop in investment can also reduce consumption. People who work for firms that produce capital equipment lose their jobs, thus, their power to buy is lost. That drop in consumption can reduce investment. This becomes a very dangerous downward spiral as the two factions of GDP depend upon each other.

When the Investment Curve shifts to the right, so too does the Aggregate Demand Curve. The opposite is also true.

GOVERNMENT SPENDING

Table 11-1 shows a list of the budgets submitted by the different presidents of the last twenty years.

TABLE 11.1 Budgets Submitted By Different Presidents

- 2016 United States federal budget – $4.0 trillion (submitted 2015 by President Obama)
- 2015 United States federal budget – $3.9 trillion (submitted 2014 by President Obama)
- 2014 United States federal budget – $3.5 trillion (submitted 2013 by President Obama)
- 2013 United States federal budget – $3.8 trillion (submitted 2012 by President Obama)
- 2012 United States federal budget – $3.7 trillion (submitted 2011 by President Obama)
- 2011 United States federal budget – $3.8 trillion (submitted 2010 by President Obama)
- 2010 United States federal budget – $3.6 trillion (submitted 2009 by President Obama)
- 2009 United States federal budget – $3.5 trillion (submitted 2008 by President George W. Bush)
- 2008 United States federal budget – $2.9 trillion (submitted 2007 by President George W. Bush)
- 2007 United States federal budget – $2.8 trillion (submitted 2006 by President George W. Bush)
- 2006 United States federal budget – $2.7 trillion (submitted 2005 by President George W. Bush)
- 2005 United States federal budget – $2.4 trillion (submitted 2004 by President George W. Bush)
- 2004 United States federal budget – $2.3 trillion (submitted 2003 by President George W. Bush)
- 2003 United States federal budget – $2.2 trillion (submitted 2002 by President George W. Bush)
- 2002 United States federal budget – $2.0 trillion (submitted 2001 by President George W. Bush)
- 2001 United States federal budget – $1.9 trillion (submitted 2000 by President Clinton)
- 2000 United States federal budget – $1.8 trillion (submitted 1999 by President Clinton)
- 1999 United States federal budget – $1.7 trillion (submitted 1998 by President Clinton)
- 1998 United States federal budget – $1.7 trillion (submitted 1997 by President Clinton)
- 1997 United States federal budget – $1.6 trillion (submitted 1996 by President Clinton)
- 1996 United States federal budget – $1.6 trillion (submitted 1995 by President Clinton)

About 67% of G from GDP is from state and local governments. Their spending is limited by tax receipts as they cannot engage in deficit spending as the federal government can.

Thus, when aggregate demand drops as a result of a drop in C and I, so, too, can G, thus, aggravating the leftward shift of the AD curve. This happens because government has less capability of collecting taxes when people are laid off by a reduction in spending by consumers and businesses. State and local governments are forced to balance their budgets even it means cutting important government functions and services. They are not permitted to borrow for operating costs. They can only borrow for capital improvements for things such as building construction and similar projects, but not for operating expenses.

This poses another problem. Since the federal government is the only government body that can engage in deficit spending, to stimulate the economy by increasing overall spending, it has to increase federal spending first to make up for the decline in spending from state and local governments. Then it must increase spending above and beyond that point if it expects G and thus GDP to rise at all.

EXPORTS

Foreign consumers and businesses (investors) behave in the same way that they do in this country, with the same determinants. In 1997, expectations were damaged by some major economic troubles in Asia. Thus, U.S. exports to those countries declined, thereby, shifting our AD curve to the left.

The silver lining about a lack of consumer confidence HERE exists when consumer confidence reduces the number of products that Americans import. Please recall that Net Exports are equal to Exports minus Imports. Therefore, if there is a decline in imports, while our export markets remain steady, there can be an increase net exports. When we do a little reality check, however, many countries abroad typically follow our economic expectations, because we are major customers of those countries.

Chapter 11 Review

QUESTIONS TO THINK ABOUT

1. Describe the consumption function and what makes it shift upward and downward.
2. What affect does the consumption function have to do to make the Aggregate Demand Curve shift right or left?
3. Use the consumption function with real numbers to make a prediction as to what consumption could be with a given marginal propensity to consume and autonomous consumption.
4. What makes the investment curve shift to the right or to the left?
5. What determinant of investment moves it along the investment curve?

TERMS TO KNOW

45-Degree Line
Autonomous Consumption
Average Propensity to Consume (APC)
Average Propensity to Save (APS)
Consumption Function
Dissaving
Fiscal Stimulus
Investment Curve
Marginal Propensity to Consume (MPC)
Marginal Propensity to Save (MPS)
Saving
Wealth Effect

CHAPTER TWELVE

How is the Economy Doing?

IN CHAPTER 2, we discussed how gross domestic product helps to tell us the current status of our economy. In Chapter 12, we will learn how there are other tools, some of which are notgenerated by our government to give us an inkling as to how the economy is performing. Many people in our society use them to tell where the economy is and where it is going. Many people have heard, for example, of the Dow Jones Industrial Average, and they will refer to it often when they discuss economic conditions, yet, they don't understand it. In many cases, people do not interpret these indexes properly. By the end of this chapter you will learn how to avoid those traps.

INDICATORS AND INDEXES

In addition to information from the Department of Labor regarding gross domestic product and employment reports, there are over 4,000 indicators that predict the future of the economy.

One of them is the stock indexes. Stock indexes give a sample of what the stock market is doing. Theindex number will be high if stocks are doing well and low numbers if not. If stocks are doing well, it can be, but is not always, a reflection of how well the economy is doing.

ECONOMIC MYTH #17	The Dow Jones Industrial Average was created by the government during the Roosevelt Administration, and the number represents the number of shares that have increased in value in a given day.

There are many misunderstandings as to what the ***Dow Jones Industrial Average (DJIA or The Dow)*** represents. When you ask the average person, you will get many different responses at to what it is, none of which is correct, and yetit is the most common report that the average person uses to get a feel for our current economic status. Most people have heard of it and watch it daily, but very few people know what it actually means.

Dow Jones & Company is a news company and a leading provider of global business news and information services. For a fee, many news providers publish its work on a minute-by-minute basis on their websites or on their news broadcasts.

It was established by two journalists and financial reporters, ***Charles Dow (1851–1902)*** and ***Edward Jones (1856–1920)***.

In November 1883, they started Dow Jones & Company which began publishing and distributing a two-page report on the financial news that was prevalent on any given day. It was distributed every afternoon, hence, the name it was given was the ***Customers' Afternoon Letter***. It gave interesting and important information regarding the overall market and stocks of particular firms. It was also the first publication to have the Dow Jones stock average, which reported the stock prices and performance of railroads, for the most part (*New World Encyclopedia*, 2017). The Customers' Afternoon Letter is still in publication today, but its name has since been changed to what we now know as ***The Wall Street Journal***. The *industrial* average did not exist until May 26, 1896, and it became what we now know as the Dow Jones Industrial Average (DJIA).

Dow Jones & Company wanted to give a regular average of stock prices to the public to give them an idea of what stock prices were doing, whether they were going up, down, or holding steady. The problem was that they could not get an average of all stocks, because in those days they did not have computers that could calculate it every nanosecond. By doing it by hand, those who computed the average would have taken a long time to do it. As a result, it would have been inaccurate by the time all of the stock prices would have been compiled. That's why they were forced to take a sample that represented the entire spectrum. Therefore, they had to track a small group of stocks (twelve in this case) that they felt represented the overall average. General Electric is the only stock tracked in recent years in the DJIA that was one of the original twelve industrials.

The first average was at 62.76. That represented the dollar average of the stocks that were tracked in the index.

Over the years, more firms were added to the index for tracking, because a larger sample size gave them more accurate results in estimating the average, and there were more industries to track. Today, they now track the stock prices of thirty corporations.

To calculate the average, you need to add up the prices of all 30 stocks and then divide it by the ***Dow divisor***. The divisor is the denominator. Rather than dividing by the thirty components, the divisor or denominator has been adjusted over these decades due to events such as stock splits or when firms are removed and replaced by others that Dow Jones & Company feel are better representatives of their industries. When stock prices are cut in half by stock splits, it is not because of bad performance but it is because firms may feel that their stock is becoming too pricey. The splits would cause the average to fall, and would often frighten those who followed the Dow Jones Industrial Average as they would think that a drop in the average was due to a drop in the value of the stocks. They would lower the denominator to put the average back up to where it would have been had there been no stock split. As a result, the average was no longer a dollar average. It was only watched to see whether or not it went up or down and by what percent it moved.

Since the index is no longer a dollar average, the percent changes each day are more relevant than the numeric size of the index. As of this writing, the DJIA is above 25,000 and is comprised of the firms in Table 12-1.

As you can see, the stocks represent a wide range of different industries to make the average a better indicator as to how all stocks are performing.

If the average changes by 1% on a given day, that is a significant change but not something that would shatter Wall Street today. That would be about 250 points, and in recent years, investors have taken that kind of change in stride. However, in the early years, that kind of point drop would have been devastating. It's the percent change, therefore, not the numeric value, that is watched. As a result of all of this, if the DOW average goes up, it means that the overall market is likely going up as well. The opposite is also true.

Other non-government statistics or indexes include the ***Standard & Poor's 500 (S&P)*** which uses, basically, the same methodology of watching stocks that the DJIA does, but it uses a bigger sample size of 500. Statisticians will tell you that a bigger sample size gives a more accurate picture of what the actual stock average is. Ironically, the DJIA still holds its own in accuracy when compared to the other indexes. The S&P 500 is also less likely to change when only a few stock prices change because of its larger sample size. Just as with the DJIA, if the S&P 500 average goes up, it means that the overall market is likely going up as well. The opposite is also true.

For many years, the ***Over-The-Counter Trade (OTC)*** of stocks was the means by which smaller firms could sell their stocks if they could not afford to purchase a seat on one of the bigger, formal stock exchanges such as the ***New York Stock Exchange (NYSE)***. Representatives of those firms would literally have to go to a brokerage house and do business "over the counter." When telephones began to be used, the need to go to a firm's office to make a transaction was no longer needed, but it was still called the Over-The-Counter Trade. In 1971, a group was formed to computerize this process where stock prices could be quoted without people having to speak to one another or play phone tag. The computer group was created by the ***National Association of Securities Dealers' Automated Quotes (NASDAQ)***. It was what we now know as the NASDAQ Stock Market. At the time that it began trading on February 8, 1971, it was

TABLE 12.1 Companies Tracked in the DJIA

COMPANY	WHERE TRADED	SYMBOL	INDUSTRY	YEAR ADDED
3M	NYSE	MMM	Conglomerate	1976-08-09
American Express	NYSE	AXP	Consumer finance	1982-08-30
Apple	NASDAQ	AAPL	Consumer electronics	2015-03-19
Boeing	NYSE	BA	Aerospace and defense	1987-03-12
Caterpillar	NYSE	CAT	Construction and mining equipment	1991-05-06
Chevron	NYSE	CVX	Oil & gas	2008-02-19
Cisco Systems	NASDAQ	CSCO	Computer networking	2009-06-08
Coca-Cola	NYSE	KO	Beverages	1987-03-12
DowDuPont	NYSE	DWDP	Chemical industry	2017-09-01
ExxonMobil	NYSE	XOM	Oil & gas	1928-10-01
General Electric	NYSE	GE	Conglomerate	1896-26-05
Goldman Sachs	NYSE	GS	Banking, Financial services	2013-09-20
The Home Depot	NYSE	HD	Home improvement retailer	1999-11-01
IBM	NYSE	IBM	Computers and technology	1979-06-29
Intel	NASDAQ	INTC	Semiconductors	1999-11-01
Johnson & Johnson	NYSE	JNJ	Pharmaceuticals	1997-03-17
JPMorgan Chase	NYSE	JPM	Banking	1991-05-06
McDonald's	NYSE	MCD	Fast food	1985-10-30
Merck	NYSE	MRK	Pharmaceuticals	1979-06-29
Microsoft	NASDAQ	MSFT	Software	1999-11-01
Nike	NYSE	NKE	Apparel	2013-09-20
Pfizer	NYSE	PFE	Pharmaceuticals	2004-04-08
Procter & Gamble	NYSE	PG	Consumer goods	1932-05-26
Travelers	NYSE	TRV	Insurance	2009-06-08
UnitedHealth Group	NYSE	UNH	Managed health care	2012-09-24
United Technologies	NYSE	UTX	Conglomerate	1939-03-14
Verizon	NYSE	VZ	Telecommunication	2004-04-08
Visa	NYSE	V	Consumer banking	2013-09-20
Walmart	NYSE	WMT	Retail	1997-03-17
Walt Disney	NYSE	DIS	Broadcasting and entertainment	1991-05-06

Source: https://en.wikipedia.org/wiki/Dow_Jones_Industrial_Average.

considered to be the world's first electronic stock market. It started out to be only a quotation system and did not provide a way to perform electronic trades, but over the years the computer group then began to facilitate sales, as well. As recently as 1987, it was still called the OTC (Over-The-Counter Trade) even though the idea of using the front counter in an office was long gone.

The stock prices of the firms traded on the NASDAQ are averaged every nanosecond. Once again, as a result of all of this, if the NASDAQ average goes up, it means that the overall market is likely going up as well, particularly the stocks that are traded on the NASDAQ which is a large part of the overall stock market activity. There is a disproportionate number of stocks traded on the NASDAQ that are called tech stocks or stocks of firms that are deeply involved in high tech industries. That's why it is not quite as objective as the other indexes, because the other index stocks are more carefully chosen to represent all industries. Therefore, when tech stocks are having a bad day on Wall Street, the NASDAQ may decline while the others remain stable or may even rise, thus have a ***mixed day*** on Wall Street.

ECONOMIC MYTH #18	The Leading Economic Indicators statistic is generated by the government.

Other than stocks, another thing that is among the most widely used and reported is ***The Leading Economic Indicators (LEI)***. It is a barometer of future economic conditions that are expected in the next three to six months. It is NOT a government statistic. It is calculated and reported by the ***Conference Board***, which is a nonprofit think tank of which any respected business leader can become a member. It is not as widely watched as stock indexes because it isn't published daily as are stocks.

It measures events and trends that will very likely have an impact on the economy such as:

1. The Average workweek (This is focused primarily on manufacturing jobs, and if this number of hours in the average workweek increases, it's an indication that there are fewer workers who have been furloughed.)
2. Initial unemployment claims
3. New orders for consumer goods
4. Delivery times (The longer it takes to deliver goods, the greater demand is assumed to be as compared to supply. As they get longer, it indicates that demand is driving sales closer to the point of full capacity.)
5. Plant and equipment orders

6. Building permits
7. Inventories (Firms build up inventories when they anticipate higher sales. This is not to be confused with undesired inventory that is unsold after a given period of time.)
8. Credit (The more that people are borrowing increases buying power and is an indication that people are indeed demanding more goods and services.)
9. Stock prices (S&P 500)
10. Real M2 (Or the money supply.)
11. Material Prices (When producers step up production, they buy more raw materials, pushing prices higher. *Fusion Investing*, 2017)

As some of them increase, they will indicate good times ahead, but that number may be adjusted downward if others increase, such as initial unemployment claims. Each is given its own weight as to how much of a good predictor it is of times ahead. Those weights may change as the predictor gains or loses its impact on the economy.

Therefore, the LEI is telling us that if these things are going up, then our economy could be looking bright within the next three to six months.

THE DOW JONES ESI (ECONOMIC SENTIMENT INDICATOR)

As we mentioned before, mood swings between business and consumers can either help or hurt our economy. ***The Dow Jones Economic Sentiment Indicator (ESI)*** is tool that is used to monitor what those moods or sentiments are. It simply tracks articles and quotes by people when they speak their thoughts about current economic times.

THE BUREAU OF ECONOMIC ANALYSIS

Let's return to the government information about the economy for a moment. The ***Bureau of Economic Analysis*** (https://www.bea.gov/) is another government agency that has a wealth of information regarding current industrial, regional, national, and international economic conditions. It will reveal things such as gross domestic product, personal income, consumer spending, corporate profits, balance of payments between countries, and much more.

The Beige Book is what they call the Summary of Commentary on Current Economic Conditions by Federal Reserve District. Eight times per year each Federal Reserve Bank gathers subjective information on current economic conditions in its District. They utilize reports obtained from bank directors as well as directors from some their branches. Each commentary is also comprised of interviews with various sources, including but not limited to major business contacts, economists, and market experts. The data is then summarized by district and sector. For example, when there was talk of tariffs in 2018, the bank officials expressed concern over the higher prices that those tariffs could cause. An overall summary of the twelve district reports is also compiled. The Fed will designate a Federal Reserve Bank to prepare it on a rotating basis. It can be found at the link: https://www.federalreserve.gov/monetarypolicy/beige-book-default.htm.

Chapter 12 Review

QUESTIONS TO THINK ABOUT

1. Describe the actual calculation of the DJIA and what it indicates.
2. Describe the actual calculation of the LEI and what it indicates.

TERMS/PEOPLE TO KNOW

Charles Dow (1851–1902)

Conference Board

Customers' Afternoon Letter

Dow divisor

Dow Jones & Company

Dow Jones Economic Sentiment Indicator (ESI)

Dow Jones Industrial Average (DJIA)

Edward Jones (1856–1920)

Leading Economic Indicators (LEI)

National Association of Securities Dealers' Automated Quotes (NASDAQ)

Over-The-Counter Trade (OTC)

Standard & Poor's 500

Wall Street Journal

CHAPTER THIRTEEN

The Multipliers

IF YOU SPEND a dollar, that one-dollar sale can lead to an additional nine dollars in sales and more. If you deposit money into a bank, that deposit can generate more than nine times itself in additional deposits. Some say that it isn't possible. But it is possible, and here in Chapter 13, you will see it happen before your mathematical eyes.

THE CONSUMPTION MULTIPLIER

ECONOMIC MYTH #19	Whenever a $1 transaction takes place, there are no other sales derived from it.

People wrongly think that each money transaction is an end unto itself. In reality, if you spend money, the person you paid it to will also likely spend it, and this process continues for many cycles unless the person you pay puts it in a shoebox in his or her closet and doesn't spend it at all. If he or she DOES spend it, more will be spent. If that same person puts it in a bank or a stock, it will be used by someone else. How? It is likely that someone may buy some product, such as a car, when he or she borrows that money from the bank in which you deposited it. A firm may buy a piece of equipment if you (the saver) use that money you received to buy its stock.

Let's look first at the chain of purchases it can create. Please recall the circular flow mentioned earlier and shown again in Figure 13-1. Also, recall the concept of the marginal propensity to consume (MPC).

Whenever you spend money, it becomes someone's income. Please observe Table 13-1. Suppose you spend $100. That would increase GDP by $100. That

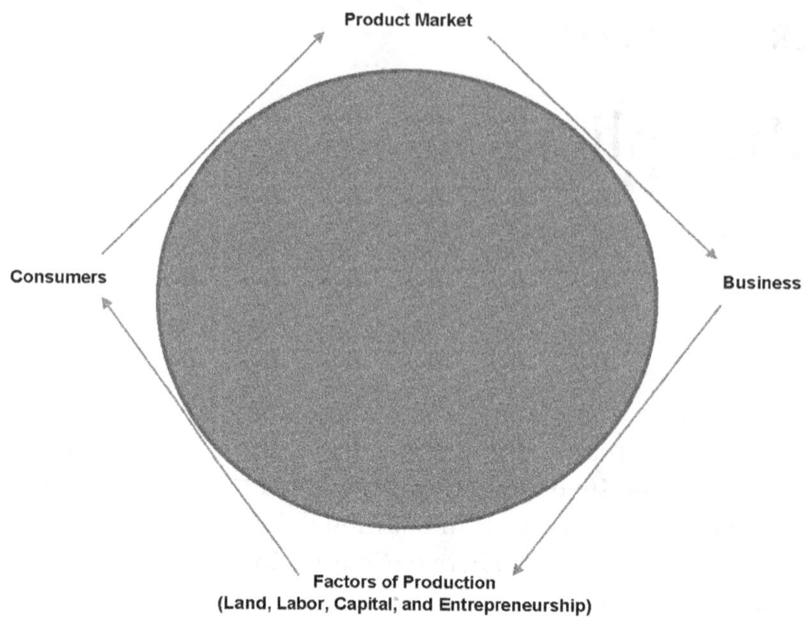

FIGURE 13.1

would be the 1st Cycle of purchases. If the people of our country have a marginal propensity to consume of 75%, then the person you paid the $100 is also likely to spend 75% of that income, or $75. The cumulative increase in GDP would now be $175. That would complete the 2nd Cycle. The recipient of that $75 would then spend 75% of that $75 or $56.25. The cumulative increase in GDP would now be

TABLE 13-1

	CYCLE CHANGE	CUMULATIVE CHANGE
1st Cycle Increase	$ 100.00	$ 100.00
2nd Cycle Increase	$ 75.00	$ 175.00
3rd Cycle Increase	$ 56.25	$ 231.25
4th Cycle Increase	$ 42.19	$ 273.44
5th Cycle Increase	$ 31.64	$ 305.08
6th Cycle Increase	$ 23.73	$ 328.81
7th Cycle Increase	$ 17.80	$ 346.61
8th Cycle Increase	$ 13.35	$ 359.95
nth Cycle		$ 400.00

$231. That would complete the 3rd Cycle. That process is going to continue *ad infinitum*. However, after a while, the amount of each incremental change that it has for GDP will be very miniscule because each time you continue to multiply a percentage times something, the number will eventually be very close to, but will never be equal to, zero.

The question becomes: At what number does that figure top out? Please observe Table 13-2. Notice that with an MPC of 75%, that change becomes close to zero but not equal to zero when the cumulative change becomes $400 at the 40th Cycle. That is not a coincidence. Through algebra, economists have found that multiplier will

TABLE 13.2 The Multiplier Effect with MPC @75%

	CHANGE	CUMULATIVE CHANGE		CHANGE	CUMULATIVE CHANGE
Cycle 1	$100.00	$100.00	Cycle 21	$0.32	$399.05
Cycle 2	$75.00	$175.00	Cycle 22	$0.24	$399.29
Cycle 3	$56.25	$231.25	Cycle 23	$0.18	$399.46
Cycle 4	$42.19	$273.44	Cycle 24	$0.13	$399.60
Cycle 5	$31.64	$305.08	Cycle 25	$0.10	$399.70
Cycle 6	$23.73	$328.81	Cycle 26	$0.08	$399.77
Cycle 7	$17.80	$346.61	Cycle 27	$0.06	$399.83
Cycle 8	$13.35	$359.95	Cycle 28	$0.04	$399.87
Cycle 9	$10.01	$369.97	Cycle 29	$0.03	$399.90
Cycle 10	$7.51	$377.47	Cycle 30	$0.02	$399.93
Cycle 11	$5.63	$383.11	Cycle 31	$0.02	$399.95
Cycle 12	$4.22	$387.33	Cycle 32	$0.01	$399.96
Cycle 13	$3.17	$390.50	Cycle 33	$0.01	$399.97
Cycle 14	$2.38	$392.87	Cycle 34	$0.01	$399.98
Cycle 15	$1.78	$394.65	Cycle 35	$0.01	$399.98
Cycle 16	$1.34	$395.99	Cycle 36	$0.00	$399.99
Cycle 17	$1.00	$396.99	Cycle 37	$0.00	$399.99
Cycle 18	$0.75	$397.74	Cycle 38	$0.00	$399.99
Cycle 19	$0.56	$398.31	Cycle 39	$0.00	$399.99
Cycle 20	$0.42	$398.73	Cycle 40	$0.00	$400.00

Multiplier = 4 =1(1-MPC)
Both increases and decreases
$398.73 $798.73

always be equal to 1 divided by (1 minus the Marginal Propensity to Consume [MPC]). In other words:

$$\text{Multiplier} = 1/(1\text{-MPC})$$

Another way of stating it is that the multiplier is equal to 1 divided by the Marginal Propensity to Save (MPS). Remember, the Marginal Propensity to save is equal to 1 minus the Marginal Propensity to Consume. That would make the Marginal Propensity to Consume in this example 25%. If you divide1 by the MPS (or 25%) you would get four. Hence, a $100 purchase will lead to many more purchases, growing to four times the original $100 purchase or $400.

Now let's apply this thinking to aggregate demand. If MPC is equal to 75% and if there is a boost in the economy to the tune of perhaps $100 billion, eventually, the cumulative change will be much larger than that and will max out at $400 billion. That number is found by multiplying 4 times $100 billion.

Let's try another example. Suppose MPC is equal to 60%. Also assume that there is a boost in the economy to the tune of perhaps $100 billion. Eventually, the cumulative change will be much larger than that and will max out at $250 billion as you can see in Table 13-3. That number is found by dividing 1 by the Marginal Propensity to Save, which in this case is 40%) That fraction would give you a 2.5 multiplier. Multiplying 2.5 times $100 billion would give you $250 billion

Sometimes the "boost" in the economy comes from the government in what is called a fiscal stimulus, which was mentioned earlier. This is something that John Maynard Keynes prescribed during bad economic times.

One of the policy levers discussed earlier deals with the use of government expenditures generated by government revenue. Please recall the differences between *government purchases* and *income transfers*. Income transfers don't become part of aggregate demand until the transfer recipients, those receiving unemployment, welfare, and Social Security, decide to spend that income. Then and only then does it become part of GDP as it then becomes a part of consumption (C).

To increase or decrease aggregate demand, the government can use fiscal policy when there has been a change in internal market forces and external shocks. They can:

1. Purchase more/less goods and services;
2. Raise/lower taxes; and/or
3. Increase/decrease the level of income transfers.

Now recall the Keynesian approach to recessionary gap. Keynesian economists feel that the government needs to get someone to spend more on goods and services, shifting the AD curve to the right, thus, ending the recession. To do this, one thing

TABLE 13.3 The Multiplier Effect with MPC @60%

	CHANGE	CUMULATIVE CHANGE		CHANGE	CUMULATIVE CHANGE
Cycle 1	$100.00	$100.00	Cycle 21	$0.00	$249.99
Cycle 2	$60.00	$160.00	Cycle 22	$ -	$249.99
Cycle 3	$36.00	$196.00	Cycle 23	$ -	$249.99
Cycle 4	$21.60	$217.60	Cycle 24	$ -	$249.99
Cycle 5	$12.96	$230.56	Cycle 25	$ -	$249.99
Cycle 6	$7.78	$238.34	Cycle 26	$ -	$249.99
Cycle 7	$4.67	$243.00	Cycle 27	$ -	$249.99
Cycle 8	$2.80	$245.80	Cycle 28	$ -	$249.99
Cycle 9	$1.68	$247.48	Cycle 29	$ -	$249.99
Cycle 10	$1.01	$248.49	Cycle 30	$ -	$249.99
Cycle 11	$0.60	$249.09	Cycle 31	$ -	$249.99
Cycle 12	$0.36	$249.46	Cycle 32	$ -	$249.99
Cycle 13	$0.22	$249.67	Cycle 33	$ -	$249.99
Cycle 14	$0.13	$249.80	Cycle 34	$ -	$249.99
Cycle 15	$0.08	$249.88	Cycle 35	$ -	$249.99
Cycle 16	$0.05	$249.93	Cycle 36	$ -	$249.99
Cycle 17	$0.03	$249.96	Cycle 37	$ -	$249.99
Cycle 18	$0.02	$249.97	Cycle 38	$ -	$249.99
Cycle 19	$0.01	$249.98	Cycle 39	$ -	$249.99
Cycle 20	$0.01	$249.99	Cycle 40	$ -	$249.99

Multiplier =2.5
Both increases and decreases
$249.99 $499999

they prescribe is to increase government purchases and to initiate tax decreases that induce increased consumption and investment.

The questions that you must then ask is how much of a shift to the right is the appropriate amount?

Now that we understand the concept of the multiplier effect with consumers, we can answer that question.

Please recall way back when macro equilibrium was discussed and how sometimes macro equilibrium GDP falls short of full employment GDP. If the GDP needs to be at $20 trillion in order to have full employment and if macro equilibrium GDP is actually only at $19.2 trillion, then the government may consider increasing G by $800 billion to close the recessionary gap. However, that could cause a problem. If it does, and if the multiplier is at 4, then the outcome would put GDP way over the needed $20 trillion, and we would then have inflationary gap.

Therefore, we must then stimulate the economy with a fiscal stimulus that is just enough to get us to full employment GDP; no more and no less.

In order to find the ***desired fiscal stimulus***, you simply divide the recessionary gap by the multiplier. For example, assuming that the multiplier is 4 and the desired fiscal stimulus was $800 billion, then the desired fiscal stimulus would be $800 billion divided by the multiplier, which would be $200 billion.

There are other ways to close the recessionary gap besides that of a government stimulus. If there is a way that the producers can be motivated to increase output, the same things can happen when the multiplier kicks in. The best way to get producers to increase output is to have more consumption. Producers aren't keen on producing things without buyers ready to purchase them.

What about a tax cut? Would that have same effect? Not quite. The reason is that when the government spends money, it is immediately in the circular flow because the government has spent it. However, a tax cut is sent to consumers but has not yet been spent. Therefore, the amount of a tax cut would not quite get us to full employment GDP if it was the same amount as the desired fiscal stimulus. The tax cut would have to be slightly more than that. Let's do some algebra again. Returning to the previous scenario, if the desired fiscal stimulus is $200 billion, we need to get consumers to spend that much in the first cycle to get the multiplier to increase it to $800 billion to close the recessionary gap. How much of a tax cut is needed? If the MPC is still 75%, we need to make the added spending as a result of the tax cut, equal to $200 billion after multiplying the tax cut by 75%. We assume that the public will spend 75% of the tax cut just as it would spend 75% of added earned income. Therefore, we set the desired tax cut equal to X. In other words, X times 75% must equal $200 billion in this example, therefore:

$$X\ 75\% = \$200 \text{ billion}$$

The way to figure out the desired tax cut, then, is to divide both sides of the equation by 75%. That would make X (or the desired tax cut) approximately equal to $200 billion divided by .75 or $266.667 billion. To see if that's correct, multiply $266.667 by 75% and that would be what consumers would spend in Cycle 1. That would come to $200 billion, and then the multiplier process would begin.

Another thing we must keep in mind here is that when we try to increase GDP by the stimulus or the tax cut, *it will only work out the way we have described if the aggregate supply curve is flat*. If the curve is sloped, however, higher GDP by means of shifting the Aggregate Demand Curve to the right will cause equilibrium prices to go higher. That means that we would need to increase the stimuli even further because the higher prices wouldn't get us to the GDP needed to get to full employment. The higher prices would impede any increases in demand.

There is a down side to all of this. If there is a drop in purchases by consumers, government, investment by business, or any one of the GDP categories to the tune of $200 billion, the downward spiral would work the same way. Therefore, if the MPC is still at 75%, it could reduce GDP by a maximum of $800 billion. The only good news is that the amount of the decline of GDP would be no greater than $800 billion and, therefore, would not reduce GDP to zero.

The Keynesian Theory prescribes that there is an adjustment process that leads to the multiplier effect when there is a cut in production. First, producers are likely to cut output and, therefore, employment when there is a recessionary gap. You could also argue that they will cut production when leakages exceed injections. Next, that loss of income causes a decline in consumer spending. Declines in consumer spending lead to further cutbacks in investment. Further declines in employment will result, with more lost income and then even further reduction in consumption. Again, the dangerous decline will stop spiraling downward when we consider the multiplier effect.

With this in mind, some economists also believe that just as there is a desired fiscal stimulus, there is also a desired fiscal restraint. If we are experiencing inflationary gap, it was prescribed that if we reduce government spending or raise taxes, then the multiplier will reduce GDP to lower rampant inflation. Many, however, feel that such a measure could cost jobs, to say nothing of the political fallout. Cutting government programs coupled with tax increases don't bode well with voters who lose jobs from cuts or have their taxes raised. In 1994, many members were voted out of Congress following the largest tax increase in its history that was passed the previous year. It was believed that one of the primary reasons that they were voted out was because of their sponsoring and voting for those tax increases.

Table 13-4 shows an example of how the fiscal stimulus or fiscal restraint via the multiplier could be used.

THE BANKING/SAVINGS AND LOAN MULTIPLIER

There is another multiplier that everyone needs to understand. It is the multiplier that takes place in the banking systems and savings and loans of the world. This multiplier actually makes it so that these institutions create money.

While these things can be done for banks or savings and loans and similar institutions, we will focus our discussion purely on banks. Here is how it works.

Every time a deposit is put into a bank, it becomes available for someone else to borrow. Please recall that there is a minimum reserve requirement for most deposits placed into banks as required by the Federal Reserve. That small portion of the deposit must be sent to the Federal Reserve and cannot be loaned out. On average, that requirement has been approximately 11%, but to show the concept with rounded

TABLE 13.4 Desired Fiscal Stimulus, Tax Cut, Restraint

	SCENARIO 1
(1) = **Given-Total Consumption In Billions**	$500
(2) = **Given-Total Disposable Income**	$600
(3) = (1)/(2) *Marginal Propensity To Consume*	0.833
(4) =1 – (3) *Marginal Propensity To Save*	0.167
(5) = 1/(4) *Multiplier*	6.000
(6) = **Given-AD Shortfall In Billions**	$40
(7) = (6)/(5) *Desired Fiscal Stimulus*	$6.67
(8) = (7)/(3) *Desired Tax Cut*	$8.00
(9) = **Given AD Excess**	$60
(10) = (9)/(5) *Desired Fiscal Restraint*	10
(10)/(3) *Desired Tax Increase*	12

numbers, we will round it to 10%. On a $1,000 deposit, only 90% of it, or $900 of it, can be loaned out.

Let us now show you a series of events that takes place when deposits are made.

Step One: Suppose, that you put $1,000 into a bank. The entire world banking system now has $1,000 more in it than it did a minute ago. Also, the entire banking system now has $900 more that it can loan out.

Step Two: Suppose that this $900 is loaned out to a person who buys a refrigerator from ACME Appliances. ACME Appliances is likely to deposit that $900 into a bank. As a result, the banking system now has two deposits in it as a result of your first deposit of $1,000: your deposit and ACME Appliances'. The total deposits have now grown to a total of $1,900 as shown in Table 13-5.

TABLE 13.5 Effect of a Bank Deposit (Cycle 1)

Your Deposit	$1,000
ACME Appliances	$900
Total	$1,900

Please recall that only 90% of the $900 of that deposit from ACME Appliances can now be loaned out in our example. That means that only $810 of it can be given out in a loan.

Step Three: Suppose that this $810 is loaned out to another consumer who buys a computer at Herzog Computer Store. That would bring the total amount in deposits added to our banking system to $2,710 as shown in Table 13-6.

TABLE 13.6 Effect of a Bank Deposit (Cycle 1)

Your Deposit	$1,000
ACME Appliances	$900
Herzog Computer Store	$810
Total	$2,710

This process will continue infinitely just as consumer purchases continue infinitely. Also, just like that of consumer purchases, there is a point that the overall change in deposits in the banking system will change but in a way that is so miniscule, it is not relevant. Again, this is because to multiplying a percentage times a number causes the numbers will dwindle and become very close to, but not equal to, zero. In this example, $1,000 times 90% becomes $900. $900 times 90% becomes $810 and so on.

Table 13-7 on the next two pages will show how the change in overall money in the banking system will occur.

By the time you get to step 138, the changes are not zero, but they are so close to zero that their changes don't have any more impact on the banking system.

Please notice three very, very important things. First, *that first $1,000 deposit created up to $10,000 in deposits*! That's a lot! That first deposit of $1,000, therefore, added $9,000 of deposits to the banking system! In other words, the first deposit of $1,000 will always grow to $10,000 if the minimum reserve requirement is 10%. It will grow up to $10,000 (not by $10,000 but up to that number). Thus, the money multiplier is found by inverting the minimum reserve requirement, or, in this case, it would be one divided by 10%, which is equal to ten.

Second, it is hugely important here is that *deposit creation is instrumental in having a healthy economy*. As one can see, if deposits become small, that means that fewer homes, cars, and appliances can be purchased because very few people can afford to pay cash for these things. If loans aren't available for those wanting to purchase them, then there is no sale. Our economy will come to a grinding halt if the banking system fails!

Third, when you return to our example of the creation of money, if the minimum reserve requirement is raised, perhaps to 15%, the multiplier will fall dramatically. If you invert 15%, it will equal 6.66667, thus, it will only multiply and ultimately raise deposits up to $6,666.67.

Notice that the minimum reserve requirement never goes below, or above, the original deposit. The fact that it never goes above the original deposit means that if everyone came to his or her banks and asked for his or her deposits, the minimum

TABLE 13.7 Effect of a Bank Deposits (Cycles 1–138)

	THE MULTIPLIER FROM BANK RESERVES	TRANSACTION	NEW DEPOSIT BALANCE	HELD IN LOANS/MONEY SUPPLY	15% RESERVE REQUIREMENT AT 0.15	REQUIRED RESERVES EXCESS TO BE LOANED OUT
Step 1	Deposit Made of $1,000	$ 1,000.00	$ 1,000.00	$ -	$ 150.00	$ 850.00
Step 2	The $850 Excess is Loaned out and is redeposited into the bank	$ 850.00	$ 1,850.00	$ 850.00	$ 277.50	$ 722.50
Step 3	The $722.5 Excess is Loaned out and is redeposited into the bank	$ 722.50	$ 2,572.50	$ 1,572.50	$ 385.88	$ 614.13
Step 4	The $614.125 Excess is Loaned out and is redeposited into the bank	$ 614.13	$ 3,186.63	$ 2,186.63	$ 477.99	$ 522.01
Step 5	The $522.00625 Excess is Loaned out and is redeposited into the bank	$ 522.01	$ 3,708.63	$ 2,708.63	$ 556.29	$ 443.71
Step 6	The $443.7053125 Excess is Loaned out and is redeposited into the bank	$ 443.71	$ 4,152.34	$ 3,152.34	$ 622.85	$ 377.15
Step 7	The $377.149515625 Excess is Loaned out and is redeposited into the bank	$ 377.15	$ 4,529.49	$ 3,529.49	$ 679.42	$ 320.58
Step 8	The $320.57708828125 Excess is Loaned out and is redeposited into the bank	$ 320.58	$ 4,850.06	$ 3,850.06	$ 727.51	$ 272.49
Step 9	The $272.490525039063 Excess is Loaned out and is redeposited into the bank	$ 272.49	$ 5,122.55	$ 4,122.55	$ 768.38	$ 231.62
Step 10	The $231.616946283203 Excess is Loaned out and is redeposited into the bank	$ 231.62	$ 5,354.17	$ 4,354.17	$ 803.13	$ 196.87
Step 11	The $196.874404340723 Excess is Loaned out and is redeposited into the bank	$ 196.87	$ 5,551.05	$ 4,551.05	$ 832.66	$ 167.34

	THE MULTIPLIER FROM BANK RESERVES	TRANSACTION	NEW DEPOSIT BALANCE	HELD IN LOANS/MONEY SUPPLY	15% RESERVE REQUIREMENT AT 0.15	REQUIRED RESERVES EXCESS TO BE LOANED OUT
Step 12	The $167.343243689614 Excess is Loaned out and is redeposited into the bank	$ 167.34	$ 5,718.39	$ 4,718.39	$ 857.76	$ 142.24
Step 13	The $142.241757136172 Excess is Loaned out and is redeposited into the bank	$ 142.24	$ 5,860.63	$ 4,860.63	$ 879.09	$ 120.91
Step 14	The $120.905493565746 Excess is Loaned out and is redeposited into the bank	$ 120.91	$ 5,981.54	$ 4,981.54	$ 897.23	$ 102.77
Step 15	The $102.769669530884 Excess is Loaned out and is redeposited into the bank	$ 102.77	$ 6,084.31	$ 5,084.31	$ 912.65	$ 87.35
Step 16	The $87.3542191012517 Excess is Loaned out and is redeposited into the bank	$ 87.35	$ 6,171.66	$ 5,171.66	$ 925.75	$ 74.25
Step 17	The $74.2510862360639 Excess is Loaned out and is redeposited into the bank	$ 74.25	$ 6,245.91	$ 5,245.91	$ 936.89	$ 63.11
Step 18	The $63.1134233006543 Excess is Loaned out and is redeposited into the bank	$ 63.11	$ 6,309.02	$ 5,309.02	$ 946.35	$ 53.65
Step 19	The $53.6464098055562 Excess is Loaned out and is redeposited into the bank	$ 53.65	$ 6,362.67	$ 5,362.67	$ 954.40	$ 45.60
Step 20	The $45.5994483347228 Excess is Loaned out and is redeposited into the bank	$ 45.60	$ 6,408.27	$ 5,408.27	$ 961.24	$ 38.76
Step 21	The $38.7595310845144 Excess is Loaned out and is redeposited into the bank	$ 38.76	$ 6,447.03	$ 5,447.03	$ 967.05	$ 32.95
Step 22	The $32.9456014218372 Excess is Loaned out and is redeposited into the bank	$ 32.95	$ 6,479.97	$ 5,479.97	$ 972.00	$ 28.00

(continue)

TABLE 13.7 Effect of a Bank Deposits (Cycles 1–138) (*continued*)

	THE MULTIPLIER FROM BANK RESERVES	TRANSACTION	NEW DEPOSIT BALANCE	HELD IN LOANS/MONEY SUPPLY	15% RESERVE REQUIREMENT AT 0.15	REQUIRED RESERVES EXCESS TO BE LOANED OUT
Step 23	The $28.0037612085616 Excess is Loaned out and is redeposited into the bank	$ 28.00	$ 6,507.98	$ 5,507.98	$ 976.20	$ 23.80
Step 24	The $23.8031970272774 Excess is Loaned out and is redeposited into the bank	$ 23.80	$ 6,531.78	$ 5,531.78	$ 979.77	$ 20.23
Step 25	The $20.2327174731858 Excess is Loaned out and is redeposited into the bank	$ 20.23	$ 6,552.01	$ 5,552.01	$ 982.80	$ 17.20
Step 26	The $17.1978098522079 Excess is Loaned out and is redeposited into the bank	$ 17.20	$ 6,569.21	$ 5,569.21	$ 985.38	$ 14.62
Step 27	The $14.6181383743767 Excess is Loaned out and is redeposited into the bank	$ 14.62	$ 6,583.83	$ 5,583.83	$ 987.57	$ 12.43
Step 28	The $12.4254176182202 Excess is Loaned out and is redeposited into the bank	$ 12.43	$ 6,596.26	$ 5,596.26	$ 989.44	$ 10.56
Step 29	The $10.5616049754872 Excess is Loaned out and is redeposited into the bank	$ 10.56	$ 6,606.82	$ 5,606.82	$ 991.02	$ 8.98
Step 30	The $8.9773642291641 Excess is Loaned out and is redeposited into the bank	$ 8.98	$ 6,615.79	$ 5,615.79	$ 992.37	$ 7.63
Step 31	The $7.63075959478949 Excess is Loaned out and is redeposited into the bank	$ 7.63	$ 6,623.43	$ 5,623.43	$ 993.51	$ 6.49
Step 32	The $6.48614565557106 Excess is Loaned out and is redeposited into the bank	$ 6.49	$ 6,629.91	$ 5,629.91	$ 994.49	$ 5.51

	THE MULTIPLIER FROM BANK RESERVES	TRANSACTION	NEW DEPOSIT BALANCE	HELD IN LOANS/MONEY SUPPLY	15% RESERVE REQUIREMENT AT 0.15	REQUIRED RESERVES EXCESS TO BE LOANED OUT
Step 33	The $5.5132238072354 Excess is Loaned out and is redeposited into the bank	$ 5.51	$ 6,635.43	$ 5,635.43	$ 995.31	$ 4.69
Step 34	The $4.68624023615009 Excess is Loaned out and is redeposited into the bank	$ 4.69	$ 6,640.11	$ 5,640.11	$ 996.02	$ 3.98
Step 35	The $3.98330420072758 Excess is Loaned out and is redeposited into the bank	$ 3.98	$ 6,644.09	$ 5,644.09	$ 996.61	$ 3.39
Step 36	The $3.38580857061844 Excess is Loaned out and is redeposited into the bank	$ 3.39	$ 6,647.48	$ 5,647.48	$ 997.12	$ 2.88
Step 37	The $2.87793728502568 Excess is Loaned out and is redeposited into the bank	$ 2.88	$ 6,650.36	$ 5,650.36	$ 997.55	$ 2.45
Step 38	The $2.44624669227182 Excess is Loaned out and is redeposited into the bank	$ 2.45	$ 6,652.80	$ 5,652.80	$ 997.92	$ 2.08
Step 39	The $2.07930968843105 Excess is Loaned out and is redeposited into the bank	$ 2.08	$ 6,654.88	$ 5,654.88	$ 998.23	$ 1.77
Step 40	The $1.76741323516639 Excess is Loaned out and is redeposited into the bank	$ 1.77	$ 6,656.65	$ 5,656.65	$ 998.50	$ 1.50
Step 41	The $1.50230124989143 Excess is Loaned out and is redeposited into the bank	$ 1.50	$ 6,658.15	$ 5,658.15	$ 998.72	$ 1.28
Step 42	The $1.27695606240772 Excess is Loaned out and is redeposited into the bank	$ 1.28	$ 6,659.43	$ 5,659.43	$ 998.91	$ 1.09
Step 43	The $1.08541265304656 Excess is Loaned out and is redeposited into the bank	$ 1.09	$ 6,660.52	$ 5,660.52	$ 999.08	$ 0.92

(continue)

TABLE 13.7 Effect of a Bank Deposits (Cycles 1–138) (*continued*)

	THE MULTIPLIER FROM BANK RESERVES	TRANSACTION	NEW DEPOSIT BALANCE	HELD IN LOANS/MONEY SUPPLY	15% RESERVE REQUIREMENT AT 0.15	REQUIRED RESERVES EXCESS TO BE LOANED OUT
Step 44	The $0.922600755089577 Excess is Loaned out and is redeposited into the bank	$ 0.92	$ 6,661.44	$ 5,661.44	$ 999.22	$ 0.78
Step 45	The $0.78421064182614 Excess is Loaned out and is redeposited into the bank	$ 0.78	$ 6,662.22	$ 5,662.22	$ 999.33	$ 0.67
Step 46	The $0.666579045552219 Excess is Loaned out and is redeposited into the bank	$ 0.67	$ 6,662.89	$ 5,662.89	$ 999.43	$ 0.57
Step 47	The $0.566592188719386 Excess is Loaned out and is redeposited into the bank	$ 0.57	$ 6,663.46	$ 5,663.46	$ 999.52	$ 0.48
Step 48	The $0.481603360411478 Excess is Loaned out and is redeposited into the bank	$ 0.48	$ 6,663.94	$ 5,663.94	$ 999.59	$ 0.41
Step 49	The $0.409362856349756 Excess is Loaned out and is redeposited into the bank	$ 0.41	$ 6,664.35	$ 5,664.35	$ 999.65	$ 0.35
Step 50	The $0.347958427897293 Excess is Loaned out and is redeposited into the bank	$ 0.35	$ 6,664.69	$ 5,664.69	$ 999.70	$ 0.30
Step 51	The $0.295764663712699 Excess is Loaned out and is redeposited into the bank	$ 0.30	$ 6,664.99	$ 5,664.99	$ 999.75	$ 0.25
Step 52	The $0.251399964155794 Excess is Loaned out and is redeposited into the bank	$ 0.25	$ 6,665.24	$ 5,665.24	$ 999.79	$ 0.21
Step 53	The $0.213689969532425 Excess is Loaned out and is redeposited into the bank	$ 0.21	$ 6,665.46	$ 5,665.46	$ 999.82	$ 0.18

	THE MULTIPLIER FROM BANK RESERVES	TRANSACTION	NEW DEPOSIT BALANCE	HELD IN LOANS/MONEY SUPPLY	15% RESERVE REQUIREMENT AT 0.15	REQUIRED RESERVES EXCESS TO BE LOANED OUT
Step 54	The $0.181636474102561 Excess is Loaned out and is redeposited into the bank	$ 0.18	$ 6,665.64	$ 5,665.64	$ 999.85	$ 0.15
Step 55	The $0.154391002987177 Excess is Loaned out and is redeposited into the bank	$ 0.15	$ 6,665.79	$ 5,665.79	$ 999.87	$ 0.13
Step 56	The $0.131232352539101 Excess is Loaned out and is redeposited into the bank	$ 0.13	$ 6,665.92	$ 5,665.92	$ 999.89	$ 0.11
Step 57	The $0.111547499658235 Excess is Loaned out and is redeposited into the bank	$ 0.11	$ 6,666.03	$ 5,666.03	$ 999.91	$ 0.09
Step 58	The $0.0948153747095001 Excess is Loaned out and is redeposited into the bank	$ 0.09	$ 6,666.13	$ 5,666.13	$ 999.92	$ 0.08
Step 59	The $0.0805930685030751 Excess is Loaned out and is redeposited into the bank	$ 0.08	$ 6,666.21	$ 5,666.21	$ 999.93	$ 0.07
Step 60	The $0.0685041082276138 Excess is Loaned out and is redeposited into the bank	$ 0.07	$ 6,666.28	$ 5,666.28	$ 999.94	$ 0.06
Step 61	The $0.0582284919934718 Excess is Loaned out and is redeposited into the bank	$ 0.06	$ 6,666.34	$ 5,666.34	$ 999.95	$ 0.05
Step 62	The $0.049494218194451 Excess is Loaned out and is redeposited into the bank	$ 0.05	$ 6,666.39	$ 5,666.39	$ 999.96	$ 0.04
Step 63	The $0.0420700854652833 Excess is Loaned out and is redeposited into the bank	$ 0.04	$ 6,666.43	$ 5,666.43	$ 999.96	$ 0.04
Step 64	The $0.0357595726454908 Excess is Loaned out and is redeposited into the bank	$ 0.04	$ 6,666.46	$ 5,666.46	$ 999.97	$ 0.03

(continue)

TABLE 13.7 Effect of a Bank Deposits (Cycles 1–138) (*continued*)

	THE MULTIPLIER FROM BANK RESERVES	TRANSACTION	NEW DEPOSIT BALANCE	HELD IN LOANS/MONEY SUPPLY	15% RESERVE REQUIREMENT AT 0.15	REQUIRED RESERVES EXCESS TO BE LOANED OUT
Step 65	The $0.0303956367486672 Excess is Loaned out and is redeposited into the bank	$ 0.03	$ 6,666.49	$ 5,666.49	$ 999.97	$ 0.03
Step 66	The $0.0258362912363671 Excess is Loaned out and is redeposited into the bank	$ 0.03	$ 6,666.52	$ 5,666.52	$ 999.98	$ 0.02
Step 67	The $0.0219608475509121 Excess is Loaned out and is redeposited into the bank	$ 0.02	$ 6,666.54	$ 5,666.54	$ 999.98	$ 0.02
Step 68	The $0.0186667204182753 Excess is Loaned out and is redeposited into the bank	$ 0.02	$ 6,666.56	$ 5,666.56	$ 999.98	$ 0.02
Step 69	The $0.015866712355534 Excess is Loaned out and is redeposited into the bank	$ 0.02	$ 6,666.58	$ 5,666.58	$ 999.99	$ 0.01
Step 70	The $0.0134867055022039 Excess is Loaned out and is redeposited into the bank	$ 0.01	$ 6,666.59	$ 5,666.59	$ 999.99	$ 0.01
Step 71	The $0.0114636996768733 Excess is Loaned out and is redeposited into the bank	$ 0.01	$ 6,666.60	$ 5,666.60	$ 999.99	$ 0.01
Step 72	The $0.0097441447253423 Excess is Loaned out and is redeposited into the bank	$ 0.01	$ 6,666.61	$ 5,666.61	$ 999.99	$ 0.01
Step 73	The $0.00828252301654095 Excess is Loaned out and is redeposited into the bank	$ 0.01	$ 6,666.62	$ 5,666.62	$ 999.99	$ 0.01
Step 74	The $0.00704014456405981 Excess is Loaned out and is redeposited into the bank	$ 0.01	$ 6,666.63	$ 5,666.63	$ 999.99	$ 0.01

	THE MULTIPLIER FROM BANK RESERVES	TRANSACTION	NEW DEPOSIT BALANCE	HELD IN LOANS/MONEY SUPPLY	15% RESERVE REQUIREMENT AT 0.15	REQUIRED RESERVES EXCESS TO BE LOANED OUT
Step 75	The $0.00598412287945084 Excess is Loaned out and is redeposited into the bank	$ 0.01	$ 6,666.63	$ 5,666.63	$ 999.99	$ 0.01
Step 76	The $0.00508650444753321 Excess is Loaned out and is redeposited into the bank	$ 0.01	$ 6,666.64	$ 5,666.64	$ 1,000.00	$ 0.00
Step 77	The $0.00432352878040323 Excess is Loaned out and is redeposited into the bank	$ 0.00	$ 6,666.64	$ 5,666.64	$ 1,000.00	$ 0.00
Step 78	The $0.00367499946334274 Excess is Loaned out and is redeposited into the bank	$ 0.00	$ 6,666.65	$ 5,666.65	$ 1,000.00	$ 0.00
Step 79	The $0.00312374954384133 Excess is Loaned out and is redeposited into the bank	$ 0.00	$ 6,666.65	$ 5,666.65	$ 1,000.00	$ 0.00
Step 80	The $0.00265518711226513 Excess is Loaned out and is redeposited into the bank	$ 0.00	$ 6,666.65	$ 5,666.65	$ 1,000.00	$ 0.00
Step 81	The $0.00225690904542536 Excess is Loaned out and is redeposited into the bank	$ 0.00	$ 6,666.65	$ 5,666.65	$ 1,000.00	$ 0.00
Step 82	The $0.00191837268861156 Excess is Loaned out and is redeposited into the bank	$ 0.00	$ 6,666.66	$ 5,666.66	$ 1,000.00	$ 0.00
Step 83	The $0.00163061678531982 Excess is Loaned out and is redeposited into the bank	$ 0.00	$ 6,666.66	$ 5,666.66	$ 1,000.00	$ 0.00
Step 84	The $0.00138602426752185 Excess is Loaned out and is redeposited into the bank	$ 0.00	$ 6,666.66	$ 5,666.66	$ 1,000.00	$ 0.00
Step 85	The $0.00117812062739357 Excess is Loaned out and is redeposited into the bank	$ 0.00	$ 6,666.66	$ 5,666.66	$ 1,000.00	$ 0.00

(continue)

TABLE 13.7 Effect of a Bank Deposits (Cycles 1–138) (*continued*)

	THE MULTIPLIER FROM BANK RESERVES	TRANSACTION	NEW DEPOSIT BALANCE	HELD IN LOANS/MONEY SUPPLY	15% RESERVE REQUIREMENT AT 0.15	REQUIRED RESERVES EXCESS TO BE LOANED OUT
Step 86	The $0.00100140253328454 Excess is Loaned out and is redeposited into the bank	$ 0.00	$ 6,666.66	$ 5,666.66	$ 1,000.00	$ 0.00
Step 87	The $0.000851192153291857 Excess is Loaned out and is redeposited into the bank	$ 0.00	$ 6,666.66	$ 5,666.66	$ 1,000.00	$ 0.00
Step 88	The $0.000723513330298078 Excess is Loaned out and is redeposited into the bank	$ 0.00	$ 6,666.66	$ 5,666.66	$ 1,000.00	$ 0.00
Step 89	The $0.000614986330753366 Excess is Loaned out and is redeposited into the bank	$ 0.00	$ 6,666.66	$ 5,666.66	$ 1,000.00	$ 0.00
Step 90	The $0.000522738381140361 Excess is Loaned out and is redeposited into the bank	$ 0.00	$ 6,666.66	$ 5,666.66	$ 1,000.00	$ 0.00
Step 91	The $0.000444327623969307 Excess is Loaned out and is redeposited into the bank	$ 0.00	$ 6,666.66	$ 5,666.66	$ 1,000.00	$ 0.00
Step 92	The $0.000377678480373911 Excess is Loaned out and is redeposited into the bank	$ 0.00	$ 6,666.66	$ 5,666.66	$ 1,000.00	$ 0.00
Step 93	The $0.000321026708317825 Excess is Loaned out and is redeposited into the bank	$ 0.00	$ 6,666.66	$ 5,666.66	$ 1,000.00	$ 0.00
Step 94	The $0.000272872702070151 Excess is Loaned out and is redeposited into the bank	$ 0.00	$ 6,666.67	$ 5,666.67	$ 1,000.00	$ 0.00
Step 95	The $0.000231941796759628 Excess is Loaned out and is redeposited into the bank	$ 0.00	$ 6,666.67	$ 5,666.67	$ 1,000.00	$ 0.00
Step 96	The $0.000197150527245684 Excess is Loaned out and is redeposited into the bank	$ 0.00	$ 6,666.67	$ 5,666.67	$ 1,000.00	$ 0.00

	THE MULTIPLIER FROM BANK RESERVES	TRANSACTION	NEW DEPOSIT BALANCE	HELD IN LOANS/MONEY SUPPLY	15% RESERVE REQUIREMENT AT 0.15	REQUIRED RESERVES EXCESS TO BE LOANED OUT
Step 97	The $0.000167577948158831 Excess is Loaned out and is redeposited into the bank	$ 0.00	$ 6,666.67	$ 5,666.67	$ 1,000.00	$ 0.00
Step 98	The $0.000142441255935007 Excess is Loaned out and is redeposited into the bank	$ 0.00	$ 6,666.67	$ 5,666.67	$ 1,000.00	$ 0.00
Step 99	The $0.000121075067544756 Excess is Loaned out and is redeposited into the bank	$ 0.00	$ 6,666.67	$ 5,666.67	$ 1,000.00	$ 0.00
Step 100	The $0.000102913807413042 Excess is Loaned out and is redeposited into the bank	$ 0.00	$ 6,666.67	$ 5,666.67	$ 1,000.00	$ 0.00
Step 101	The $0.000087476736301086 Excess is Loaned out and is redeposited into the bank	$ 0.00	$ 6,666.67	$ 5,666.67	$ 1,000.00	$ 0.00
Step 102	The $7.43552258559231E-05 Excess is Loaned out and is redeposited into the bank	$ 0.00	$ 6,666.67	$ 5,666.67	$ 1,000.00	$ 0.00
Step 103	The $6.32019419775346E-05 Excess is Loaned out and is redeposited into the bank	$ 0.00	$ 6,666.67	$ 5,666.67	$ 1,000.00	$ 0.00
Step 104	The $5.37216506809044E-05 Excess is Loaned out and is redeposited into the bank	$ 0.00	$ 6,666.67	$ 5,666.67	$ 1,000.00	$ 0.00
Step 105	The $4.56634030787687E-05 Excess is Loaned out and is redeposited into the bank	$ 0.00	$ 6,666.67	$ 5,666.67	$ 1,000.00	$ 0.00
Step 106	The $3.88138926169534E-05 Excess is Loaned out and is redeposited into the bank	$ 0.00	$ 6,666.67	$ 5,666.67	$ 1,000.00	$ 0.00
Step 107	The $3.29918087244104E-05 Excess is Loaned out and is redeposited into the bank	$ 0.00	$ 6,666.67	$ 5,666.67	$ 1,000.00	$ 0.00

(continue)

TABLE 13.7 Effect of a Bank Deposits (Cycles 1–138) (*continued*)

					15%	REQUIRED RESERVES
	THE MULTIPLIER FROM BANK RESERVES	TRANSACTION	NEW DEPOSIT BALANCE	HELD IN LOANS/MONEY SUPPLY	RESERVE REQUIREMENT AT 0.15	EXCESS TO BE LOANED OUT
Step 108	The $2.80430374157488E-05 Excess is Loaned out and is redeposited into the bank	$ 0.00	$ 6,666.67	$ 5,666.67	$ 1,000.00	$ 0.00
Step 109	The $2.38365818033865E-05 Excess is Loaned out and is redeposited into the bank	$ 0.00	$ 6,666.67	$ 5,666.67	$ 1,000.00	$ 0.00
Step 110	The $2.02610945328785E-05 Excess is Loaned out and is redeposited into the bank	$ 0.00	$ 6,666.67	$ 5,666.67	$ 1,000.00	$ 0.00
Step 111	The $1.72219303529468E-05 Excess is Loaned out and is redeposited into the bank	$ 0.00	$ 6,666.67	$ 5,666.67	$ 1,000.00	$ 0.00
Step 112	The $1.46386408000047E-05 Excess is Loaned out and is redeposited into the bank	$ 0.00	$ 6,666.67	$ 5,666.67	$ 1,000.00	$ 0.00
Step 113	The $0.000012442844680004 Excess is Loaned out and is redeposited into the bank	$ 0.00	$ 6,666.67	$ 5,666.67	$ 1,000.00	$ 0.00
Step 114	The $1.05764179780034E-05 Excess is Loaned out and is redeposited into the bank	$ 0.00	$ 6,666.67	$ 5,666.67	$ 1,000.00	$ 0.00
Step 115	The $8.98995528130291E-06 Excess is Loaned out and is redeposited into the bank	$ 0.00	$ 6,666.67	$ 5,666.67	$ 1,000.00	$ 0.00
Step 116	The $7.64146198910748E-06 Excess is Loaned out and is redeposited into the bank	$ 0.00	$ 6,666.67	$ 5,666.67	$ 1,000.00	$ 0.00
Step 117	The $6.49524269074136E-06 Excess is Loaned out and is redeposited into the bank	$ 0.00	$ 6,666.67	$ 5,666.67	$ 1,000.00	$ 0.00

	THE MULTIPLIER FROM BANK RESERVES	TRANSACTION	NEW DEPOSIT BALANCE	HELD IN LOANS/MONEY SUPPLY	15% RESERVE REQUIREMENT AT 0.15	REQUIRED RESERVES EXCESS TO BE LOANED OUT
Step 118	The $5.52095628713015E-06 Excess is Loaned out and is redeposited into the bank	$ 0.00	$ 6,666.67	$ 5,666.67	$ 1,000.00	$ 0.00
Step 119	The $4.69281284406063E-06 Excess is Loaned out and is redeposited into the bank	$ 0.00	$ 6,666.67	$ 5,666.67	$ 1,000.00	$ 0.00
Step 120	The $3.98889091745153E-06 Excess is Loaned out and is redeposited into the bank	$ 0.00	$ 6,666.67	$ 5,666.67	$ 1,000.00	$ 0.00
Step 121	The $3.3905572798338E-06 Excess is Loaned out and is redeposited into the bank	$ 0.00	$ 6,666.67	$ 5,666.67	$ 1,000.00	$ 0.00
Step 122	The $2.88197368785873E-06 Excess is Loaned out and is redeposited into the bank	$ 0.00	$ 6,666.67	$ 5,666.67	$ 1,000.00	$ 0.00
Step 123	The $2.44967763467992E-06 Excess is Loaned out and is redeposited into the bank	$ 0.00	$ 6,666.67	$ 5,666.67	$ 1,000.00	$ 0.00
Step 124	The $2.08222598947793E-06 Excess is Loaned out and is redeposited into the bank	$ 0.00	$ 6,666.67	$ 5,666.67	$ 1,000.00	$ 0.00
Step 125	The $1.76989209105624E-06 Excess is Loaned out and is redeposited into the bank	$ 0.00	$ 6,666.67	$ 5,666.67	$ 1,000.00	$ 0.00
Step 126	The $1.50440827739781E-06 Excess is Loaned out and is redeposited into the bank	$ 0.00	$ 6,666.67	$ 5,666.67	$ 1,000.00	$ 0.00
Step 127	The $1.27874703578814E-06 Excess is Loaned out and is redeposited into the bank	$ 0.00	$ 6,666.67	$ 5,666.67	$ 1,000.00	$ 0.00
Step 128	The $1.08693498041992E-06 Excess is Loaned out and is redeposited into the bank	$ 0.00	$ 6,666.67	$ 5,666.67	$ 1,000.00	$ 0.00

(continue)

TABLE 13.7 Effect of a Bank Deposits (Cycles 1–138) (*continued*)

	THE MULTIPLIER FROM BANK RESERVES	TRANSACTION	NEW DEPOSIT BALANCE	HELD IN LOANS/MONEY SUPPLY	15% RESERVE REQUIREMENT AT 0.15	REQUIRED RESERVES EXCESS TO BE LOANED OUT
Step 129	The $9.23894733356929E-07 Excess is Loaned out and is redeposited into the bank	$ 0.00	$ 6,666.67	$ 5,666.67	$ 1,000.00	$ 0.00
Step 130	The $7.85310523353389E-07 Excess is Loaned out and is redeposited into the bank	$ 0.00	$ 6,666.67	$ 5,666.67	$ 1,000.00	$ 0.00
Step 131	The $6.67513944850381E-07 Excess is Loaned out and is redeposited into the bank	$ 0.00	$ 6,666.67	$ 5,666.67	$ 1,000.00	$ 0.00
Step 132	The $5.67386853122824E-07 Excess is Loaned out and is redeposited into the bank	$ 0.00	$ 6,666.67	$ 5,666.67	$ 1,000.00	$ 0.00
Step 133	The $4.822788251544E-07 Excess is Loaned out and is redeposited into the bank	$ 0.00	$ 6,666.67	$ 5,666.67	$ 1,000.00	$ 0.00
Step 134	The $4.0993700138124E-07 Excess is Loaned out and is redeposited into the bank	$ 0.00	$ 6,666.67	$ 5,666.67	$ 1,000.00	$ 0.00
Step 135	The $3.48446451174054E-07 Excess is Loaned out and is redeposited into the bank	$ 0.00	$ 6,666.67	$ 5,666.67	$ 1,000.00	$ 0.00
Step 136	The $2.96179483497946E-07 Excess is Loaned out and is redeposited into the bank	$ 0.00	$ 6,666.67	$ 5,666.67	$ 1,000.00	$ 0.00
Step 137	The $2.51752560973254E-07 Excess is Loaned out and is redeposited into the bank	$ 0.00	$ 6,666.67	$ 5,666.67	$ 1,000.00	$ 0.00
Step 138	The $2.13989676827266E-07 Excess is Loaned out and is redeposited into the bank	$ 0.00	$ 6,666.67	$ 5,666.67	$ 1,000.00	$ 0.00

The New Balance = Multiplier × Original Deposit

Deposit Creation Added To Money Supply

The Required Reserve Never dips below the original deposit.

TABLE 13.8 The Multiplier from Bank Reserves

Step 116	The $7.64146198910748E-06 Excess is Loaned out and is redeposited into the bank	$0.00	$6,666.67	$5,666.67	$1,000.00	$0.00
Step 117	The $6.49524269074136E-06 Excess is Loaned out and is redeposited into the bank	$0.00	$6,666.67	$5,666.67	$1,000.00	$0.00
Step 118	The $5.52095628713015E-06 Excess is Loaned out and is redeposited into the bank	$0.00	$6,666.67	$5,666.67	$1,000.00	$0.00
Step 119	The $4.69281284406063E-06 Excess is Loaned out and is redeposited into the bank	$0.00	$6,666.67	$5,666.67	$1,000.00	$0.00
Step 120	The $3.98889091745153E-06 Excess is Loaned out and is redeposited into the bank	$0.00	$6,666.67	$5,666.67	$1,000.00	$0.00
Step 121	The $3.3905572798338E-06 Excess is Loaned out and is redeposited into the bank	$0.00	$6,666.67	$5,666.67	$1,000.00	$0.00
Step 122	The $2.88197368785873E-06 Excess is Loaned out and is redeposited into the bank	$0.00	$6,666.67	$5,666.67	$1,000.00	$0.00
Step 123	The $2.44967763467992E-06 Excess is Loaned out and is redeposited into the bank	$0.00	$6,666.67	$5,666.67	$1,000.00	$0.00
Step 124	The $2.08222598947793E-06 Excess is Loaned out and is redeposited into the bank	$0.00	$6,666.67	$5,666.67	$1,000.00	$0.00
Step 125	The $1.76989209105624E-06 Excess is Loaned out and is redeposited into the bank	$0.00	$6,666.67	$5,666.67	$1,000.00	$0.00
Step 126	The $1.50440827739781E-06 Excess is Loaned out and is redeposited into the bank	$0.00	$6,666.67	$5,666.67	$1,000.00	$0.00
Step 127	The $1.27874703578814E-06 Excess is Loaned out and is redeposited into the bank	$0.00	$6,666.67	$5,666.67	$1,000.00	$0.00

(continue)

TABLE 13.8 The Multiplier from Bank Reserves (*continued*)

	THE MULTIPLIER FROM BANK RESERVES	TRANSACTION	NEW DEPOSIT BALANCE	HELD IN LOANS/MONEY SUPPLY	15% RESERVE REQUIREMENT AT 0.15	REQUIRED RESERVES EXCESS TO BE LOANED OUT
Step 128	The $1.08693498041992E-06 Excess is Loaned out and is redeposited into the bank	$0.00	$6,666.67	$5,666.67	$1,000.00	$0.00
Step 129	The $9.23894733356929E-07 Excess is Loaned out and is redeposited into the bank	$0.00	$6,666.67	$5,666.67	$1,000.00	$0.00
Step 130	The $7.85310523353389E-07 Excess is Loaned out and is redeposited into the bank	$0.00	$6,666.67	$5,666.67	$1,000.00	$0.00
Step 131	The $6.67513944850381E-07 Excess is Loaned out and is redeposited into the bank	$0.00	$6,666.67	$5,666.67	$1,000.00	$0.00
Step 132	The $5.67386853122824E-07 Excess is Loaned out and is redeposited into the bank	$0.00	$6,666.67	$5,666.67	$1,000.00	$0.00
Step 133	The $4.822788251544E-07 Excess is Loaned out and is redeposited into the bank	$0.00	$6,666.67	$5,666.67	$1,000.00	$0.00
Step 134	The $4.0993700138124E-07 Excess is Loaned out and is redeposited into the bank	$0.00	$6,666.67	$5,666.67	$1,000.00	$0.00
Step 135	The $3.48446451174054E-07 Excess is Loaned out and is redeposited into the bank	$0.00	$6,666.67	$5,666.67	$1,000.00	$0.00
Step 136	The $2.96179483497946E-07 Excess is Loaned out and is redeposited into the bank	$0.00	$6,666.67	$5,666.67	$1,000.00	$0.00

THE MULTIPLIER FROM BANK RESERVES		TRANSACTION	NEW DEPOSIT BALANCE	HELD IN LOANS/MONEY SUPPLY	15% RESERVE RE-QUIREMENT AT 0.15	REQUIRED RESERVES EXCESS TO BE LOANED OUT
Step 137	The $2.51752560973254E-07 Excess is Loaned out and is redeposited into the bank	$0.00	$6,666.67	$5,666.67	$1,000.00	$0.00
Step 138	The $2.13989676827266E-07 Excess is Loaned out and is redeposited into the bank	$0.00	$6,666.67	$5,666.67	$1,000.00	$0.00

The New Balance = Multiplier × Original Deposit

Deposit Creation Added To Money Supply

The Required Reserve Never dips below the original deposit.

reserve requirement would never be able to cover those requests. *That is why we say that the minimum reserve requirement is NOT there in case of bank failures. It is imposed by the Federal Reserve only as a tool to control money supply.*

The money supply, therefore, rises dramatically when there is deposit creation, but it drops significantly if there is not.

FDIC AND OTHER FINANCIAL INSURANCE

It is highly unlikely but not impossible for everyone to go to his or her bank and demand the money he or she has deposited. Everyone has the legal right to do so, and that is why they are often called ***demand deposits***. However, this has been a problem in certain banks. When it happens, it is called a ***run on the bank***. If depositors demand more money from their banks than the bank holds, the only way to give depositors their money back is by the ***Federal Deposit Insurance Corporation (FDIC)*** or in the case of savings and loans, the ***Federal Savings and Loan Insurance Corporation (FSLIC)***. Most of the banks and savings and loan institutions pay a premium for such insurance just as you would pay car insurance or life insurance premiums. If the banks are forced to close due to a run on them, the FDIC would bail them out and give depositors their money back. In this case, they would give the other 90% of their deposits that the banks could not cover. It will either close the bank and give deposits to its customers or close the bank temporarily and then reopen it under a new name, again, making sure all depositors receive their funds.

The FDIC is actually a United States Government corporation. It provides deposit insurance to depositors only in American banks. The ***Banking Act of 1933*** during the Great Depression created it because more than a third of American banks went bankrupt at its outset. Between 1930 and 1933, 9,000 banks failed. President Franklin Roosevelt was trying to encourage Americans to create bank deposits while also trying to convince them that those deposits would be safe. He gave his ***fireside chats*** on the radio during the Great Depression, and he would talk about this situation. However, the only way that Americans could be convinced that it was safe to make those deposits was through the creation of the FDIC. Up to that point, there were many runs on banks, and many people lost their deposits. This also caused people to lose their homes because when their deposits were gone, they could not pay their mortgages; thus, they then lost their homes to foreclosures. Initially, depositors were only guaranteed to receive $2,500 by the FDIC in the event of a bank failure, but as of 2011, that number has grown to $250,000 per ownership category.

While the FDIC is funded by premiums paid by banks and not by public funds, the federal government will come to their rescue if they fall short, thus, they cannot go bankrupt unless the federal government goes bankrupt. As of this writing, they have a $100 billion line of credit with the United States Department of the Treasury.

Credit unions are also insured up to that same deposit limit of $250,000 per ownership category by the ***National Credit Union Administration (NCUA)***, which is also a federal government agency. Credit unions will be discussed later.

In 1988, 200 banks failed, and, until then, that was the worst since the Great Depression of 1929. Later, between 2007 and 2008 an even worse problem emerged with many people losing their homes during many layoffs. When the banks foreclosed on borrowers with home loans, many of those homes were worth less than what the banks were owed for them. Therefore, the banks took some heavy losses as they attempted to sell them to recover their money. During that same period, there was also a crisis with financial institutions that had extended risky loans to many borrowers. This is called the ***subprime market***. When a borrower has a very good credit rating and it is believed that the borrower is all but certain to pay back his or her loans, those loans are said to be a part of the ***prime lending market***. Any loans given to anyone with a credit rating below that is said to be a part of the ***subprime market***. Many of the borrowers in that subprime market defaulted on those loans as well, and it left many lenders insolvent. The bank crisis was caused by the economy's layoffs, but the seriousness of the economy was aggravated when these financial institutions closed. As emphasized before, the banking industry is crucial to maintain a healthy economy. When the economy got bad, banks closed. When banks closed, the economy got worse. When the economy got worse, more banks closed, and the dangerous downward spiral began, which became a deep recession, creating nearly 11% unemployment.

To give you an idea as to how badly the FDIC was affected by the crisis, there were only 27 bank closures from October 2000 to January of 2008. But bank closures between January of 2008 and August of 2013 totaled 490, more than 18 times the rate of the years previous!

As of May 1, 2017, the FDIC was insuring 5,844 institutions. Hence, more than 8% of the banks protected by the FDIC failed during that bank crisis that began between 2007 and 2008.

The FDIC also examines and supervises financial institutions to make sure that banks are being operated in a safe manner. The FDIC also performs consumer-protection functions for depositors.

Bank deposit-creation activities are regulated by government agencies, the most important of which is the ***Federal Reserve System***, or the Fed, as mentioned earlier. We will be talking about the banking system in much more depth later, but it is important to understand the concept of these two multipliers: the one for consumption and the one for banking deposits.

Chapter 13 Review

QUESTIONS TO THINK ABOUT

1. List the different reasons that our banking system is so important in regard to our macro economy.
2. What is the economic danger that we face if our banking system loses the trust of the people?
3. Recommend economic policy if someone wants to stimulate the economy with a given MPC and a given GDP shortfall.

TERMS TO KNOW

Banking Act of 1933
Demand Deposits
Desired Fiscal Restraint
Desired Fiscal Stimulus
Desired Tax Cut
Desired Tax Increase
Federal Deposit Insurance Corporation (FDIC)
Federal Reserve System
Federal Savings and Loan Insurance Corporation (FSLIC)
National Credit Union Administration (NCUA)
Prime Lending Market
Run on the Bank
Subprime Market

CHAPTER FOURTEEN

Government Spending and Deficits

WITH GOVERNMENT PLAYING such a major role in GDP, we often have to ask ourselves if it's not a very dangerous road we are on when we rely on it so much. We may also ask ourselves if government is spending and ultimately borrowing too much. Chapter 14 will discuss with you the amount that government spends here in America, how much it has borrowed, and whether or not economists feel that it is appropriate.

THE EFFECTS OF GOVERNMENT SPENDING

Sometimes there are problems with the policy levers we have discussed before, particularly with government spending. Many economists believe that it can cause ***crowding out***. Crowding out exists when government borrows to finance its spending, leaving very little money left for businesses to borrow for expansion and leaving very little for consumers to borrow to buy homes, cars, and appliances. When government goes on a spending spree or a binge of lowering taxes (the kind that could lower government revenue), it creates a greater need for it to borrow. Therefore, some economists argue that investment (I) or consumption (C) won't increase and may even shrink as result of government spending and borrowing (G) going up. Others argue, however, that if there is a shortage of funds needed for borrowing, businesses and consumers can also seek resources abroad. Some counter that type of thinking with the notion that worldwide resources of loans can also become diminished if the U.S. Government's borrowing is not kept in check and if it thus causes foreign lenders to be skeptical of America's ability to pay back loans.

Sometimes spending takes place in the form of what is known as ***pork barrel projects***, which often win out over needed spending cuts for fiscal restraint when the economy is booming. Pork barrel is a term used, some say, to describe government spending for localized projects in a politician's district. They are projects such as the building of bridges or expandling local colleges and the list is endless. Such projects often bring nice things to a politician's district while also creating jobs. Thus, they are often used for winning votes and praise from the politicians' constituents. It has been said that the term is used because when politicians do this they are "bringing home the bacon." The term is often used in derogatory context to attack politicians who, according to some, are just using taxpayers' money to get reelected. However, scholars also use it as a technical term regarding legislative appropriations.

Deficit spending in the context of government spending exists when government spends more money than it receives in tax revenues. Thus, it requires the government officials to finance their spending and borrowing when their spending exceeds revenue. It is a process. On the other hand, the ***budget deficit*** is the *amount by which* the government spending exceeds revenue *in a given time*. The opposite is a ***budget surplus***. In Table 14-1, you can see that the budget deficit has been steadily climbing for many decades, with a few exceptions during the times that there was a surplus. The deficits became particularly high primarily in the days of the implementation of Keynesian Economics. Keynes believed that a balanced budget was only necessary when the economy was at full employment, but a deficit was acceptable if it would permit government to spend in a way that a recession, deep recession, or depression could be ended. His thinking was that it was more important to balance the economy before worrying about balancing the budget. Regardless of what you hear at election time, members of Congress and presidents of both political parties have contributed significantly to the size and persistent increases of the deficit over the years, even though they have condemned each other for it. The last time we have had a surplus was during the boom times of the late 1990s.

The Keynesian view also prescribed that the deficits and surpluses are by-products of the countercyclical fiscal policy. Why?

First, during bad times, it requires more transfer payments for those in need of unemployment benefits, welfare, and Social Security. Second, due to fewer people working and fewer profits across the country, tax revenues fall because there is less income that can be taxed. Third, government also begins to engage in fiscal stimulus. More transfer payments paid out, fewer tax dollar revenue coming in, and more money paid out by government for fiscal stimulus will create a significant deficit.

The opposite is also true once the economy gets back on its feet, and the good times return. During good times with full employment, tax revenues start to rise, less money is needed for transfer payments, and no stimulus is needed, thus, there is potential for creating government spending surpluses. Those surpluses can help to pay off the debt that was incurred during the bad times. That is something the Keynes prescribed, but politicians seldom take those measures.

There is an important point to be made here about Social Security. Much of Social Security is from workers and their employers who have paid into the system over the years. There are some who get aid from it who have not paid into it, but much of that

TABLE 14.1 Federal Government Deficit History

1929	($1)	($1)	(0.7%)	Market crash
1930	($1)	($1)	(0.8%)	Smoot-Hawley
1931	$0	$1	0.6%	Dust Bowl
1932	$3	$3	4.5%	Hoover tax hike.
1933	$3	$3	4.5%	FDR. New Deal
1934	$4	$5	5.4%	GDP up 10.8%.
1935	$3	$2	3.8%	Social Security. WPA.
1936	$4	$5	5.1%	Tax hikes renewed depression
1937	$2	$3	2.4%	
1938	$0	$1	0.1%	Depression ended
1939	$3	$3	3.0%	Dust Bowl ended
1940	$3	$3	2.8%	Defense increased
1941	$5	$6	3.8%	Pearl Harbor
1942	$21	$23	12.3%	Defense tripled
1943	$55	$64	26.9%	
1944	$48	$64	21.2%	Bretton-Woods
1945	$48	$58	20.8%	WWII ended.
1946	$16	$11	7.0%	Recession.
1947	($4)	($11)	(1.6%)	Cold War.
1948	($12)	($6)	(4.2%)	Recession.
1949	($1)	$0	(0.2%)	
1950	$3	$5	1.0%	Korean War
1951	($6)	($2)	(1.7%)	
1952	$2	$4	0.4%	
1953	$6	$7	1.7%	Korean War ended
1954	$1	$5	0.3%	Recession
1955	$3	$3	0.7%	
1956	($4)	($2)	(0.9%)	
1957	($3)	($2)	(0.7%)	Recession
1958	$3	$6	0.6%	
1959	$13	$8	2.4%	Fed raised rates
1960	$0	$2	(0.1%)	Recession.
1961	$3	$3	0.6%	JFK and Bay of Pigs
1962	$7	$10	1.2%	Cuban Missile Crisis
1963	$5	$7	0.7%	U.S. aids Vietnam. JFK killed *(continue)*

Source: https://www.thebalance.com/us-deficit-by-year-3306306.

TABLE 14.1 Federal Government Deficit History (*continued*)

FISCAL YEAR	DEFICIT (IN BILLIONS)	DEBT INCREASE (BY FY)	DEFICIT /GDP	EVENTS AFFECTING DEFICIT
1964	$6	$6	0.9%	LBJ War on Poverty.
1965	$1	$6	0.2%	Medicare. Medicaid.
1966	$4	$3	0.4%	Vietnam War
1967	$9	$6	1.0%	
1968	$25	$21	2.6%	Moon landing.
1969	($3)	$6	(0.3%)	Nixon took office.
1970	$3	$17	0.3%	Recession
1971	$23	$27	1.9%	Wage price controls.
1972	$23	$29	1.9%	Stagflation.
1973	$15	$31	1.8%	End of gold standard.
1974	$6	$17	1.0%	Budget process created.
1975	$53	$58	0.4%	First Ford budget.
1976	$74	$87	3.1%	Stagflation.
1977	$54	$78	3.9%	Stagflation.
1978	$59	$73	2.5%	First Carter budget.
1979	$41	$55	1.5%	Volcker raised rates to 20%.
1980	$74	$81	2.6%	Recession. Iran oil embargo.
1981	$79	$90	2.4%	Reagan tax cut.
1982	$128	$144	3.8%	Reagan's 1st budget.
1983	$208	$235	5.6%	Jobless rate 10.8%.
1984	$185	$195	4.5%	Increased defense spending.
1985	$212	$256	4.8%	
1986	$221	$297	4.8%	Tax cut.
1987	$150	$225	3.1%	Market crash
1988	$155	$252	2.9%	Fed raised rates.
1989	$153	$255	2.7%	S&L Crisis.
1990	$221	$376	3.7%	Desert Storm.
1991	$269	$432	4.3%	Recession.
1992	$290	$399	4.4%	
1993	$255	$347	3.7%	Clinton signed Balanced Budget Act.
1994	$203	$281	2.8%	First Clinton budget.
1995	$164	$281	2.1%	

TABLE 14.1 Federal Government Deficit History (*continued*)

FISCAL YEAR	DEFICIT (IN BILLIONS)	DEBT INCREASE (BY FY)	DEFICIT /GDP	EVENTS AFFECTING DEFICIT
1996	$107	$251	1.3%	Welfare reform
1997	$22	$188	0.3%	
1998	($69)	$113	(0.8%)	LTCM crisis
1999	($126)	$130	(1.3%)	Glass-Steagall repealed
2000	($236)	$18	(2.3%)	Surplus.
2001	($128)	$133	(1.2%)	9/11 attacks. EGTRRA
2002	$158	$421	1.4%	War on Terror.
2003	$378	$555	3.2%	JGTRRA
2004	$413	$596	3.3%	
2005	$318	$554	2.4%	Katrina. Bankruptcy Act
2006	$248	$574	1.8%	Bernanke chairs Fed
2007	$161	$501	1.1%	Iraq War cost
2008	$459	$1,017	3.1%	Bank bailout. QE
2009	$1,413	$1,632	9.8%	Stimulus Act
2010	$1,294	$1,905	8.6%	Obama tax cuts. ACA. Simpson-Bowles
2011	$1,300	$1,229	8.3%	Debt crisis
2012	$1,087	$1,276	6.7%	Fiscal cliff
2013	$679	$672	4.1%	Sequester. Government shut-down
2014	$485	$1,086	2.8%	Debt ceiling
2015	$438	$327	2.4%	Defense = $736.4 b
2016	$585	$1,423	3.1%	Defense = $767.3 b
2017	$666	$672	3.4%	Defense = $812.3 b
2018 (est)	$440	NA	NA	Defense = $824.7 b

money it is from contributors and the return on those funds that have been loaned out with interest. They question is, then, why would it pay more out during a recession or bad economic times if it is designed to give us a retirement income? The answer is that when people in their sixties lose their jobs, they often opt to draw from their Social Security accounts if they can't find any other work. Many prefer to wait until they are older to draw from their accounts because waiting longer gives them higher benefits. But if older people can't find work, it often leaves them little other choices but to draw from Social Security right away. Another thing to remember is that Social Security is really a separate system from our typical government's financial resources.

Keynes wouldn't have been surprised at the change in significant deficits we have seen over the years when there were serious recessions. He would have considered the deficits as a routine by-product of counter-cyclical fiscal policy.

Many argue that the government can't control spending that much anyway due to automatic spending, and, for the most, part they are correct.

ECONOMIC MYTH #20	When the federal government sets the budget, all of the budget is fair game.

When the federal government decides that budget cuts are necessary, there are some funds that it cannot touch. Those funds represent about 80% of the federal budget. A big part of that sector of the budget is often known as the ***automatic spending***. It is uncontrollable or untouchable because it is that which resulted from commitments made over the years by prior Congresses and/or prior presidential administrations. Examples include Social Security payments, veterans' benefits, and interest from debts that the government incurred. The government can't simply decide to pull the rug out from these people to whom it made commitments long ago. Most of the money is, in fact, automatic stabilizers (discussed earlier) that respond to cyclical changes in the economy. People who are eligible for transfer payments when they are out of work will receive those funds as a means of stabilizing their family financial status as well as trying to give some level of stability to our economy.

It is important to note here that budget cuts in some areas are not an indication that politicians don't care about the people who need the programs where budget cuts take place. State and local governments have no choice but to balance their budgets. But governments also will often find ways to become more efficient in the administration of those programs and have cut budgets in that regard rather than that of cutting services.

The automatic stabilizers imply that the government lacks control of the budget and that, in reality, the size of the federal deficit or surplus is more sensitive to the economy, be it in economic expansion (full employment) or contraction (during a recession).

Discretionary spending for the federal government is similar to that of a person's spending. It can be spent at the discretion of the government. The other 20% of the budget is what the government may spend at its discretion. This is the money more likely to be used for fiscal restraint and fiscal stimulus. It may include things such as military equipment, grants for different social needs and studies, education, road repair, and other needed projects.

Let's discuss a little bit now about the counter cyclical changes to the deficit that Keynes talked about.

For every 1% that *GDP decreases*, it has been found through research and study that it will cause two major things to happen. First, it will cause government spending to *automatically* increase by $2 billion as it will cost that much to pay unemployment, welfare, Social Security, and Medicaid benefits to those who are out of work. The reverse is also true. When we get near full employment, the need to spend for those things will be reduced. Second, a 1% decline in GDP will also cause government revenues to *automatically* decline by $28 billion in individual and corporate income taxes and Social Security taxes because there will be less income of business and individuals to tax. When you add the loss of revenue to the added costs of spending, it will create a deficit increase of $30 billion.

Ironically, for every 1% *increase in inflation*, the deficit will actually decline. While it will compel government spending to *automatically* increase by $35 billion in retirements, Social Security, and interest (due to cost of living allowances (COLAs)) in those benefits, government revenue will increase by $42 billion *automatically. Why? Because inflation can create motivation for producers to increase output and thus jobs as mentioned before. More jobs translate into more taxable income. There will also be an increase* in corporate taxes and Social Security taxes by the higher prices when and if they generate more income and profits. Therefore, when you subtract the added costs of $35 billion from the added revenue of $42 billion driven by inflation, you will still have $7 billion remaining by which you can lower the deficit. The reverse is also true.

There is a thing called the ***cyclical deficit***. It is the portion of the government budget balance that is a result of these short-run changes in these economic conditions. It only occurs during bad economic times. Therefore, based upon what was said earlier, there are two things that will increase the deficit: GDP decreases or slowdowns and lower inflation. And, therefore, the *cyclical deficit* decreases with GDP increases and higher inflation. Remember that cyclical unemployment exists when the economy is in a slump. They call that deficit the cyclical deficit, because higher unemployment causes a greater deficit.

The remaining changes in the deficit are the result of fiscal policy such as changes in tax rates and spending patterns by Congress. These are called the ***structural deficit***. This is the deficit that the federal government may incur even when we are at full employment. It is equal to the federal revenues at full employment minus expenditures at full employment as a result of the fiscal policy at that time.

If you have a checkbook account or savings account at a bank, you will likely hold an account ***balance***. That is equal to what's left over after money paid out is subtracted from your deposits that were paid in. In the same way, during a recession, the federal government has a balance after subtracting government expenditures from government revenue. One of them is called the ***cyclical balance***. It is the *revenue changes* minus the *expenditure changes* as a result of *cyclical growth or cyclical slowdowns* in our economy.

A ***structural balance*** is the *revenue changes* minus the *expenditure changes* resulting from all other changes in government spending.

The ***budget balance***, therefore, is equal to the cyclical balance (from the business or economic cycle) plus the structural balance (from fiscal policy).

The structural balance is what the fiscal stimulus is affecting. Therefore, measures of thrust of fiscal policy (in either its ability to create GDP growth or slowdowns) are measured in the ***structural budget balance***.

You can also assume then that the fiscal stimulus (or dollars spent to stimulate the economy) is measured by how much the structural deficit rises (or by the reduction of any structural surplus). Fiscal restraint is measured by how much the structural deficit has been reduced (Schiller, 2016).

So, what are the economic effects of deficits? Are they good news or bad news? As mentioned before, many argue that crowding out can occur, creating less borrowing by the private sector and, thus, less private sector output if foreign resources have been used up by our government. Some also argue that the production possibilities curve is not as good if there fewer private goods due to more government output. This can create a great deal of opportunity costs as many will question whether this shrinkage of output in the private sector is worth the amount increased by government spending. Another by-product of deficits can be higher interest rates. Just like anything else, if there are more people borrowing or a greater demand for borrowable money, it will drive up the price or, in this case, interest rates. Higher interest rates lower the money supply and can hurt the economy with fewer purchases of house, cars, and appliances. It is important to point out here, however, that many economist believe that crowding out is no longer an issue, people can simply borrow abroad and borrow as much as they want at the rates they want.

What about the economic effects of surpluses when government takes in more money in taxes than it spends? It's important to note that, for the most part, a surplus will not llikely happen unless we are at or near full employment for the reasons mentioned earlier. Some economists say that surpluses will cause what they refer to as ***crowding in***. This exists when surpluses add to the leakages in the circular flow. If the surpluses are too large to put in any one bank, the government can act, using one of four choices.

First, the government can spend it. This is not recommended as it would be a stimulus, and crowding in happens usually at or near full employment when we need to be slowing down the growth rate and not increasing it. The government should not give a stimulus at full employment. At full employment, the government needs to be sure that supply is keeping up with demand. Added spending of a surplus will most likely cause rampant inflation. However, some politicians have been known to spend it anyway as spending money in their districts helps their reelections.

A second option would be to *reduce taxes* in order to remove the surplus. A lot of taxpayers would like that, but one must remember that tax cuts are also a form of economic stimulus and, again, stimulus is bad economics at full employment.

Third, government could *increase transfers payments*, but this probably is the most absurd of all of these options. At full employment who needs more transfer payments? Who needs more welfare and unemployment benefits and the like if almost everyone is working? Some will need transfer payments, but there would likely be less need and not more need of such payments.

Fourth and finally, many feel that the most logical option is to pay off old debt with the surplus. This will cut interest costs with fewer loans and it will reduce the government's demand for borrowable funds. It will also open up more money for consumers and business to borrow. It is particularly good that business can borrow more in order to keep expanding output to keep up with the demand of goods and services at full employment.

What happens if the federal deficit continues to increase? That will cause the government to borrow more, which would then increase our ***national debt***. That is accumulated debt of the federal government and has existed since the end of the Revolutionary War as shown in Table 14-2. The lowest debt that our federal government ever had was in 1835 when it was a mere $33,733.05!

WHO OWNS THE DEBT?

ECONOMIC MYTH #21	The U.S. Federal Government owes most of its debt to China and other foreign countries.

The fact is that not even one third of the U.S. Government's debt is owed to people outside our country. Table 14-3 shows a breakdown of who we owe as of 2015.

As you can see, the federal government owes nearly half of its debt to itself. The largest bondholder of government bonds is ... the government, holding nearly 50% (45% to be exact) of the national debt. Anytime the government owes money to other government entities, we call that ***internal debt***. The largest debt we owe is to Social Security, which, in turn, gives the interest it earns from that debt to people like you and me to enhance our retirements and other benefits. That way, we don't get just what we pay in but a little extra at retirement, as well.

While it is true that much more than that is owed to foreign countries, much of it is owed, not by our government but by Americans when they buy imports. As Americans continue to import, other nations lend us money to buy those goods.

TABLE 14.2 U.S. National Debt History

9/30/2015	18,150,617,666,484.30	9/30/1981	*997,855,000,000.00	6/30/1947	258,286,383,108.67
9/30/2014	17,824,071,380,733.80	9/30/1980	*907,701,000,000.00	6/28/1946	269,422,099,173.26
9/30/2013	16,738,183,526,697.30	9/30/1979	*826,519,000,000.00	6/30/1945	258,682,187,409.93
9/30/2012	16,066,241,407,385.80	9/30/1978	*771,544,000,000.00	6/30/1944	201,003,387,221.13
9/30/2011	14,790,340,328,557.10	9/30/1977	*698,840,000,000.00	6/30/1943	136,696,090,329.90
9/30/2010	13,561,623,030,891.70	6/30/1976	*620,433,000,000.00	6/30/1942	72,422,445,116.22
9/30/2009	11,909,829,003,511.70	6/30/1975	*533,189,000,000.00	6/30/1941	48,961,443,535.71
9/30/2008	10,024,724,896,912.40	6/30/1974	475,059,815,731.55	6/29/1940	42,967,531,037.68
9/30/2007	9,007,653,372,262.48	6/30/1973	458,141,605,312.09	6/30/1939	40,439,532,411.11
9/30/2006	8,506,973,899,215.23	6/30/1972	427,260,460,940.50	6/30/1938	37,164,740,315.45
9/30/2005	7,932,709,661,723.50	6/30/1971	398,129,744,455.54	6/30/1937	36,424,613,732.29
9/30/2004	7,379,052,696,330.32	6/30/1970	370,918,706,949.93	6/30/1936	33,778,543,493.73
9/30/2003	6,783,231,062,743.62	6/30/1969	353,720,253,841.41	6/29/1935	28,700,892,624.53
9/30/2002	6,228,235,965,597.16	6/30/1968	347,578,406,425.88	6/30/1934	27,053,141,414.48
9/30/2001	5,807,463,412,200.06	6/30/1967	326,220,937,794.54	6/30/1933	22,538,672,560.15
9/30/2000	5,674,178,209,886.86	6/30/1966	319,907,087,795.48	6/30/1932	19,487,002,444.13
9/30/1999	5,656,270,901,615.43	6/30/1965	317,273,898,983.64	6/30/1931	16,801,281,491.71
9/30/1998	5,526,193,008,897.62	6/30/1964	311,712,899,257.30	6/30/1930	16,185,309,831.43
9/30/1997	5,413,146,011,397.34	6/30/1963	305,859,632,996.41	6/29/1929	16,931,088,484.10
9/30/1996	5,224,810,939,135.73	6/30/1962	298,200,822,720.87	6/30/1928	17,604,293,201.43
9/29/1995	4,973,982,900,709.39	6/30/1961	288,970,938,610.05	6/30/1927	18,511,906,931.85
9/30/1994	4,692,749,910,013.32	6/30/1960	286,330,760,848.37	6/30/1926	19,643,216,315.19
9/30/1993	4,411,488,883,139.38	6/30/1959	284,705,907,078.22	6/30/1925	20,516,193,887.90
9/30/1992	4,064,620,655,521.66	6/30/1958	276,343,217,745.81	6/30/1924	21,250,812,989.49
9/30/1991	3,665,303,351,697.03	6/30/1957	270,527,171,896.43	6/30/1923	22,349,707,365.36
9/28/1990	3,233,313,451,777.25	6/30/1956	272,750,813,649.32	6/30/1922	22,963,381,708.31
9/29/1989	2,857,430,960,187.32	6/30/1955	274,374,222,802.62	6/30/1921	23,977,450,552.54
9/30/1988	2,602,337,712,041.16	6/30/1954	271,259,599,108.46	7/1/1920	25,952,456,406.16
9/30/1987	2,350,276,890,953.00	6/30/1953	266,071,061,638.57	7/1/1919	27,390,970,113.12
9/30/1986	2,125,302,616,658.42	6/30/1952	259,105,178,785.43	7/1/1918	14,592,161,414.00
9/30/1985	*1,823,103,000,000.00	6/29/1951	255,221,976,814.93	7/1/1917	5,717,770,279.52
9/30/1984	*1,572,266,000,000.00	6/30/1950	257,357,352,351.04	7/1/1916	3,609,244,262.16
9/30/1983	*1,377,210,000,000.00	6/30/1949	252,770,359,860.33	7/1/1915	3,058,136,873.16
9/30/1982	*1,142,034,000,000.00	6/30/1948	252,292,246,512.99	7/1/1914	2,912,499,269.16
7/1/1913	2,916,204,913.66	07/01/1877	2,205,301,392.10	01/01/1842	13,594,480.73

Source: https://www.treasurydirect.gov/govt/reports/pd/histdebt/histdebt_histo4.htm.

DATE	DOLLAR AMOUNT	DATE	DOLLAR AMOUNT	DATE	DOLLAR AMOUNT
7/1/1912	2,868,373,874.16	07/01/1876	2,180,395,067.15	01/01/1841	5,250,875.54
7/1/1911	2,765,600,606.69	07/01/1875	2,232,284,531.95	01/01/1840	3,573,343.82
7/1/1910	2,652,665,838.04	07/01/1874	2,251,690,468.43	01/01/1839	10,434,221.14
7/1/1909	2,639,546,241.04	07/01/1873	2,234,482,993.20	01/01/1838	3,308,124.07
7/1/1908	2,626,806,271.54	07/01/1872	2,253,251,328.78	01/01/1837	336,957.83
7/1/1907	2,457,188,061.54	07/01/1871	2,353,211,332.32	01/01/1836	37,513.05
7/1/1906	2,337,161,839.04	07/01/1870	2,480,672,427.81	01/01/1835	33,733.05
7/1/1905	2,274,615,063.84	07/01/1869	2,588,452,213.94	01/01/1834	4,760,082.08
7/1/1904	2,264,003,585.14	07/01/1868	2,611,687,851.19	01/01/1833	7,001,698.83
7/1/1903	2,202,464,781.89	07/01/1867	2,678,126,103.87	01/01/1832	24,322,235.18
7/1/1902	2,158,610,445.89	07/01/1866	2,773,236,173.69	01/01/1831	39,123,191.68
7/1/1901	2,143,326,933.89	07/01/1865	2,680,647,869.74	01/01/1830	48,565,406.50
7/1/1900	2,136,961,091.67	07/01/1864	1,815,784,370.57	01/01/1829	58,421,413.67
07/01/1899	1,991,927,306.92	07/01/1863	1,119,772,138.63	01/01/1828	67,475,043.87
07/01/1898	1,796,531,995.90	07/01/1862	524,176,412.13	01/01/1827	73,987,357.20
07/01/1897	1,817,672,665.90	07/01/1861	90,580,873.72	01/01/1826	81,054,059.99
07/01/1896	1,769,840,323.40	07/01/1860	64,842,287.88	01/01/1825	83,788,432.71
07/01/1895	1,676,120,983.25	07/01/1859	58,496,837.88	01/01/1824	90,269,777.77
07/01/1894	1,632,253,636.68	07/01/1858	44,911,881.03	01/01/1823	90,875,877.28
07/01/1893	1,545,985,686.13	07/01/1857	28,699,831.85	01/01/1822	93,546,676.98
07/01/1892	1,588,464,144.63	07/01/1856	31,972,537.90	01/01/1821	89,987,427.66
07/01/1891	1,545,996,591.61	07/01/1855	35,586,956.56	01/01/1820	91,015,566.15
07/01/1890	1,552,140,204.73	07/01/1854	42,242,222.42	01/01/1819	95,529,648.28
07/01/1889	1,619,052,922.23	07/01/1853	59,803,117.70	01/01/1818	103,466,633.83
07/01/1888	1,692,858,984.58	07/01/1852	66,199,341.71	01/01/1817	123,491,965.16
07/01/1887	1,657,602,592.63	07/01/1851	68,304,796.02	01/01/1816	127,334,933.74
07/01/1886	1,775,063,013.78	07/01/1850	63,452,773.55	01/01/1815	99,833,660.15
07/01/1885	1,863,964,873.14	07/01/1849	63,061,858.69	01/01/1814	81,487,846.24
07/01/1884	1,830,528,923.57	07/01/1848	47,044,862.23	01/01/1813	55,962,827.57
07/01/1883	1,884,171,728.07	07/01/1847	38,826,534.77	01/01/1812	45,209,737.90
07/01/1882	1,918,312,994.03	07/01/1846	15,550,202.97	01/01/1811	48,005,587.76
07/01/1881	2,069,013,569.58	07/01/1845	15,925,303.01	01/01/1810	53,173,217.52
07/01/1880	2,120,415,370.63	07/01/1844	23,461,652.50	01/01/1809	57,023,192.09
07/01/1879	2,349,567,482.04	07/01/1843	32,742,922.00	01/01/1816	127,334,933.74
07/01/1878	2,256,205,892.53	01/01/1843	20,201,226.27	01/01/1815	99,833,660.15
01/01/1814	81,487,846.24	01/01/1806	75,723,270.66	01/01/1798	79,228,529.12

(continue)

TABLE 14.2 U.S. National Debt History (*continued*)

DATE	DOLLAR AMOUNT	DATE	DOLLAR AMOUNT	DATE	DOLLAR AMOUNT
01/01/1813	55,962,827.57	01/01/1805	82,312,150.50	01/01/1794	78,427,404.77
01/01/1812	45,209,737.90	01/01/1804	86,427,120.88	01/01/1793	80,358,634.04
01/01/1811	48,005,587.76	01/01/1803	77,054,686.40	01/01/1792	77,227,924.66
01/01/1810	53,173,217.52	01/01/1802	80,712,632.25	01/01/1791	75,463,476.52
01/01/1809	57,023,192.09	01/01/1801	83,038,050.80	01/01/1790	71,060,508.50
01/01/1808	65,196,317.97	01/01/1800	82,976,294.35		
01/01/1807	69,218,398.64	01/01/1799	78,408,669.77		*Rounded to Millions

TABLE 14.3 Those Owed, What Percent, and Their Categories

THOSE OWED, WHAT PERCENT, AND THEIR CATEGORIES
Social Security owns 17% (Internal)
Federal Agencies own 16% (Internal)
Federal Reserve 7% (Internal)
State and Local Governments 5% (Internal)
Foreigners 31% (External Debt)
Banks, corporations, insurance companies, individuals 24% (External Debt)

External debt, therefore, is debt that is owed to someone other than government itself. What we owe to people outside the United States is only 31%.

Since banks and individuals own 24%, we say individuals hold the debt directly or indirectly because when you put money into banks, buy stock, or buy insurance, some of your money that you put into these institutions is often loaned out again to the federal government.

To the government, the debt is a ***liability*** or something owed and to be paid back, but to those who lend to the government by purchasing the issued bonds, it is an ***asset***. Thus, the national debt *creates debt for the government* but *wealth for the bondholders*. This is not always a bad thing as you or many other American taxpayers can obtain wealth. When you loan money to the government or own an asset of value, you get a relatively decent return on the debt, and the value of the asset adds to your wealth.

Historically, our government has piled up debt *without* creating economic damage. As debts become due, the government does not default, it just borrows more to pay off that which is due now, which is considered refinancing. Many argue that as long as this process continues, the government can borrow eternally *as long as no one demands more of his or her money back than the government is able to borrow, which is highly unlikely*. Even still, things comparable to that have already happened as some countries have had economic problems by doing the same thing. A few years ago, the country of Greece experienced very difficult hardships as its continuous piling up of debt made its lenders very nervous. Greece, as of this writing, still has not completely resolved this issue.

But what about interest and cost to our economy? The U.S. Treasury paid over $200 billion in interest costs in 2005. High interest costs remove the government's ability to balance the budget and fund needed programs. However, some are quick to argue that because nearly 70% of the money owed is to Americans and/American institutions, we are often the beneficiaries, either directly or indirectly, of many of those interest payments.

The cost of the debt to our economy is only affected with opportunity costs when resources or factors of production are used. When this happens, and if money is taken away from out private sector, it can cause a problem if that government money is spent on interest, thus, reducing the possibility for using it for economic growth, transfer payments, other government purchases, or debt repayment.

On the flip side, one advantage here is that it permits us to get more public-sector goods without cutting back on private sector production, thereby, pushing out the production possibilities curve and expanding the economy. The national debt is never going to stop climbing, obviously, as long as there is a deficit. That is another reason why some say paying off debt with a surplus is good as it not only stops the debt from rising, but it reduces it when there is the opportunity to do so.

The ***Gramm-Rudman-Hollings Act of 1985*** was passed in order to lower the ceiling of each year's deficits until a balanced budget was achieved and to impose automatic cutbacks if Congress did not stay below the ceiling. Those cutbacks were aimed at hurting many vital government programs. The law did this with the hope that it would scare Congress and the president into being more fiscally responsible, but Congress put many amendments into it over the years that basically made the law useless. Debt ceilings are also used to keep the debt under control, but those are often a joke as Congress and the White House usually ignore them or they simply raise those ceilings.

Chapter 14 Review

QUESTIONS TO THINK ABOUT

1. Who owns the debt that our country has borrowed over the years?
2. What is the best way to resolved the issue of crowding in and why?

TERMS TO KNOW

Automatic Spending

Asset

Balance

Budget Balance

Crowding In

Cyclical Balance

Cyclical Deficit

Discretionary Spending

External Debt

Gramm-Rudman-Hollings Act of 1985

Internal Debt

Liability

National Debt

Structural Balance

Structural Budget Balance

Structural Deficit

CHAPTER FIFTEEN

Money, Money, Money, and Banking

IN CHAPTER 15, you will now learn how we really define what money is and what it is not. You will see a little history on how trade was conducted before money existed. You will also see what we consider to be the money supply and how it is measured. Finally, you will get a brief look at what banking institutions exist and how they operate from your neighborhood bank all the way up to the United States Federal Reserve.

MONEY DEFINED

So, what is ***money***? It is three things. First, it is a *medium of exchange* and is accepted as payment for goods, services, and debts. Until money existed, people had to carry gold or things of value if they wanted to get other things they needed. It became very impractical when a person traveled as he or she had to carry so much with him or her, hoping to find someone who had what he or she needed and needed what *he or she* had. Money made it possible to simply put valuables in your pocket and then buy what you needed. Second, money is also a *standard of value*. It is the yardstick of the value of a good or service. When we talk about the net worth of a thing or a person, that worth is expressed in money terms, usually in the currency of the country in which you are. Third, it stores value for future purchases. For example, if I had been an egg farmer, and if I needed a doctor's services, I had to hope that the doctor needed eggs at the same time that I needed a cure. If it took me time to find that doctor, or if I didn't need the doctor's services for a few weeks after I produced the eggs, the eggs might no longer be edible and I would have been out of luck. *Storage of value* with money makes it so I can wait years before spending it. This old way of doing things, known as the ***bartering system***, was replaced by money.

For many years, people would use coins as currency that would represent gold which backed it up. But the coin mint became very expensive to operate, and the government then began to look for ways to reduce the cost of creating our money. As mentioned earlier, paper money was not allowed by the Constitution until 1861.

At this point in time, we consider currency and all ***checking accounts*** to be money. That's because, in either case, when we write a check or give cash, we are saying that someone will back up what we are handing out as money, either by the balance in my checking account when I write a check or by the government backing up my cash with its gold reserves. Your checking account is considered money just as much as currency is, but some bank accounts are better substitutes for cash than others, depending upon who may be writing bad checks. ***Credit cards*** are a medium of exchange, but *they are not money* because cash or checking must be used to pay the balance on credit; however, you are never in debt when you use currency or write a check.

Once we have an understanding of what money is and isn't, it helps us to better define what we mean by the money supply.

The narrowest definition of the money supply is called ***M1***. It includes currency now in circulation and ***transaction account balances***. Transaction account balances are checking accounts or the equivalent that are readily accessed by a check or debit card or wherever direct payment is permitted to a 3rd party without you, the payor, having to make a trip to the bank.

When we talk about the money supply that the government wants to increase or decrease in order to manage the economy, ***M2*** is the mostly widely watched to measure it. It is equal to all of M1 plus most ***savings, time deposits*** of less than $100,000, and ***money market accounts***. These are typically short-term, low-risk investments. An example of a time deposit is a certificate of deposit (CD) issued and sold by banks to those who wish to loan money to banks on a long-term basis. A ***jumbo CD*** would be one that has a very high value such as the $100,000 CD mentioned earlier. Sometimes the buyers of CDs own them for as little as seven days or up to more than one year. ***Money market accounts (MMAs)***, also known as ***money market deposit accounts (MMDAs)*** are non-financial accounts that pay interest based upon whatever the current interest rates are in the money markets. They usually pay a better return to their buyers, but they require a higher minimum balance, ranging from $1,000 to $25,000.

All of these types of investments, compared to stocks and bonds, pay a lower return to those who own them because people demand less reward or return when there are fewer risks, and these are, indeed, less risky than most stocks and bonds.

Measuring these items of the money supply gives an understanding of consumers' purchasing power. When people go to financial institutions to borrow for purchasing things, such as cars, appliances, and housing, many lenders will use these accounts to lend to these buyers.

The remaining liquid assets are not as likely to be used for purchases and, thus, are not as much of a concern when deciding purchasing power of the consumer.

M3 is equal to M2 plus time deposits that have a value greater than $100,000, ***repurchase agreements***, and ***overnight Eurodollars***. Repurchase agreements are the sale of stocks with the understanding for the seller to buy them back at a later date (http://gcl.nu/forms/all%20in%20one.docx). A ***security*** is any tradable financial asset of value such as stocks or bonds. ***Eurodollars*** are time deposits denominated in U.S. dollars at banks outside the United States and, thus, are not under the jurisdiction of the Federal Reserve; therefore, no minimum reserve requirement exists for them. The term ***Euro*** implies that it is only denominated in U.S. dollars in Europe, but over the years, the term applies to any bank outside of the U.S.

Last but not least, ***L*** is equal to all of M3 plus all remaining liquid assets. They include things such as ***treasury bills (T-bills), U.S. savings bonds, banker's acceptances, commercial paper, and term Eurodollars***. A T-bill is a very short-term debt loaned to the U.S. Government that it must pay back to the lender within one year. The date that it is due to be paid in full is called the maturity date as is with most bonds. T-bills are sold in denominations ranging from $1,000 up to $5 million. The most common are due to be paid back within four weeks, thirteen weeks, and twenty-six weeks. U.S. savings bonds allow you to receive a guaranteed return for your investment while you help the government to raise money. Banker's acceptances, also called BAs, are a promised future payment, which is accepted and guaranteed by a bank and drawn on a deposit at the bank.

Commercial paper is short-term, unsecured (having no collateral) promissory notes issued by a firm, expecting to pay it back quickly. For example, car dealers often borrow to fill up their showrooms but pay back the notes quickly when the cars are sold as do farmers when they borrow to plant and they pay back such debt when they are paid for their harvest.

So, the money supply is mostly in the category of M2, but there are many other liquid assets within our financial institutions. It is now important to take a look at some of those institutions.

THE DIFFERENT TYPES OF FINANCIAL INSTITUTIONS

As of this writing, there are about 8,000 ***commercial banks*** in the United States. They offer any and all financial services available. They hold nearly all demand deposits (transaction accounts) and half of all savings in this country. You can get anything you need at one of them, including checking accounts, savings accounts, loans of all types, and even retirement accounts and mutual funds.

There are approximately 500 ***savings and loans (S&Ls)*** left in this country after surviving some very turbulent times over the years. They were originally used to pool resources of a neighborhood, offering only savings accounts to their depositors and home loans to their borrowers. Originally, there were no checking accounts, no car loans, and no appliance loans. They have also been called thrifts and building and loans.

As the industry became more competitive and deregulated, it began to offer many of the other services found at a commercial bank. Now it acts so much like the commercial banks, offering so many commercial bank services, to many, it is difficult to distinguish between them.

In the 1970s through the 1990s, there was a savings and loan crisis. Nearly half of them failed during that time, and nearly one third of the over three thousand S&Ls failed in the United States between 1985 and 1995 alone. Some of them were protected by the FSLIC, but some were protected by their own state insurance funds that quickly went insolvent as the crisis unfolded.

In 1979, inflation became rampant. Therefore, our Federal Reserve System raised the interest rates in an effort to reduce inflation (more on that later). Interest rates also went up because, as mentioned earlier, interest rates will rise with inflation because they include the inflation premium. Many of the S&Ls already had outstanding long-term loans at much lower fixed interest rates set by the Fed in earlier years. The S&Ls thrived on deposits, and they had to pay very high interest rates to get people to make deposits. That rate was often higher than what the borrowers were paying them as the loans were initiated during the years when interest rates were low. Thus, many S&Ls became insolvent. With fewer regulations and government oversight, many began to invest in very risky investments that collapsed, making some of the S&Ls insolvent.

In Ohio, most of the S&Ls converted to banks in 1985 due to the failure of ***Home State Federal*** and the ***Ohio State Insurance Fund***, which went bankrupt. Many of Ohio's S&Ls did not use the FSLIC but, rather, they used an insurance fund that was completely underfunded. It was immediately wiped out in their crisis. Then, Governor ***Richard Celeste*** of Ohio declared his own savings and loan holiday when one of the Home State Savings and Loan, went bankrupt, touching off a domino effect that sank many of Ohio's other S&Ls. He closed all Ohio S&Ls until they could reopen as a bank with FDIC insurance.

Another problem facing both commercial banks and the S&Ls in this country during those times was their high investment in firms exploring for oil. In the mid-1970s, with high oil prices, it was considered a safe bet to loan money to any firm involved with the exploration and production of oil. In the late 1980s, the price of oil plummeted, and the oil exploration and production came almost to a complete halt. Many of the firms defaulted on the loans held by those banks and S&Ls. This wreaked more havoc on the financial institution market.

There are about 1,000 ***mutual savings banks*** in the United States, located primarily in New York, Massachusetts, Connecticut, Pennsylvania, and New Jersey. They were originally created for small savers, but now their deposits are used for more things such as investment bonds and blue-chip stocks. This makes the deposits riskier, but returns are also better than that of a conventional commercial bank of savings and loan.

A ***credit union*** is often referred to as a financial cooperative because it is a nonprofit, member-owned institution, democratically controlled by its members. Its intent was to be able to be more concerned about the depositors rather than profits, thus, giving its depositors high rates of return on their savings and low interest rate loans. There are about 10,000 in this country today, representing about 5% of total savings in this country. The depositors are people who have been formed by a common tie, such as employment by a certain company or government agency or enrollment at a given educational institution. You cannot be a depositor unless you belong to one of these groups. Some of them are struggling due to competition from bigger banks. Those who wish to use the automatic teller machines at banks in which they do not do banking, often have to pay a fee. Credit unions aren't big enough to have ATMs everywhere asthe bigger banks are, thus credit union customers are more likely to have to pay those high transaction fees.

BANKS' ESSENTIAL FUNCTIONS

Regardless of what type of bank you have, in general, they perform two essential functions for the macro economy. First, they transfer money from savers to spenders by lending their reserves held on deposit, *creating a reinjection into the economy, which counters the savings leakage.* They also create additional money by making loans in excess of total reserves as we have mentioned earlier.

Also, as previously mentioned, deposit creation is crucial if we want to have a strong economy. We must have the banking system create money! There are three major constraints on deposit creation. The first is deposits themselves. It seems like a no brainer, but you need to remember that one deposit creates more deposits. Thus, if people make fewer and/or smaller deposits, the additional deposits generated will also be fewer and smaller. When the number and dollar amount of deposits decrease, the multiplier will reduce them exponentially. Few deposits are made when people prefer to hold on to their cash.

Second, just as fewer depositors bring down deposits, fewer borrowers bring down deposits. Remember, a deposit doesn't create more money unless it is loaned out. Thus, fewer loans mean that there will be fewer cycles in which money is created in banks. If nobody borrows, then the deposits stop multiplying.

So, what can create a financial atmosphere that has fewer depositors and borrowers? Fewer depositors will exist if they don't feel that the banks are giving them *adequate return on their savings* or if they question the *solvency or stability of the financial institutions* in our country. That is why a solid FDIC and the like is crucial. Fewer borrowers will exist if *interest rates are high*, if the credit rating *lending standards are too stringent* to have people qualify for loans, or if there is *low consumer confidence in the economy*. There will also be fewer loans available if the Fed's regulating of the *minimum reserve requirement, interest rates, and lending standards* makes loans less likely. Increasing the minimum reserve requirement can truly put the brakes on the economy.

The minimum reserve requirement has actually been used rarely to change the money supply because it is so powerful. Other countries have used it, but not all countries do. In the United States, it has averaged approximately 11%, ranging from approximately 8.5% to 12% over the last several decades.

Overnight funds or ***federal funds*** are used by banks to borrow overnight when their cash balances fall below the minimum reserve requirement. They can also borrow funds from the Fed to simply loan out to customers when they lack enough deposits to make loans. Sometimes money doesn't come into banks as quickly as banks would like. If for any reason there is a dry spell where depositors don't make deposits as usual or if payments due from loans are delayed, the banks may slightly miss the reserves they are supposed to have. No bank wants to be short on its reserves to the Fed. Therefore, the Fed can impact the money supply here, too, by changing the rate for borrowing such funds.

For example, if the Fed is trying to increase the money supply, it will want to encourage loan creation, which dramatically increases deposit creation. Loans are more likely to be granted if banks feel safe in pushing the envelope, loaning out their deposits right up to, but not including, any of the funds that they need for their reserves. If banks come close being short on their reserves, they know they can borrow from the Fed overnight to keep their reserves where they belong if the overnight rate is low. Banks don't want to keep any more deposits in their banks than they have to because they are paying interest to the depositors. If they pay interest on deposits that they have not loaned out, there is no income from them, and every second that it continues, the banks are taking a loss.

If the Fed is trying to reduce the money supply and, therefore, loans or deposits, it can raise these rates, so banks won't be able to afford to borrow as much overnight. This will reduce their likelihood to push the envelope in risking becoming reserve poor, thus, they will loan out less, and, thus, there will be a smaller money supply.

Please recall that those federal funds are also used by banks to loan out to other borrowers. If the rate to borrow those funds goes up, the banks would have to raise their rates, but making the loan less affordable and reducing the number of loans that can be created. The opposite of all of this is also true.

Chapter 15 Review

QUESTIONS TO THINK ABOUT

1. What is considered a form of money?
2. What is NOT considered a form of money?
3. How important is the money supply, and what level or category of money represents the money supply?

TERMS/PEOPLE TO KNOW

Bartering System
Banker's Acceptances
Checking Accounts
Commercial Banks
Commercial Paper
Credit Cards
Credit Union
Euro
Eurodollars
Home State Federal
Jumbo CD
L
M1
M2
M3
Money
Money Market Accounts (MMAs)
Money Market Deposit Accounts (MMDAs)
Mutual Savings Banks
Ohio State Insurance Fund
Overnight Eurodollars
Overnight Funds or Federal Funds
Post-Dated Check
Repurchase Agreements
Richard Celeste
Savings and Loans (S&Ls)
Security
Term Eurodollars
Time Deposits
Transaction Account Balances
Treasury Bills (T-Bills)
U.S. Savings Bonds

CHAPTER SIXTEEN

The Fed

IN CHAPTER 15, we introduced the Federal Reserve. Now in Chapter 16, we will cover it in more depth because it has such a huge impact on our macro economy every minute of every day. Many of its decisions have, in the past, and will, in the future, determine whether or not many people will be employed or out of work.

THE ROLES OF THE FED

Besides managing the money supply, as we have previously discussed, the Federal Reserve also manages the *clearing of checks* in our country. There are more than 40 billion checks per year that have to be processed, and the Federal Reserve has to make sure that it is performed quickly. If not, the banking process becomes sluggish and slow. Therefore, as one can imagine, if transactions aren't happening quickly, it can also cause delays in commerce, which can lead to a slow economy.

There are twelve ***Federal Reserve Districts*** as shown in Figure 16-1. ***Federal Reserve Banks*** exist all over the country, thus, the Fed's check-clearing capabilities make it so that a member bank in California can clear a check from New York without having to wait for the check to travel across the country by plane or truck. There are check-clearing locations in each district to make that happen.

Each district has its own routing number, and the routing number of any check (seen in Figure 16-2) will reference the Federal Reserve district in which the checks are cleared.

For example, in Boston (District 1), a check drawn on a bank from San Francisco (District 12) used to take weeks to cash. That is now streamlined with the system that is now in place.

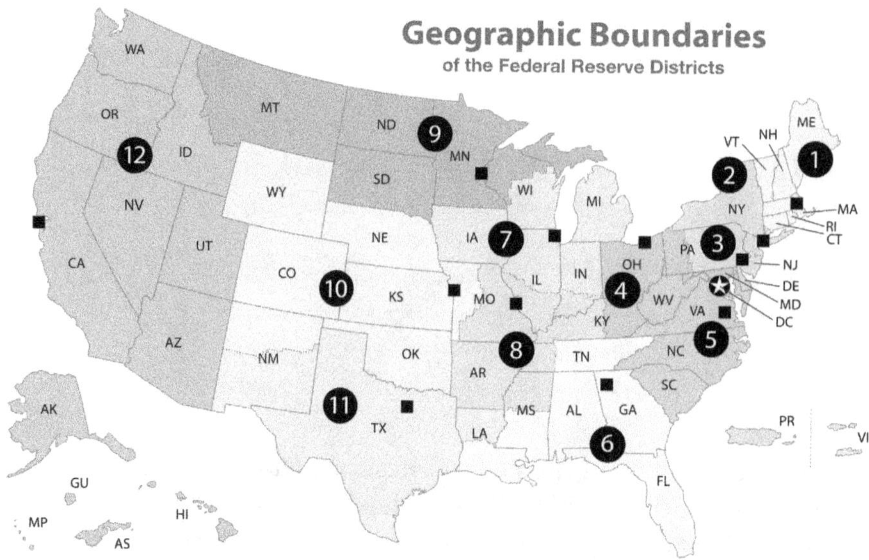

FIGURE 16.1 Federal Reserve Bank Districts

Source: Copyright © Nkocharh (CC BY-SA 2.5) at https://commons.wikimedia.org/wiki/File:Federal_Reserve_Districts_Map.svg

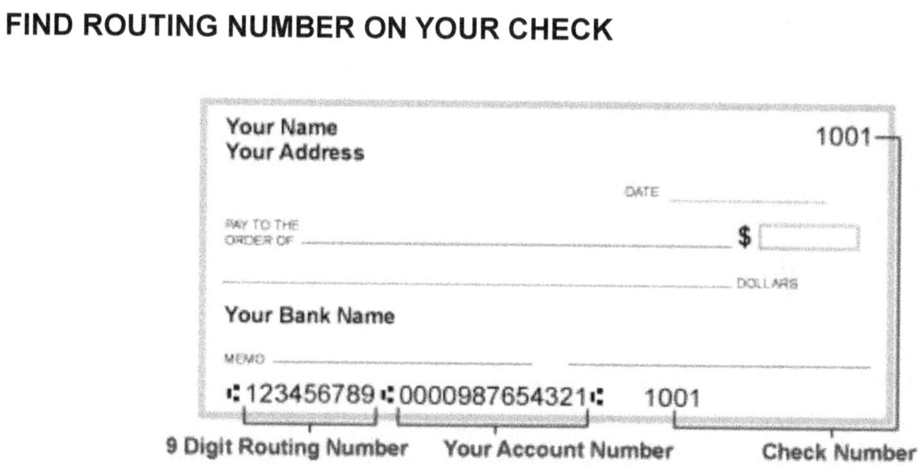

FIGURE 16.2 Elements of a Check

Source: https://www.treasurydirect.gov/govt/reports/pd/histdebt/histdebt_histo4.htm

The second major function of the Fed, as mentioned earlier, is the *holding of bank reserves*. Only small amounts of bank reserves are held in their vaults. The rest is held by the Fed (which allows the Fed to monitor actual reserve levels).

The Fed also orders the production of currency. When banks need money, the Fed will make sure that the correct amount is obtained from our ***National Mint***. Every year, currency is removed from circulation when it becomes tattered and hard to use in vending machines or wherever they are passed. Each dollar retired from the system must then be replaced. If the Fed wants to increase the money supply, it will print more money than was removed from circulation. That money finds its way into our economy through member banks.

Banks seldom hold much cash, but they often need it for sporadic demand such as holidays, and such cash can be provided by the Fed. Such cash is delivered by armored truck, and the amount of it is deducted from the reserves just mentioned. When the holidays are over, the vendors who are paid the cash return it to the banks in deposits a few days later. The excess cash is then sent back to the Fed.

Providing loans, as mentioned before, is crucial to the money supply, and the Fed provides loans to private banks to make this happen. This is called discounting because the banks are loaned this money at a lower rate, or a discount, than what they will charge their customers who borrow it.

THE ORGANIZATION OF THE FED

The Federal Reserve is run by a ***Board of Governors*** which has seven members. Each is appointed by the president and confirmed by the Senate. They each have 14-year terms. That way it keeps them independent of any given administration or political party. They cannot be reappointed.

One of the governors is appointed/reappointed by the president to be the chairperson, and that chairperson must report to Congress at least once every six months. As of this writing, the current chairperson is Jerome Powell, preceded by ***Janet Yellen***, the first woman to hold the position. She began her term on February 1, 2014, and previously served as the vice chair under ***Ben Bernanke*** from 2010 to 2014. Table 16-1 shows the chairpersons of the Fed since 1979.

THE FEDERAL OPEN MARKET COMMITTEE (FOMC)

The ***Federal Open Market Committee (FOMC)*** is responsible for the Fed's daily activity in financial markets, setting up short-term interest rates and the level of reserves held by private banks. The membership of the FOMC includes all of the board of governors and five of the twelve regional Federal Reserve bank presidents. They meet in Washington, D.C. every month to review the economy's performance. It recommends changes in monetary policy to the chairperson based upon the country's economic status, but the Fed chairperson has the final say as to what policy will be set.

In addition to setting the minimum reserve requirements mentioned earlier, there are other monetary tools used to control the money supply.

Discount rates are the interest rates discussed earlier that are charged to banks that wish to borrow from the Fed to either increase their business in loan creation or when they push the envelope and lend out until there are no excess funds above and

TABLE 16.1 Past and Current Chairpersons

Chairperson	Term
 Paul Volcker	August 6, 1979–August 11, 1987
 Alan Greenspan	August 11, 1987–January 31, 2006
 Ben Bernanke	February 1, 2006–January 31, 2014
 Janet Yellen	February 1, 2014–February 4, 2018
 Jerome Powell	February 5, 2018–Present

Source: United States Federal Reserve, a) https://bit.ly/2r8iGSf; b) https://bit.ly/2FTzuqu; c) https://bit.ly/2TTlxvg; d) https://bit.ly/2TQ0daf; e) https://bit.ly/2zvxjnd.

beyond the minimum reserve requirement. These loans are called federal funds, or overnight funds, as discussed previously.

Banks may also buy government bonds, but when they become reserve-poor, they can sell those securities and deposit the proceeds in a regional Federal Reserve bank. Each bank has an account, much like regular bank depositors, and they can borrow from those accounts when they are reserve-poor. By raising the discount rate, the amount of the money supply again decreases because there will be fewer loans due to higher monthly payments on those loans and, thus, less deposit creation. The opposite is also true.

The ***open market operations*** of the Fed, by far, have the greatest impact on the economy compared to the others mentioned before. They are the *principal* mechanism for directly altering the reserves of the banking system and are used in lieu of changing minimum reserve requirements.

HERE IS HOW IT WORKS

When people decide where to invest idle or excess funds, they make what is called the ***portfolio decision***. If you have savings accounts, stocks, bonds, certificates of deposit, rental properties, or any other investments, the combination of these investments is referred to as your ***investment portfolio***. You will decide what combination of investments will meet your needs. If you wish to move money from your savings to stocks or bonds, for example, you have just made a portfolio decision.

The Fed's open market operations focus on the portfolio decisions while people try to decide whether to put money in bank accounts or in government bonds. If the people keep their money in banks, that increases the money supply because it keeps deposit balances high, but if they move their accounts to bonds, then deposits and, therefore, the money supply will decline. If the Fed is trying to make this happen, perhaps during booming economies when it wants to slow down the growth of GDP as it fears that inflation is imminent, it will make bonds more attractive to investors. Doing so will prompt people to move their money out of their banks to buy those attractive bonds, thus lowering their deposit balances.

The question is: How do they make a bond more attractive? There are several ways to do this. One way is to offer the buyers of bonds more return without raising the price. For example, if a $1,000 bond is giving a 5% return, the Fed may choose to pay more than 5%. Another way would be to leave the return rate as is and then offering buyers a lower price for the bonds. The Fed could also do a combination of these two thnigs. Offering the bonds at a lower price gives it higher yield if the bonds are paying a set amount of money in the way of returns. For example, if you are receiving a cash flow of $50 from a $1,000 bond, then you would obviously be receiving a 5% return. If, however, the bond price was lowered to $900 while still paying you a $50 yield or return, then your return rate would jump to 5.56% ($50/$900). The less you pay for a bond, the higher its yield all the way up to maturity, unless the dollar return you get is reduced; Thus, the Fed can induce people to buy bonds by offering to sell them at a lower price, such as a $1,000 bond yielding 5% for a price of $900. The opposite is also true. The Fed could raise the price for the same bond, and, therefore, new buyers may be charged $1,100. If that happened, the yield would now drop to 4.55%. Such an unattractive bond would compel investors to keep their money in their savings accounts, thus making the money supply in the way of bank deposits and excel reserves higher.

The Fed can also buy bonds from the public. That means that it is lending more to the people and business, and when loans are made, more deposits happen, not just when people deposit the loans upon receiving them but when they take the loans and buy things such as houses, cars, and appliances with them.

The daily volume of the bond market exceeds $500 billion. Bonds are IOUs and can be sold and resold before maturity. Typically, they only pay interest or a yield until maturity (or when the loan or bond is due to be paid off).

Sometimes the value and, therefore, the price of bonds change without the Fed directly changing its prices. The value of the bonds goes up as interest rates fall. Why? Because when you buy a bond, there is an agreed-upon price that is paid and a rate of return that cannot usually be changed, unless the bond is a variable rate bond.

Suppose, for example, that you loan the government $1,000 in the way of buying a bond that promises to pay you 6% interest. If all interest rates drop around the country or if the Fed offers NEW bonds for sale paying a lower interest rate, other investors will covet the bond you have that is locked in at paying you a higher rate. They will covet it so much that they are likely to offer you more than what you paid for it.

The fact that a bond value rises as interest rates fall can also be proven mathematically when you consider the time value of money.

A main objective of the Federal Reserve open market activity is to alter the price of bonds. By doing that, it also changes their yields. For example, if you are being paid $1,000 for a bond for which you paid $10,000, you are getting a 10% yield. If the price of those bonds goes up to perhaps $12,000, assuming your yield (or interest) remains the same, your yield rate would drop to just over 8%. That would make the bonds less attractive. The opposite is also true. If the Fed lowers the cost to perhaps $5,000, your yield rate would be 20%. Another thing to consider is the fact that if the Fed pumps more reserves into the banking system by buying bonds, the interest rate for borrowing overnight funds or federal funds will likely decline (Schiller, 2016). Why? Because banks would not have as great of a need to borrow those funds. They would be swimming in the money given to them by the Fed when they buy the bonds. There would be less demand for borrowing overnight funds, thus, rates will fall. Hence, the federal funds rate is a good indicator of the open market operations.

Chapter 16 Review

QUESTIONS TO THINK ABOUT

1. What are the major duties of the Federal Reserve Board?
2. What is the impact on our economy and our money supply from the Open Market Committee as opposed to other elements of the Federal Reserve?
3. Who makes up the Open Market Committee?
4. Who are the most recent of the Federal Reserve Chairpersons, and what impact did they have on our economy during their tenures?
5. Describe the Federal Reserve Districts, and indicate the one in which you live.

TERMS/PEOPLE TO KNOW

Board of Governors

Discount Rates

Federal Open Market Committee (FOMC)

Federal Reserve Banks

Federal Reserve Districts

Investment Portfolio

National Mint

Open Market Operations

Portfolio Decision

CHAPTER SEVENTEEN

The Supply and Demand for Money

JUST LIKE THERE is a supply and demand for goods and services (as discussed in Chapter 4), there is a supply and demand for money, as well. Chapter 17 will define what the supply and demand for money is and show how changing interest rates determine them.

THE SUPPLY AND DEMAND FOR MONEY

There is a ***supply and demand for money*** just like any other goods and services, with price being the interest rate.

The ***demand for money*** can be measured by the quantity of money people are willing and able to hold or borrow as interest rates fall (Schiller, 2016).

If you put money into things such as transaction accounts (checking accounts), you get a much lower return. You are then experiencing opportunity cost for not having taken the higher risk with investments such as stocks and bonds. The opportunity cost is the difference between the higher and lower returns. The quantity of money that people are willing and able to hold in their pockets or borrow increases as interest rates fall.

For example, if interest rates are very low, it isn't worth tying up your money in a bank or in a certificate of deposit. ***Liquidity*** is having quick access to money if and when you need it, and it is a very valuable thing. Do you want to forgo liquidity to get a measly .5% return on a checking or saving account? If an emergency comes up, such as an unexpected repair bill, and if I don't have enough money in my checking account to take care of it, I may have to start selling the stocks and bonds that I have to take care of that expense. In some cases, I may have to take losses when I sell those stocks and bonds. The value of stocks and bonds rollercoasters up and down, depending upon how the market is doing, which depends on how the economy is doing. People own stocks and bonds for the long haul because usually in the long haul, the average price stay above what they paid for them. Sometimes you get lucky, but other times, losses occur when you want to draw money out of your stocks and bonds at a time when their value has dropped below the price you paid for them.

TABLE 17.1 Risk vs. Required Rates of Return

Transaction accounts	Savings	Stocks and Bonds
Lower returns required	Moderate returns required	Higher returns required

Please remember that people accept lower rates of return from banks than from stocks and bonds because bank investments are so much less risk. This is illustrated in Table 17-1. As a society, people are risk averse. They don't mind taking risks, but when they do, they want to be rewarded handsomely for it.

Another thing to consider is the forgone interest that becomes the opportunity cost of money when people choose to hold money in their wallets.

DEMAND FOR MONEY

There are three circumstances under which people will demand money. The first is ***transactions demand for money***. That is money demanded, needed, or held in their checking accounts or their wallets for daily transactions, such as car payments, utilities, groceries, and the like. Second, ***precautionary demand for money*** is what people keep in case an unexpected expense emerges, such as a doctor bill or home repair. (Schiller, 2016) People usually make sure that their wallets and their checking accounts have enough to cover these two needs. Third, ***speculative demand for money*** is money demanded in addition to the previous two circumstances or held for possible financial opportunities that could also come up. In all of these cases, people fear that if they don't have quick access to funds such as these, they might have to tap into their stocks and bonds or retirements and, again, doing so is with a big risk. Some retirement accounts even penalize you, and the government may tax you if you withdraw money from them before you reach a certain age.

People hold or demand more of money as interest rates fall, therefore, because the opportunity cost of holding it is less. The extremely small amount of interest they lose by holding on to it isn't worth worrying about. It is not worth giving up liquidity for it.

The Fed's goal of using monetary policy is to alter macroeconomic outcomes, specifically prices, output, and employment. Monetary stimulus is often used to increase aggregate demand. One way is to lower interest rates. According to economists, this is how it could work. If the Fed lowers interest rates:

1. That will lower the cost for consumers and for investment by business.
2. That in turn will lower the opportunity cost of holding inventories.

3. Businesses will then hire more people to produce and/or buy more goods.
4. The added hiring from that creates more income in our society to spend.
5. The jump in spending means more money will be in the circular flow.
6. More deposits are then created.
7. The multiplier then kicks in and makes deposits rise even more.

According to Keynesians and other economists, therefore, the Fed can stimulate the economy with monetary policy by doing the following in this succession:

1. It can increase the money supply by making more money available for borrowing in our banking system.
2. With all of that money waiting to be borrowed, banks will likely lower their interest rates to get people to borrow it all, or, with that huge supply of money that can be loaned out, there would be a reduction in interest rates. Remember, when supply of anything goes up, the market is often glutted, and, thus, prices do down.
3. This could create an increase in aggregate demand.

The reverse of all of this is also true.

Former Fed Chairperson ***Alan Greenspan*** used a policy guide which stated that lowering long-term interest by 1% could create approximately $100 billion in fiscal stimulus. He also felt that it was linear. In other words, he believed that lowering long-term interest by .1% would only bring a $10 billion fiscal stimulus.

The stimulus may be used to either correct an existing recession, or it may be an attempt to counter a downward spiral of demand. Sometimes it doesn't work. When terrorist attack took place on September 11, 2001, the stock market was closed for a few days until things could settle down. The Monday morning after 9/11, just prior to the reopening of the stock market, interest rates were slashed by a full percentage point in the hope of heading off a recession and preventing a stock market meltdown. Very seldom does the Fed reduce interest rates that much and that quickly, but it was done in the hope of preventing economic chaos. Some argue that the measure did help a little as they felt that stocks could have plummeted much more than they did that day, but a recession still followed those days in spite of the interest rate reduction.

SHORT VS. LONG-TERM RATES

Short-term rates are overnight rates, and they are the rates charged for loans that will be paid back quickly. Banks borrow money charging short-term rates when they become reserve poor, but they can also loan them out for things such as cars, vacations, appliances. Banks can borrow from the Fed at a very low rate and then charge a higher rate to their borrowers without having to use deposits for such loans. ***Long-term rates*** are the rates charged on loans to buy things that will last much longer than cars or appliances. Real estate loans are a good example of loans that charge a long-term rate and are often used for mortgages. Therefore, it's important to make this distinction because the money raised on loans that use these rates, as you can now see, are for different product market types.

Remember when it was said earlier that raising the money supply to lower interest rates can create higher aggregate demand? Unfortunately, sometimes the process does not work. Why? First of all, when the short-term rates are lower, *long-term rates often don't fall at the same rate*. They often fall much slower than the short-term rates. For example, in 2001, the Fed lowered the federal fund (overnight) rate by 3%, but during the same period, 30-year rates dropped by only ½ %.

Another reason is that you may have *unwilling lenders*. If the Fed is trying to increase aggregate demand by lowering interest rates while the economy is experiencing a recession, private banks are less willing to lend money during a recession. When people's jobs are at risk, there is a higher probability that there will be more people losing jobs and then defaulting on their loans. Banks are often hurt financially when a borrower defaults on a loan.

Third, there is the problem of the ***liquidity trap***. When interest rates drop, the opportunity cost to hold money is cheap, as mentioned before. At such times, people hold all the money they can in their pockets (or maintain liquidity) in order to have it available for later opportunities or needs. This causes fewer deposits because their money is "trapped" in their wallets until things change. If this happens, further increases in the money supply don't have an effect on interest rates. Keynes himself actually coined the term liquidity trap, therefore, even he acknowledges that the process doesn't always flow as he would hope. If people keep holding money, deposits don't increase, and the multiplier doesn't kick in, thus, aggregate demand does not increase.

Low expectations are often experienced during bad economic times when we are trying to stimulate the economy. Investment (business) decisions are motivated not only by interest rates but by expectations, as well. Firms have little incentive to invest in new equipment for expansion in output when the economy outlook is bleak no matter how low interest rates fall. Low expectations also cause consumers to reduce their purchases when people are pessimistic about the economy's foreseeable future.

Time lags are often another reason that policies of lower interest rates don't meet objectives. It takes time for people to "get it" when the Fed takes measures to encourage borrowing and spending. There is often a time lag that could last as long as six to twelve months between the moment that there is a lowering of interest rates and the time when people going out and begin borrowing.

When the economy is booming at full employment or when we are near full employment, we don't want aggregate demand to get ahead of aggregate supply. Restraint in the economy is often needed to slow down the growth of GDP but not to decrease GDP. Keynesian Economics says that the government must do the opposite of what is needed to stimulate the economy when we are trying to restrain growth. To restrain the economy, Keynesians suggests that:

1. We must lower the money supply.
2. That will in turn raise interest rates.
3. That will then restrain aggregate demand.

Sometimes, monetary restraint doesn't slow down the economy. Why?

First of all, during such times, there are very *high expectations* of rising sales and profits for businesses and more jobs for consumers. Businesses want to cash in on the boom while consumers begin to buy the things they wanted or needed that they previously couldn't afford while there were out of work. Even higher interest rates won't stop many of them from buying more. Remember, expectations are a major determinant of aggregate demand, and high expectations will shift the Aggregate Demand Curve to the right. High expectations will also shift the investment curve to the right. Even Keynes himself says that higher interest rates and higher prices often don't stop demand if people's income is rising.

Time lags work in the opposite direction during boom times. People don't quickly reduce their spending when government wants them to.

Global resources of money will also compel people to go to another country for loans when the Fed raises interest rates, raises the credit rating standards for loans, or takes measures to have less loans available. American financial institutions are no longer the only game in town. If businesses or consumers wish to borrow at a low rate when the Fed raises interest rates, they can go outside the U.S. to borrow with the click of a mouse.

Chapter 17 Review

QUESTIONS TO THINK ABOUT

1. What is the process that Keynesians believe will happen when the money supply is increased or decreased?
2. What are often the reasons that the process from Question 1 doesn't happen?
3. How does the supply and demand of money compare to the supply and demand of goods and services?
4. What kind of returns do investors expect or demand when they have a low- or high-risk investment?

TERMS TO KNOW

Liquidity

Liquidity Trap

Long-Term Rates

Precautionary Demand for Money

Short-Term Rates

Speculative Demand for Money

Supply and Demand for Money

Transactions Demand for Money

CHAPTER EIGHTEEN

Monetarist and Keynesian Sniping

IN CHAPTER 10, we discussed the major economic theories that are prescribed for use in managing the macro economy. It was made very clear that there are many differences of opinion about them. The many tools that the economic theorists use are defined in more depth in the subsequent chapters that follow. Here, in Chapter 18, we will take a closer look at the two major theories that are among the furthest apart, specifically in the area of the use of the money supply (M).

MONETARISTS VS. KEYNESIANS

Monetarists contend that you must increase the money supply (M) at a predictable rate. Why? Because they say that the long-run Aggregate Supply Curve is vertical. They feel that there is no reason for producers to depart from this "natural" level of output when aggregate demand (AD) increases. It is unnatural to expand a business's output capacity unless the business owners are absolutely sure that the increase in demand is going to last. The Monetarists believe that producers are smart enough to know that both costs and prices will rise when spending increases because higher demand drives up prices. Thus, even though the law of supply says that higher prices will give more incentive to supply, rising prices won't create any new incentive to produce, because the profit remains the same as long as costs go up at the same rate as prices.

If, for example, the market is paying $10 for a pizza that costs me $6 to produce, I am not going to raise output when prices rise to $11 per pizza because I know that the cost to produce them will likely rise to $7. In either case, my profit per pizza remains at $4 each, and my motive to increase output is gone.

The Monetarists contend that a quick fix won't work. If you increase M too quickly, it will increase AD by shifting the curve out, thus, you will cause rampant inflation. The only way to prevent rampant inflation would be to match that added demand with added supply. But added supply will not likely happen if costs to produce rise and, thus, even with a price increase, no incentive to produce more exists.

The Monetarists also do not share the beliefs of Keynes when he suggests that we must raise or lower the money supply to manage economy in light of the limitations already discussed. As mentioned in a different discussion, the Monetarists see such quick-fix changes in the money supply as *unpredictable and ineffective* and that real levels of output are not affected by monetary stimulus. Only prices change. They DO see it as a powerful tool for managing inflation. Recall *the Equation of Exchange*.

$$MV = PQ \text{ (Money Supply} \times \text{Velocity of Money)}$$
$$= \text{(Price} \times \text{Quantity Produced and Purchased)}$$

This equation is not disputed. If the money supply increases, the Monetarists feel that only prices will rise, because they contend that the velocity of money, and thus the quantity of goods sold, is stable, depending upon the structure of the money markets as well as peoples' habits.

They feel that Q is stable if producers cannot increase output to meet demand. Thus, only prices, not output, will rise. An outward shift of the Aggregate Demand Curve will only cause equilibrium prices to rise, causing rampant inflation as shown in Figure 18-1.

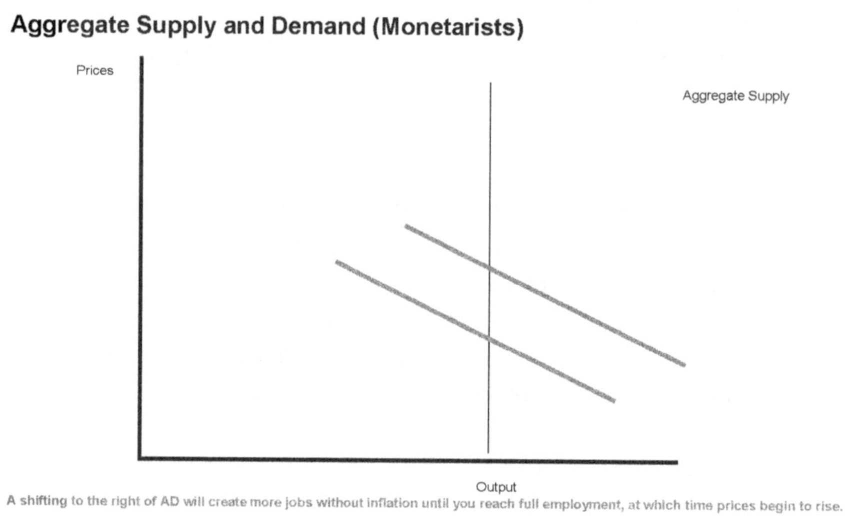

FIGURE 18.1 Aggregate Supply and Demand (Monetarists)

The Monetarists also believe that *interest rate* movements are secondary to the thrust of monetary policy and should not be its primary focus. They feel that the most important thing to happen are *changes in the money supply* to alter total spending regardless of how interest rates move.

Monetarists feel that all of these facts will typically bring producers' output to the level of what is known as the ***natural rate of output***. It is the rate at which you produce without having to push production to the envelope and/or without having to increase capacity. It is the structure of the organizations that determines their output. Producers don't like to rock the boat by adding capacity only for the economy to later stall, maybe even before the costly expansion is fully operational. Producers take a big risk with expansion, and many would naturally want to hold fast to their current capacity and just rake in the profits at that level. When there begins to be a shortage of their goods, prices will often rise, thus, giving them the ability to cash in without costly expansion.

If the natural rate of output does not rise, you can have what is defined as ***natural unemployment***. These structural forces establish what is, therefore, referred to as the ***natural rate of unemployment***. Earlier, the idea of structural and frictional unemployment was discussed. They exist even when the economy is booming and when GDP is growing dramatically. During such times, many jobs go unfilled because those experiencing structural unemployment lack the skills to work those jobs. In addition, frictional unemployment includes those who are not seriously looking for work either because they have something lined up or they are looking for something better to come along. They choose not to take the jobs offered. When we reach this point of unemployment, many argue that the government has done all it can to help the economy. Its strategies to stimulate the economy have achieved their objectives.

There is no reason for producers to depart from the natural rate of output when the money supply increases. Monetarists proclaim that producers are smart enough to know that *both prices and costs will rise* when spending increases *at the same rate*. When this happens, profits remain the same, thus, giving no profit incentive to increase output.

What about Keynesians and the Monetarists and their views on restraint? The Monetarists feel that Keynes's view that reducing the money supply to drive up interest rates to slow the economy or to reduce government spending won't work for several reasons. Some of these reasons are those mentioned earlier.

For one thing, when we reach full employment, business investment (I) will often increase because business owners are likely to have high hopes of future sales, and they will need better technology to keep up with demand. They are likely to become more capital intensive because there are fewer people they can hire at full employment.

When this happens, there is a process that unfolds. First, the aggregate demand curve shifts out to the right. Next, available inventories shrink. When inventory depletion takes place, it is often a sign of shortages and, thus, impending inflation. Third, household incomes will get a boost due to more hiring. This often will even lure some people out of retirement and some workers out of their stay-at-home cycle, and it has even encouraged some to work extended hours or weekends. Next, the added household income creates induced consumption as we said earlier. Increases in income shift the Aggregate Demand Curve outward. Fifth, the multiplier effect will begin. When that happens, prices will rise due to demand-pull inflation. Finally, this rise in inflation creates an inflationary gap (mentioned earlier).

The Keynesian analysis of leakages, injections, and the multiplier concludes that the economy is vulnerable to abrupt changes in spending behavior and won't self-adjust to a desired macro equilibrium. As a result, Keynesians feel that we must decrease GDP to react.

If we do, there are two problems. The first is that reducing GDP can cause job losses. Second, when this happens, and then the government increases GDP to put those people back to work, we begin to have booms and busts, especially when we cause a more than proportional adjustment of increasing GDP to the point that we cause inflation.

Monetarists believe that lowering interest rates for economic restraint won't work because *nominal rates are already likely to be high because inflation drives them up* and that an effective anti-inflation policy (if adopted) would drive interest rates down. Please recall how interest rates are decided by investors and lenders. What borrowers are charged is called the nominal rate of interest. It is equal to the real rate plus expected inflation rate plus risk premium.

Monetarists feel that the real rate of interest is fairly stable, thus, changes in the nominal rate reflect changes in anticipated inflation, and, therefore, they feel that *high interest rates are a symptom of inflation, not a cure*.

Both Keynesians and the Monetarists agree that tightening the money supply is needed to slow down the economy, but the Monetarists claim that Keynesians rely on a quick fix of higher interest rates to slow consumption. Keynesians feel that interest rates *will fall* with a tight money supply because people will anticipate less inflation with a tight money supply and reduce nominal rates.

Recall that long-term interest rates don't mirror the short-term rates when they fall. If you loan money to someone and expect that same interest rate for the length of the loan, a lot can happen in thirty years. Therefore, if people anticipate no inflation, in the long run, long-term rates will fall. They will increase if market participants believe that inflation will worsen in the long term.

Therefore, Monetarists believe that you may have to stall the economy to reduce interest rates and inflation, but rather than take that risk, they prefer to recommend *steady, predictable changes in the money supply, reducing uncertainties and stabilizing long-term interest rates* and GDP growth.

Monetarists feel that to stimulate employment, raising M in order to lower rates (as Keynes advocates) would have the opposite effect. They feel that it will only raise prices, and if everyone foresees this happening, nominal interest rates would then go up (not down) in anticipated inflation, defeating the purpose of monetary stimulus.

They feel that it could actually create inflation on top of our unemployment woes (creating stagflation) as we saw in the late 1970s.

Predictable increases in M would allow firms to plan years in advance for such increases so that a higher M would create a higher Q and not a higher P. Monetarist believe that we need to get producers into the habit of increasing output at all times, thus when we reach full employment, output capacity will continue to rise.

Other problems with tight money include the fact that higher interest rates hit many industries harder than others disproportionately, such as housing, automotive, and appliances. Remember, many industries, such as food and low-cost consumer goods, don't require their customers to obtain affordable loans. Also, higher interest rates not only hurt the economy but reduce the share of housing, automotive, and appliances in GDP spending. All related fields and suppliers to the firms in those industries are also affected, and these industries need stability. If they are not stable, the boom times will quickly become a bust.

Another problem exists with tight money as it tends to be available for larger firms rather than smaller firms. Smaller firms would then have a disproportionate disadvantage when such policies are imposed.

A summary of these views between Keynesians and the Monetarists are seen in Table 18-1.

TABLE 18.1 Summary of Economic Views Toward Policy Levers

POLICY	KEYNESIAN VIEW	MONETARIST VIEW
Government Spending (G)	Increase it to increase the velocity of money to increase GDP.	Higher government spending (G) will NOT increase velocity of money (V) because V is stable and will be unchanged. Thus, it won't reduce unemployment nor inflation. Nominal interest rates will rise but real rates won't.
Taxes	Lower them to increase the velocity of money to increase GDP.	Lower taxes will NOT increase velocity of money (V) because V is stable and will be unchanged. Thus, it won't reduce unemployment nor inflation. Nominal interest rates will rise but real rates won't.
Money Supply	Increase it to make interest rates fall to increase GDP.	If it goes up, prices go up, thus, interest rates go up, but aggregate demand is unchanged.

In either case, many economists believe that the closer we are to capacity, the greater the risk that fiscal or monetary stimulus will spill over into inflation. They feel that demand stimulus would cause inflation, and restraint would cause decreases in output and, therefore, would cause decreases in employment when the supply curve is upward sloping.

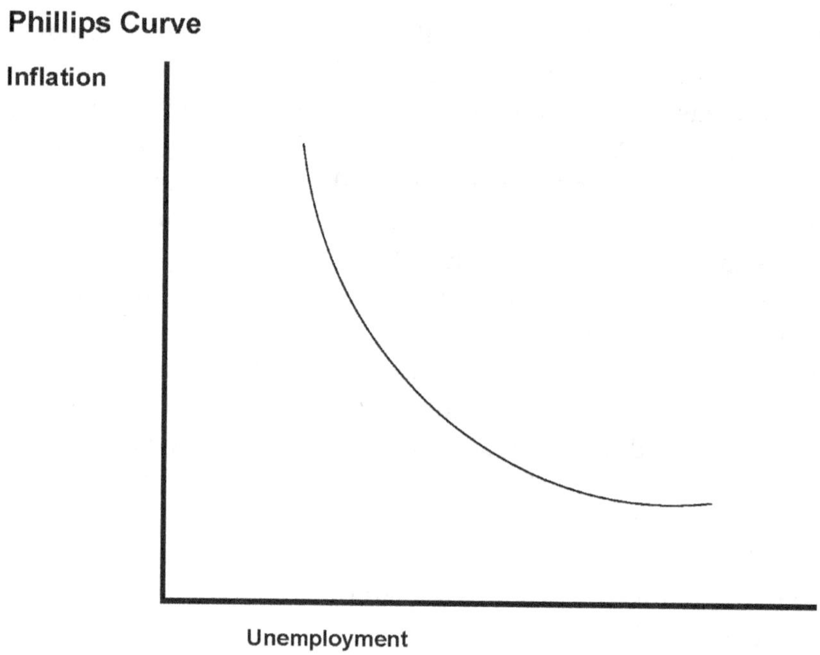

FIGURE 18.2 Phillips Curve

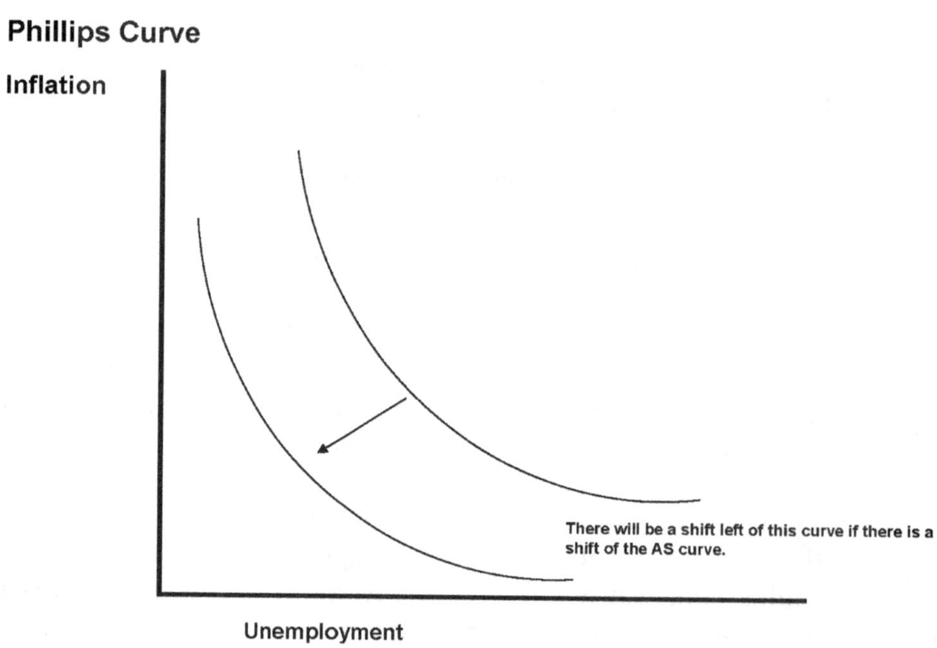

FIGURE 18.3 Phillips Curve (Shifted Left)

The ***Phillips Curve*** illustrates the tradeoff between inflation and employment. ***William Phillips (1914–1975)***, an economist from New Zealand, wrote a paper in 1958 titled, *The Relation between Unemployment and the Rate of Change of Money Wage Rates in the United Kingdom*. It explained how he noticed an inverse correlation between money wage changes and unemployment in the British economy. The curve has become known as the Phillips Curve, and many have added their own belief that all prices rise as unemployment falls. It is shown in Figure 18-2.

Supply-Side economists have taken issue with it, however, as they feel that rightward shifts of the aggregate supply curve can reduce both inflation and unemployment. It can also, therefore shift the Phillips Curve to the left. That would give us the better of both worlds of lower unemployment and lower prices as illustrated in Figure 18-3.

Chapter 18 Review

QUESTIONS TO THINK ABOUT

1. In your own words, describe the main differences between the Monetarist and the Keynesian Economics theorists.
2. Which theory do you agree with at each difference and why?

TERMS/PEOPLE TO KNOW

Natural Rate of Output

Natural Rate of Unemployment

Natural Unemployment

Phillips Curve

William Phillips (1914–1975)

CHAPTER NINETEEN

Bringing It All Together

AFTER DISCUSSING ALL of the theories and the tools in managing our economy, this is the moment you have been waiting for! Chapter 19 will now help you to see what economic theory economists believe should be applied at any given stage of any economic cycle, whether it be depression, deep recession, mild recession (or recovery), and full employment (or prosperity). If you have a firm understanding of each of the theories and their tools, this chapter will make you a very good economic advisor. Would you be qualified to advise any given president? Perhaps. Whatever the case, all of the major topics of this textbook will now fall into place.

THE ECLECTIC (HYBRID) LONG-RUN AGGREGATE SUPPLY CURVE

As said earlier, economists tend to agree that the application of some economic theories work better in certain circumstances, such as deep recession or depression, while others are more effective in a recovering economy and full employment. As a result, the idea of the ***Eclectic (Hybrid) Long-Run Aggregate Supply Curve*** has been created by economists to summarize when they feel these things are true.

There are many versions of the curve, but the one in Figure 19-1 is the one that we will study.

THE KEYNESIAN SEGMENT/DEPRESSION/DEEP RECESSION SECTOR

Notice the part of the Eclectic (Hybrid) Long-Run Aggregate Supply Curve that is labeled as the ***Keynesian Segment/Depression/Deep Recession*** sector. It is called that because it is during deep economic recession or depression that economists believe that the Keynesian Theory will be the best remedy to heal the economy during those times. At that point, as mentioned earlier,

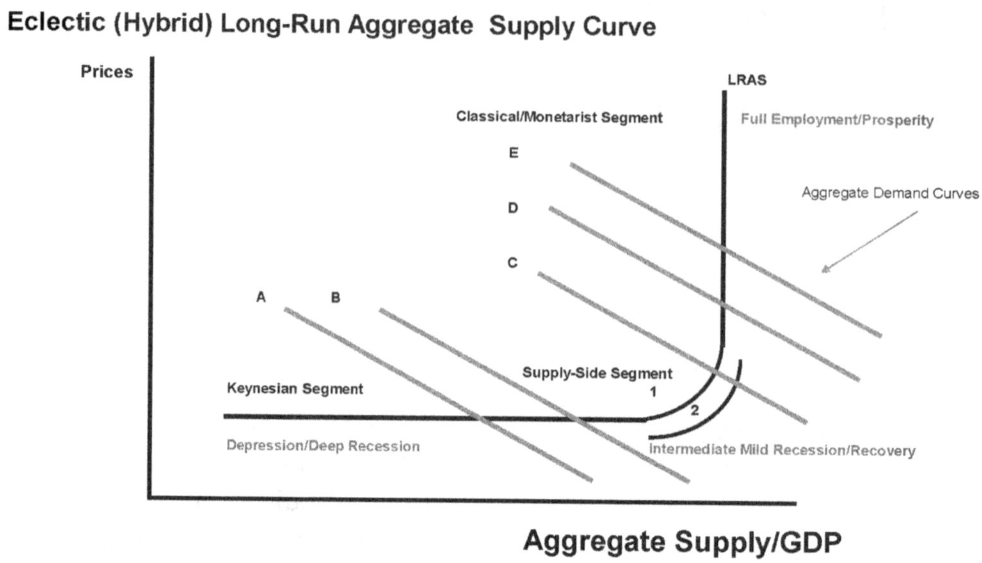

FIGURE 19.1 The Eclectic (Hybrid) Long-Run Aggregate Supply Curve

the Aggregate Supply Curve is typically flat because during bad times, people will be more than happy to supply more and without requiring more pay per hour or per unit produced.

During deep recessions, factories are just happy to get work. They usually have a great deal of idle areas in their factories, and idle factories are costly. Workers are the same way. They are just happy to get back to work. and they will not demand a larger wage as more of their time is needed, thus, they will supply more at the same wage.

It is also flat during depression or deep recessions because suppliers of resources to factories in businesses often lower their prices to get business volume back to where it was before the bad times set in. If suppliers lower their prices, producers can actually make more money per unit produced, thus producing more can mean more profits per sale.

Keynesians prescribe the shifting of the Aggregate Demand Curve to the right by government's use of both fiscal and monetary policies as shown in Figure 19-1. Normally when the aggregate demand is shifted out, it will increase equilibrium prices. Please remember that equilibrium prices are at the point where the Aggregate Demand and the Aggregate Supply Curves intersect. With the curve being flat during deep economic recession or depression, however, a shift of the Aggregate Demand Curve will not cause inflation. Notice in Figure 19-1, when the Aggregate Demand Curve moves from Point A to Point B, equilibrium pricing remains the same. Therefore, you can aggressively increase aggregate demand and put people back to work without having to worry about inflation.

THE SUPPLY-SIDE SEGMENT/INTERMEDIATE MILD RECESSION/RECOVERY SECTOR

As output increases from increasing aggregate demand/GDP, as more people begin to find work, and as factories are increasing their output, eventually, workers and producers are going to get to the place that they will, once again, begin to demand higher wages and prices in order to be motivated to increase aggregate supply. When that happens, the Aggregate Supply Curve will start to slope upward again as is normal. When that happens, you can no longer shift the Aggregate Demand Curve outward or to the right without having a problem with inflation. In Figure 19-1, you can see that if demand is shifted outward to the point of Aggregate Demand Curve C, then inflation will start to become a problem.

At that time, we have to STOP shifting the Aggregate Demand Curve out, and we need to START shifting the Aggregate Supply Curve out in order to stop inflation from rising and to maintain continued growth in GDP. That is why it is also called the Intermediate/ Mild Recession Curve. That is what the curve looks like during such times. The virtual consensus of economists is that Supply-Side Economics is the best theory to apply at such times. The reason for this is that it prescribes the shifting of the Aggregate Supply Curve to the right instead of the Aggregate Demand Curve. Please remember that doing so still allows GDP to rise but without inflation.

During such times, the economy is improving, and so the recession is now mild. The economy is not truly having a deep recession or depression, but it's not quite back to prosperity or to full employment either. Therefore, the name of that segment of the curve is called the ***Supply-Side Segment/Intermediate Mild Recession/Recovery*** sector of the Eclectic (Hybrid) Long-Run Aggregate Supply Curve.

It is also important to understand here that the intermediate/mild recession economy can exist under two circumstances. The first circumstance exists when the economy is falling after having had a period of prosperity or full employment. In the summer of 2000, we had full employment, but then a mild recession began, and we fell down into the intermediate segment, but the economy soon began to recover from there.

The second circumstance under which we find ourselves in that segment with is when we are recovering from a deep recession or recession. That's why the segment is also labeled as recovery.

THE CLASSICAL/MONETARIST SEGMENT/FULL EMPLOYMENT/PROSPERITY SECTOR

When the economy reaches full employment, many ask why the government needs to get involved with the economy anymore. If everyone is working, we don't need to fix something that isn't broken. Economists feel, however, that the government may want to take measures to *maintain* a good economy. Remember, to many, the patient is the economy, and the medication is economic theory implemented by the government through the advisement of economists. A healthy person must still take measures to remain healthy, and, in the same way, economists feel that there should be measures taken to keep the economy prosperous.

The Classical/Monetarist Segment/Full Employment/Prosperity sector of the Eclectic (Hybrid) Long-Run Aggregate Supply Curve is called that because during prosperity it becomes vertical. That is what the Monetarists say the curve looks like. Please remember why.

Even if prices go sky-high, businesses don't increase supply to cash in on those prices because they can't. They are at full capacity. Thus, supply stays put as prices continue to rise. If we are at full employment, there are very few people a business can hire, which forces it to resort to adding machinery or capital equipment and factory space. But it is reluctant to do that unless it is certain that prosperity is here to stay. It is costly to add capital equipment, and if prosperity is short-lived and things quickly return to bad times in our economy, these firms find themselves with a lot of costly capital equipment that is now idle and no longer paying for themselves. The problem is that if more are buying and, thus, if aggregate demand continues to shift outward on its own, it can jump from Point D to Point E, thus, causing rampant inflation as seen in Figure 19-1.

The important thing to remember here, therefore, is that at full employment everyone is buying. Consumers are now working so they can now buy what they couldn't afford during the bad times. This is all fine and good as long as aggregate supply can keep up with that demand. Otherwise, shortages will occur, and rampant inflation can then happen. If it does, people would not be able to afford to buy many things, aggregate demand would fall, and our prosperity would be quickly gone. Therefore, we must make sure that aggregate supply will keep up with aggregate demand during prosperity and full employment.

So how do we do it? Many argue that the Classical Theory is correct, that we should leave businesses to find ways of increasing output, and that they will do so. They feel that it is inherent, therefore, that self-correction will take place. In many ways, the Monetarists agree with the Classical Theory. They, too, have given arguments, as mentioned earlier, that government intervention will not work and that, in many cases, it makes things worse.

There is one significant area, however where the Monetarist and the Classical Theorists differ. As mentioned earlier, the Monetarists profess that the government can maintain a prosperous economy if it increases the money supply slightly with ample notice to producers. They suggest, for example, that government could increase the money supply by perhaps 3% with a one-year notice and then do the same each year thereafter, using any of the means that were discussed earlier.

We can *slow down growth of GDP and not reduce it*. Reduction of GDP means some may have to lose their jobs, and nobody wants that. By slowing the growth of GDP but still, in fact, keeping GDP growing, *the Monetarists feel some businesses make take a leap of faith to buy more capital equipment, thus, consumption and investment will rise, causing more aggregate demand that can be satisfied with adequate supply*. They feel that if producers know that strong current demand could improve in a year with an increase in the money supply that they can cash in. A year's notice would give them the ability to buy more capital equipment. *They believe that we need to get producers into the habit of increasing output at all times, thus when we reach full employment, output capacity will continue to rise*.

The, Eclectic (Hybrid) Long-Run Aggregate Supply Curve, therefore, becomes the most important part of macroeconomics. It tells any presidential administration, any Congress, any Federal Reserve Board member what needs to be done during any economic condition. I have coined the curve, ***The Steering Wheel of the Economy***. It becomes our guide as to what procedure to follow when we find the economy in any given situation.

Will the government use the curve as many economists believe it should? We hope so. We hope that politicians will put politics aside and practice good economics in its place.

Chapter 19 Review

QUESTIONS TO THINK ABOUT

In your own words, describe what economists feel are the best policy levers for the government to apply and why they should be applied under the following circumstances (please remember that the policy levers applied must be those recommended by the economic theory economists recommended during these circumstances):

1. Depression/Deep Recession
2. Mild Recession/Recovery
3. Full Employment/ Prosperity

TERMS TO KNOW

Eclectic (Hybrid) Long-Run Aggregate Supply Curve

The Classical/Monetarist Segment/ Full Employment/Prosperity Sector

The Keynesian Segment/Depression/Deep Recession Sector

The Steering Wheel of the Economy

The Supply-Side Segment/Intermediate Mild Recession/Recovery Sector

CHAPTER TWENTY

International Economics

IN ALL PREVIOUS chapters, we talked about the American economy. But should we only be concerned about our own economy? Economists make a good case that we should be concerned with all economies. Even though there are downsides to having what we will define as an open economy, Chapter 20 will show you why and what tools we have internationally to make sure that all economies are running well.

THE NEED TO BECOME INTERNATIONALLY INVOLVED

ECONOMIC MYTH #22	We should stop giving other countries our attention and our financial aid and just take care of ourselves.

Not only is it rather selfish and egocentric to put only our own needs ahead of that of the rest of world, but it has also been found to be bad economics. Believe it or not, we often help our own economy when we give foreign/financial aid to other countries. People often forget that one of the four major components of gross domestic product is net exports. If we lose our customers abroad, we lose a lot of jobs here. Of course, some economists and politicians who prefer isolationism feel that would be just fine in that we could also stop importing, thinking that if we do that, the jobs lost with no exports would be gained in more sales here and, thus, more jobs here when people stop importing goods from those countries and start buying them at home.

Many times, our country has given help to nations and propped up other economies because the people and businesses and even the governments in those countries were major purchasers of American goods. If their economies collapse, ours could, too. One must remember that when global protectionism became prevalent in the late 1920s, economists of those days felt that it caused our export market to collapse, which was believed to be among the things that led to the Great Depression of the 1930s. Many fear that we could make that happen again.

In 2017, talk of tariffs and trade wars began and often sent Wall Street scrambling as well as other economies in countries around the world.

In recent decades, America has been experiencing what is called a ***trade deficit***. It exists when a country consumes more than it produces. As mentioned before, trade deficits occur when the leakage of imports exceeds the reinjection of exports. We make up for that shortage of reinjection in our circular flow by the fact that banking and government spending reinjections are far greater than the leakages they create when people save, invest, or pay taxes.

In one sense, ***isolationism*** is what people are endorsing when they want to stop imports or exports. This philosophy endorses no economic cooperation or trade with any other country except our own. It creates what is called a ***closed economy***. However, isolationism has both advantages and disadvantages, the but the disadvantages far outweigh the advantages. that An ***open economy***, by which we do permit cooperation and economic trade with countries around the world, also has advantages and disadvantages.

How can isolationism be harmful to our economy and why is an open economy better? First, if we stop importing from other countries, we cannot sustain our economy because there are many goods that we need from other countries. If we become a closed economy, we would either be in short supply of those goods, or we would have to do without them altogether. These things include items such as sugar, coffee, and oil. While America is now among the leaders in oil production around the world, we still cannot manage if we stop buying oil from other countries. Another problem is that without an open economy, as our domestic living standards exceed domestic output (or when American consumption exceeds American output) we would have not options as consumers to buy what we need by going abroad.

Third, even when we are at full employment, an open economy can reduce domestic crowding out when increased government spending could otherwise supplant consumption and investment. We have stated many times that our ability to borrow money abroad has eased the idea of crowding out.

Fourth, an open economy can keep other countries' economies with a trade surplus and, thus, healthy enough to buy our products.

Also, open economies discourage other countries from setting tariffs on our goods that we export.

Yes, there are some disadvantages of an open economy. First, it causes much of our capital money to leave our country and go to other countries by buying the foreign products. It can also send more capital money abroad when we buy more investments overseas than what foreign consumers buy from our corporations. This is called a ***capital deficit***.

The only other disadvantage to an open economy is that exports and imports are not a factor in a country's GDP. Therefore, fiscal stimulus has to be increased to have the same effect as it would have if we had a closed economy. Any government stimulus can directly help our economy here as long as we can assume that the marginal propensity to consume here in our country will translate into purchases ofy American goods. But that is not the case. With the purchase of imports, much of those dollars spent in fiscal stimuli buy goods abroad and not here. That spending is called the ***marginal propensity to import (MPM)***.

Using the example in Table 20.1, let's assume, for a moment, that our country's marginal propensity to consume (MPC) is 80% while the marginal propensity to import (MPM) is 5%. Please remember that this would mean that the marginal propensity to save would be 20%. In a closed economy, the multiplier would be the same as stated before: one divided by 20% or 1/20%, which would give a multiplier of 5. Now let's assume that the government implements a $10 billion fiscal stimulus. If so, the added savings in our country would be $2 billion (20% times $10 billion). With no imports in a closed economy, the multiplier would be 5 (1/MPS = 1/.20 = 5), and the added consumption would be $8 billion ($10 billion stimulus times MPC of 80%). The multiplier-induced consumption would be $40 billion (5 × $8 billion added consumption). The cumulative change in our GDP from consumption would be $50 billion (original $10 billion + $40 billion of multiplier induced consumption) = $50 billion).

With an open economy, however, if we needed $50 billion to close the recessionary gap, we would fall short if we used that same amount in fiscal stimulus. Assuming again that the marginal propensity to import (MPM), as mentioned earlier, was 5%; keeping all other assumptions intact, we would gain only $42 billion. The reason is that the multiplier would have to be recalculated to now include the *leakage of imports* to be added to the *leakage of savings*. The formula for the multiplier would now be written as:

$$\text{Multiplier} = 1/(\text{MPS} + \text{MPM}) = 1/(20\% + 5\%)$$

In this case, the imports spending would not be zero, but it would be $500 million (or .05 times $10 billion). Also, we would add the marginal propensity to save of 20% to the marginal propensity to import of 5%. Thus, instead of a multiplier of 5 (1/.20), it would be a multiplier of only 4 (1/.25). Added consumption, before the multiplier takes effect for our economy, will now be $7.5 billion, because 5% of the Marginal Propensity to Consume would be spent abroad. Once the new multiplier of 4 is applied, we would now have $30 billion in Multiplier Induced Consumption instead of $50 billion. Therefore, the same stimulus with an open economy would only give us $40 billion in an increase to GDP rather than $50 billion. This example shows that an open economy does reduce the impact of fiscal stimuli. But you must still remember that the problems we would have with no ability to buy needed goods for our economy that are not available in enough quantities here, far outweighs the problem with more needed fiscal stimuli.

TABLE 20.1 Closed Economy vs. Open Economy Impact of Fiscal Stimulus

EXAMPLE: ASSUME 80% MPC, 20% MPS IN EITHER CLOSED OR OPEN ECONOMY AND ASSUME 5% MPM IN AN OPEN ECONOMY. ASSUME AN ADDED FISCAL STIMULUS OF $10 BILLION.

	CLOSED ECONOMY	OPEN ECONOMY
Added Government Spending	$10 billion	$10 billion
Added Savings	$2 billion	$2 billion
Imports Spending	0	$.5 billion (or $500 million)
Multiplier	5 (1/MPS=1/.20)	4 (1/(MPS+MPM)=1/(.20+.05))
Added DOMESTIC Consumption	$8 billion ($10 billion x (1-.20)	$7.5 billion ($10 billion × (1-.25))
Multiplier Induced Consumption	$40 billion (5 × $8 billion added consumption)	$30 billion (4 × $7.5 Billion Consumption)
Cumulative Change	$50 billion ($10 billion + $40 billion)	$40 billion ($10 billion + $10 billion)

It is important to note here that foreign economies also suffer when we stop importing or when our economy suffers bad times. Countries that tend to be hardest hit by economic slowdowns in our country are those that produce major import of ours, such as cars and high-tech equipment.

GLOBAL COORDINATION AND COOPERATION

As we, therefore, feel the need to remain an open economy, we find it helpful to seek some level of coordination and cooperation from the other countries engaged in the global economy. ***The International Monetary Fund (IMF)*** which has been a good *resource for many of the statistics and information* in this textbook, is used to help all economies in several ways. First, it provides surveillance "of economic and financial developments, as well as the provision of policy advice, aimed especially at crisis-prevention. The IMF also lends to countries with balance of payments difficulties, providing temporary financing and to support policies aimed at correcting the underlying problems." They provide loans to low-income countries in an effort to reduce world poverty. The IMF "provides countries with technical assistance and training. Supporting all three of these activities is the IMF work that involves economic research and statistics. [...] The IMF also plays an important role in the fight against money-laundering and terrorism" (Schiller, 2016).

The IMF has come under fire over the years as many social justice activists feel that countries that cannot pay back loans to the Fund should be excused from those debts as they put pressure on those countries that already struggle with poverty and serious social problems. This debate has been going on for many years.

The Group of Eight (G8) (or what many call the G8) is a forum for governments of eight nations of the Northern Hemisphere. Those countries are Canada, France, Germany, Italy, Japan, Russia, the United Kingdom, the European Union, and the United States. G8 can refer to the member states or to the annual summit meeting of the G8 heads of government. They come together to discuss trade issues, and they attempt to come to some understanding and agreement as to how to address issues in order to make world trade fair and more beneficial to all member nations and to keep it free flowing.

The ***World Bank*** is another international financial institution. It provides leveraged loans to developing countries for capital improvements. Much like the IMF, its goal is also to reduce poverty around the world. It, too, has had many who have demanded the forgiveness of many loans to countries experiencing economic poverty (Schiller, 2016).

The ***United Nations*** is the most well-known organization of international economic cooperation. Its precursor was ***The League of Nations (LON)***. The League of Nations was initiated by the work of President ***Woodrow Wilson (1856–1924)*** and was founded as a result of the ***Treaty of Versailles***. The United Nations' major goals include preventing war and the settling of international disputes through negotiation (Schiller, 2016).

Chapter 20 Review

QUESTIONS TO THINK ABOUT

1. What are the advantages of having a trade deficit?
2. What are the advantages and disadvantages of having an open economy?
3. What happens to government stimulus plans with an open economy?
4. Do you feel that the United States should remain active in its cooperation efforts with other countries regarding international economic balance? Why or why not?

TERMS/PEOPLE TO KNOW

Trade Deficit

Isolationism

Closed Economy

Open Economy

Capital Deficit

The International Monetary Fund (IMF)

The Group of Eight (G8)

Outreach Five (O5) or the Plus Five

World Bank

United Nations

The League of Nations (LON)

Treaty of Versailles

Woodrow Wilson (1856–1924)

Epilogue

There you have it. It is my hope that everything written here will give insight to all readers as to how a macro economy can be managed to reach the objectives of all.

By now you should have a genuine understanding of how our macro economy works and what it needs in order to continue working. A very small percentage of people in this country know what you now know, and, yet, nearly everyone has an opinion about it. When you talk with others about these issues, you will be one of the few who will have an educated viewpoint. It is my hope that you use it well and for the betterment of your careers, your families, and for society.

References

"Council of Economic Advisers." *Wikipedia*. https://en.wikipedia.org/wiki/Council_of_Economic_Advisers.

"Dow Jones Industrial Average." *Wikipedia*. https://en.wikipedia.org/wiki/Dow_Jones_Industrial_Average.

Durden, Tyler. "Guest Post: The Global Endgame in Fourteen Points." *The Balance*. http://www.zerohedge.com/news/2013-02-15/guest-post-global-endgame-fourteen-points

"ESI." *Dow Jones*. http://dowjones.com/esi.

Gregory, Paul R. Essentials of Economics. Pearson Publishing, Upper Saddle River, NJ, 2005.

"GDP, CPI and other key economic reports." *Bank Rate*. https://www.bankrate.com/rates/economic-indicators/reports.aspx.

"How the Government Measures Unemployment." *U.S. Bureau of Labor Statistics*. https://www.bls.gov/cps/cps_htgm.pdf (pages 1–2).

"ICT Business Law Economy." GCL. http://gcl.nu/forms/all%20in%20one.docx.

Langdana, Farrokh K. *Macroeconomic Policy: Demystifying Monetary and Fiscal Policy*. Switzerland: Springer International Publishing. 2016. https://link.springer.com/book/10.1007%2F978-3-319-32854-6.

McConnell, Campbell R., *Economics*. McGraw Hill Book Co., New York, NY 1984.

Peach, Richard W. and Karen Alverez. "Core CPI: Excluding Food, Energy ... and Used Cars?" *Current Issues in Economics and Finance,* Volume 2, No. 4. April 1996. https://www.newyorkfed.org/medialibrary/media/research/current_issues/ci2-4.pdf.

"Relative Price." *Wikipedia*. https://en.wikipedia.org/wiki/Relative_price.

"Return to a Recession is a Real Risk According to Dow Jones Economic Sentiment Indicator." *Cision PR Newswire*. https://www.prnewswire.com/news-releases/return-to-a-recession-is-a-real-risk-according-to-dow-jones-economic-sentiment-indicator-126529688.html.

"Savings and Loan Crisis." *Wikipedia*. https://en.wikipedia.org/wiki?curid=896632.

Schiller, Bradley, R. *The Macro Economy Today*. McGraw-Hill Irwin, New York, NY 2016.

"The International Man's Glossary: A–Z." *The International Man*. https://www.theinternationalman.com/texts/glossary.php.

"Top 5 Causes of the Great Depression." *Beacon Historical Society*. http://www.beaconhistoricalsociety.org/top-5-causes-of-the-great-depression./

"Unemployment Rate by Year Since 1929 Compared to Inflation and GDP." *The Balance*. https://www.thebalance.com/unemployment-rate-by-year-3305506.

"Understanding The "Official" 17 Key Economic Indicators and How They Move the Stock Market." *Fusion Investing*. 21st Century Investor Publishing, Inc. http://www.fusioninvesting.com/Files/reading/economic-indicators.pdf.
"United States Federal Budget." *Wikipedia*. https://en.m.wikipedia.org/wiki/United_States_federal_budget#.
"What the IMF does." *International Monetary Fund*. http://www.imf.org/external/work.htm.

Index

CPSIA information can be obtained
at www.ICGtesting.com
Printed in the USA
FSHW010028171219
65149FS